Life Dancing
Mastering Life's Movement

*A Program for Self-Directed, Wholistic,
Integral Well-Being*

Linda L. Lawless, LMFT, LMHC

BALBOA
PRESS

A DIVISION OF HAY HOUSE

Balboa Press books may be ordered through booksellers or by contacting:

Balboa Press
A Division of Hay House
1663 Liberty Drive
Bloomington, IN 47403
www.balboapress.com
1 (877) 407-4847

Because of the dynamic nature of the Internet, any web addresses or links contained in this book may have changed since publication and may no longer be valid. The views expressed in this work are solely those of the author and do not necessarily reflect the views of the publisher, and the publisher hereby disclaims any responsibility for them.

The author of this book does not dispense medical advice or prescribe the use of any technique as a form of treatment for physical, emotional, or medical problems without the advice of a physician, either directly or indirectly. The intent of the author is only to offer information of a general nature to help you in your quest for emotional and spiritual well-being. In the event you use any of the information in this book for yourself, which is your constitutional right, the author and the publisher assume no responsibility for your actions.

ISBN: 978-1-5043-4669-6 (sc)
ISBN: 978-1-5043-4670-2 (e)

Library of Congress Control Number: 2015920020

Print information available on the last page.

Balboa Press rev. date: 12/15/2015

ACKNOWLEDGMENTS

First and foremost, heartfelt thanks to the family, friends, and colleagues who dance in my life!

Glen Speckert, my wonderful husband, who remains tried and true through all of our life changes.

Gretchen Burgess, my gift of a daughter who is also my best friend.
Maximilian Rex, a very wise grandson.

Anthony Shannon, who loves and cares for Gretchen and Maximilian and keeps my website humming.

Stephanie Wood, my coach, who moved with me through the incubation, slow and fast steps.

Carolyn Flynn, my editor, who asked many hard questions and helped integrate my thoughts.

Judy Irvin, who patiently edited every line.

Clients who keep showing up and working hard to create healthier lives. I thank them all for enriching my life.

Teachers who appear in many guises. Some more obvious than others. There are the ones everyone recognizes and ones (like Max) who teach by being.

Gods and Goddesses - and all the other forces of the universe that keep us all dancing.

All hummingbird images captured by Glen Speckert, copyright 2015.

Contents

Table of Contents

Enhancing this book

THE MASTER CLASS WORKBOOK

THE LIFEDANCING JOURNAL

Find these books at www.lifedancing.com

A note to my readers

His or Her, That is the Question!

I remember, when I was a much younger, and quite the avid reader, I wondered why all the people in the books I read in my room under the covers, were written by men. Yes, I did notice, and I concluded that all of the writers were either men, or that men had all of the really cool experiences. For heaven's sake, the U.S. Declaration of Independence that I was learning about in school said, "... all MEN are created equal," so I could only guess that our forefathers included women in that statement. I mean, why would only men be equal?

Then as I matured, I discovered that earlier female authors actually used male names on their work because they wanted to be published. They knew that if they were known as a female author, their work would NEVER be seen by others outside of their personal circles.

Having been published by big publishing houses before this first self-publishing event, knowing that words do matter, I'm making my own choices regarding the use of gender in my work. So, you'll find that I use "she" rather than "he" when the content is not gender-specific. You'll see female nouns and pronouns when the gender of the subject(s) is unclear, varies, or when a group to which I'm referring contains members of both sexes.

As I wrote this introduction, I renewed my curiosity about other authors' personal and public use of gender. I discovered that many authors still use "pen" names to branch out into new literary genres so they won't jeopardize their current gender-based reputations. I mean, what would you think of a male science fiction writer who wrote a romance novel? Maybe a little differently?

Devolving into a discussion about how erasing women from our language makes it easier to continue gender inequality is tempting, but that is not my major thesis, yet – rather, I simply want to use "she" rather than "he" in this book. Because there does not appear to be any current "hard" rules about this issue, and because I'm female, I used "she" as the default gender identifier. If you find this offensive, DON'T READ THE BOOK – or on a more positive note, explore your discomfort.

Personally I believe we, men and women, are different, yet equal. Anyone who says we're all the same simply needs to notice that there are usually two doors to bathrooms in most public places. Our brains are different, our bodies are different, and our values and priorities are often different. Yet, we are equal in that we all have the right to a life well-lived.

I invite you to your own individual dance of life in whatever gender form it manifests!

Warmly,

THE BIRTHING OF LIFEDANCING

If you are not interested in the birthing of LifeDancing, you can skip this section. The wisdom of dance begins and ends with knowing where your center lies. Physically, that means your bodies center of gravity, psychologically your sense of self, and spiritually your relationship to that which is bigger than you are. To know your center is to liberate you and give you the gift of dance. When you dance from your center, you move fearlessly, open to change, and are always amazed and curious about what unfolds.

Movement points us to the awareness of our individual centerpoint/s. Movement also keeps us from becoming rigid and brittle so we don't break when hit by change. Movement teaches us flexibility – in our physical bodies, in our thoughts, in our emotions, in and our concept of who we are.

LifeDancing is not only about dancing. Rather, it's about tuning in to the movement of life, turning into our center of being, so that we may turn confidently to face the world. LifeDancing uses dance as a metaphor because dancing captures the way our hearts are moved, and the way our visions take shape.

Early in my life, I deeply understood the power of movement. When things were bad, to ease my angst, I ran or jumped. As an adult, time and time again, I have turned to the discipline of movement and dance as a way to manage life's changes. I have a dance therapy background, but more importantly, I have learned a set of techniques. LifeDancing is the movement process I created for dancing with life; it is the choreography of change.

THE EVOLVING DANCE

The moment I published this book, it needed updating. That is often the case with the nonfiction books. I have a curious mind and am always discovering new information and ways of looking at things. To keep my Editor happy, and knowing updates are endless for me, I refer you to a webpage that I'll now shift my additions and editions to. Please visit www.LifeDancing.com/updates to continue your exploration of LifeDancing. If you discover something you believe can enhance this dance, send them to Linda@LifeDancing.com and put LifeDancing in the subject line.

Onward!

Linda

Introduction

DANCER-IN-TRAINING

*Y*ou may have many reasons for picking up this book. You may be focused on what you want, what you don't have, or you may only be able to focus on your current pain and struggles. Fortunately, LifeDancing teaches you how to meet any life challenge at any stage of your life. LifeDancing gives you a new way of moving through life no matter where your needs fall, from survival to self-transcendence.

I know that today many of you are bombarded with other people's solutions for creating the life they believe you should live. I'm suggesting that you are the expert on your life and might first look inward, because resources and answers lie within you that you may have never known, or used.

Each of us carries inside of ourselves the tools and wisdom we need to create a unique, joyful dance of life. Unfortunately, sometimes we don't use these resources wisely because we look for answers outside.

LifeDancing hands you the keys to your inner wisdom and unique solutions to a joyful life. LifeDancing brings peace of mind because it shows you that you have the power – the tools, the vision, the goals and the plans – to create your best life possible. You'll discover your unique life's movement, and following that, you'll discover your center, your inner source of joy, lasting peace and well-being.

YOUR INVITATION TO THE DANCE

Life is a dance of constant change.

In every life, there are dances of joy and sorrow, beauty and horror, tribulation and peace.

That's life.

But we can dance with the grand symphony of it all when we know how to move with the music of life.

> "

A journey
of a thousand miles must
begin with a single step.

LAO TSU

> "

What we have
currently available is what
we have available.

PAUL BROWN

LifeDancing is a way to live and be.

This book teaches you simple ways to live in harmony with all around you, to be in the world but not controlled by it.

When you live in harmony with yourself, you invite more joy, beauty and peace into your life, creating a well-being lifestyle.

LifeDancing enhances your ability to attract peace and joy. The research of Martin Seligman, author of *Authentic Happiness*, shows us that people with a happy outlook on life live longer, have better relationships, do better work ... and on and on. For me, there is no other option but to experience and enjoy the life I'm living. Suffering is my cue to let go and dance on.

LifeDancing teaches you how to live authentically so that you tap into that deep place of peace that you may be surprised to find resides within. It has taken much courage and determination for me to be able to access this place. Now, peace is always available to me when I notice it missing. It's available to you as well!

In this book, I'll share with you how you can find that deep place within whenever you choose. It will no longer elude you; it will always welcome you home.

Using the principles of LifeDancing; the assessments that deepen your self-understanding; the **MASTER CLASS WORKBOOK** that supports this book; and your **LIFEDANCING JOURNAL**, I'll show you how you can dance on the razor's edge of life in dynamic balance. This is the ever-moving place on which we balance between the then, the now, and the new, the person we believe we are and the person we are becoming.

Before I understood how to dance with life, I tumbled and stumbled many times not knowing what to do next. Understand that when we hit bumps in the road, these are the intersections where "life happens." Full, authentic living happens at these junctures of change, where there is no stasis, no resting on your laurels. I know about embracing the new, accepting change, being centered – and uncentered – through it all. I know the dance I can trust, my LifeDance. Through LifeDancing, I have dreamed of impossible things – and lived those dreams, with hard work, enthusiasm and vision. It's how I've risen from the ashes when my life went up in flames. Dancing with Life is the way of living that assures me that I will continue to live life with no regrets and a sense of passion and adventure for each day.

LifeDancing is why I continue to dare to dream. I invite you to dance your best possible Dance of Life.

THE ESSENCE OF LIFEDANCING

LifeDancing is for everyone who wonders how to experience joy in her life. It doesn't matter who or where you are. Right here, right in this moment, if you are breathing, you can experience joy. You can even design a life that's centered in this joy.

It does not matter if your circumstances are not ideal. You do not have to have the perfect job or the perfect relationship. As life coach Pat McHenry Sullivan, founder of Work With Meaning and Joy, says so well:

> *Dare to dream,*
> *to speak the language of your heart,*
> *to shape its longings into clear visions with*
> *solid goals and objectives.*

> *Dare to do,*
> *to build your visions with integrity, and the*
> *joys of stretching your skills far beyond their*
> *present capacity.*

LifeDancing is a way to live your life, much like the steps of a dance. The essential steps include:

- **DISCOVERING YOUR AUTHENTIC SELF**. This happens by opening your awareness to your inner dancer with a neutral/noncritical compassionate eye. This is the center from which all movement originates.

- **FINDING THE COURAGE TO HONOR YOUR DREAMS**. Many times I've thought, felt or imagined something I thought others would not agree with or support. It takes courage and a willingness to stand fast and to honor what emerges from within.

- **BEING OPEN TO JOY, LOVE AND COMPASSION**. Often it is eas-

"

The question is not whether we will die, but how we will live.

JOAN BORYSENKO

"

It is no doubt possible to fly - but first you must know how to dance like an angel.

FRIEDRICH NIETZSCHE

"

Bravery is stability, not
of legs and arms,
but of courage and the soul.

MICHEL DE MONTAIGNE

ier to find compassion for everyone except ourselves. The world needs more of these qualities, and it can happen one person at a time. Live authentically and move from your center at all times. This is the essence of LifeDancing.

THE MAKING OF A LIFEDANCER OR, IF I CAN DO IT SO CAN YOU!

I've been there, done that, tie-dyed T-shirts and written journals full of great stories about amazing adventures. I know survival firsthand, personally and professionally. Working in state mental hospitals for 18 years, I know life at the bottom of the bucket. I discovered that no matter how low you go, there can be compassion, light and joy, when you are open to it. LifeDancing is the integration of what I learned as a teen parent, welfare mother, working mother, student, professional, spiritual seeker and student of life.

To give you a sense of how LifeDancing emerged, here's my story: I grew up with a single parent who periodically brought in boyfriends and stepfathers for flavor. It made for a life fraught with chaos and rocky with change. I always knew there had to be an easier way to live. My escape to a place of joy and peace was at the beach listening to the ocean and finding that sweet spot in the water where I could float and gently feel the rhythm and flow of the sea. The rest of the time I did the best I could to keep my eyes open, watching the changes, honoring what I knew and was drawn to, and trying to be as honest with myself as I could, amidst the chaos called my life.

I got out of a difficult home life by getting pregnant at 16. My peers thought I was cool marrying the handsome champion surfer and living at the beach, but teenagers' raising a baby with no family help – that's a difficult road to walk. Divorce came quickly, and I had to figure out how to support my beautiful daughter and myself, alone, at the age of 18. It was clear that lying on the beach all day was not an option. I had to work as hard as I could to survive. While my peers were off to college and supported by their parents, I worked as a waitress. Yes, there was intermittent joy, peace and beauty, but life mostly was struggling to survive. This was a time when being a welfare teen parent and divorcee was greeted with suspicion, something like walking around with the plague in earlier times. Hard work paid off though. I finished my high school degree and kept looking for better jobs.

In my mid-20s, I was working in aerospace in a job I hated and was spiraling downward in a difficult relationship while raising a small child on my own. My emotional confusion and pain became so overpowering that I knew I needed help. I sought out a psychiatrist, Dr. B., who I thought would heal me. Instead, he told me I was the creator of my own world and would have to, with guidance, fix it myself. Darn, no heroes in that office! Step one was to take complete responsibility for the mess I had created. Step two was to discover what I wanted and third, to make it so.

I remember walking out of my first therapy session, I saw the world in a new light. Dr. B's message was so simple, yet so very powerful: You can create any life you want!

Eventually, I left my aerospace job and went to work for the psychiatrist, wanting to learn everything I could about being human. But soon after that, Dr. B. unexpectedly downsized his practice. Suddenly, I was a welfare mother once again. I couldn't go back to aerospace; my spirit was dying there. I knew life could be good, so I went to school at the Fashion Institute of Merchandising and Design in Los Angeles and began designing clothes and jewelry. My clothing line's tag was: "Clothes that are as beautiful on the inside as the outside." The pieces I created sold well and soon other designers were stealing them and making their own knock-offs. I was too young and naive to take them to task for it, so I changed fields.

In those years, the late '60s, the state of California offered a program that would pay for school and child care if you committed to working in the California state mental hospitals for a year after receiving your degree. Little did I know that I was looking at an education on just how low people could go – staff and clients!

It was during this stressful, overscheduled time that I came to believe that to reach my goals, I had to take control of every aspect of my life. I was a single welfare mother, working part-time, going to school full-time, raising my daughter and juggling all of the other daily chores necessary to keep us afloat. This was when LifeDancing emerged.

My LifeDancing approach was a synthesis of inner work, creativity, time and energy management, intuitive guidance, cognitive growth and accountability. I found LifeDancing worked very, very well. There was virtually no problem that

"

Follow what you are genuinely passionate about and let that guide you to your destination.

DIANE SAWYER

> "
>
> Leadership is the capacity to translate vision into reality.
>
> WARREN BENNIS

arose – and they did all the time – that I could not sort out and move through. Over the many years that have followed those times, the LifeDancing way of living has deepened into a Dance of Being.

LifeDancing saw me through disastrous relationships, raising a happy daughter, completing my psychotherapy degree, remarrying, getting licensed as a psychotherapist in California and Massachusetts, writing three books and starting three successful practices. I have created a positive psychology and pro-fessional life coaching business, become trained as a Mindfulness-Based Stress Reduction (MBSR) educator and continue to grow, change and love my life and work.

LifeDancing includes the fundamentals of personal organization and self-leadership, integrates positive psychology and the emerging fields of coach-ing, mindfulness and neuroscience. LifeDancing gives you the tools you need to create the life of your dreams. At first it takes commitment and hard work on your part, but eventually it becomes second nature, and, believe me, it's worth it. The voyage for me has not always been smooth. I have traveled to the depths of depression and back again. At the bottom I found I had a choice – death or not. I chose life, and life is movement.

Finally, life continues to change, and my dance with life is choreographed every day.

With LifeDancing, you'll live life with no regrets. I offer **LIFEDANC-ING**, the **MASTER CLASS WORKBOOK**, and the **LIFEDANCING JOURNAL** to help you discover how to create your own joyful LifeDance.

YOUR PERSONAL INVITATION

Over the years, I've held a constant, abiding belief about the beauty of each person and her ability to discover and champion her individuality, strengths and unique gifts. Words cannot completely capture the magnificence of being with people as they discover themselves, and take responsibility and control of their LifeDance.

For professionals reading this book, LifeDancing is a tool to be used when clients are ready to take on the responsibility of being the leader of their own lives. I know by experience, it is no small feat to expand from the allopathic, disease- or problem-oriented medical model, most every psychotherapist is taught in order to obtain a professional license, to a wholistic or homeopathic approach. It takes faith and work to move to a strengths and values-based orientation. An integral positive psychology approach is generally not supported in our field or by our professional associations, but a values-based, mindful, client-directed approach is gaining credence as research is proving how well it works. LifeDancing gives you, and your clients, the tools you need for healthy personal and professional change.

In the pages that follow, you will see that the dance of life takes place on many stages. The tools I give you will help you weave the interplay of movements into an integral Dance of Self. As you create a dialogue between your inner and outer worlds, you'll discover a center in yourself from which all movement and action originates. What follows is a sense of authenticity, trust in yourself, and peace of mind in all that you are and do.

"

He who avoids complaint invites happiness.

ABU BAKR

Beyond the Book LifeDancing

THE MASTER CLASS WORKBOOK, THE LIFEDANCING JOURNAL

THE BOOK. LifeDancing is the master plan. It's a guidebook that provides resources and assessments that help you develop the essential concepts of Life-Dancing – authenticity, centering, dreaming and living in joy, beauty, compassion and peace. First, you step within, and then you look to how the Inner Dancer expresses itself out in the world. I then give you guides and resources as you perform your LifeDance in and on the stages of life. Finally, I leave you with ways to keep performing and perfecting your LifeDance, long after you lay this book down. Within the chapters, the appendices, **MASTER CLASS WORKBOOK** and your **LIFEDANCING JOURNAL** you'll find practical information and references to more resources. There's also room in the margins to include your own resources and ideas. Keep this book where you can easily find it. Use sticky notes or a beautiful bookmark to help you find your favorite pages or exercises you're working on. Read this book as you would eat a fine meal, slowly and with relish. It's not the kind of book to savor in one sitting.

To get your copies of the **MASTER CLASS WORKBOOK** and the **LIFEDANCING JOURNAL**, go to www.lifedancing.com.

GOING DEEPER

MASTER CLASS WORKBOOK. In Master Class: The Authentic Dancer Workbook, you deepen and expand your explorations. Master Class gives you a place to capture your experiences, explore, deepen and experiment with ideas in this book.

"

The good life is one inspired by love and guided by knowledge.

BERTRAND RUSSELL

"

The act of putting pen to paper encourages pause for thought, this in turn makes us think more deeply about life, which helps us regain our equilibrium.

N. PLATT

YOUR COMPANION

Your LIFEDANCING JOURNAL. The personal journal has been used as a tool for self-exploration since ancient times. Many journal records have created insights so universal that they have survived to present day.

Many different people in different cultures and times chose to journal their inner voyages because journaling is a free-flowing and effective way to make the invisible real and the unknown known.

When you write in your journal, write what you want and when you want. Don't allow anyone, **and that includes you**, to judge or edit the content. Thus, there are only two rules:

1. Your journal must be a protected environment in which you suspend self-judgment.

2. Your journal must also be protected from the eyes of others. If it is a book, lock it or keep it in a safe place; if it is on the computer, password-protect it.

Use your **LIFEDANCING JOURNAL** as a companion to LifeDancing and Master Class. If you are going to include pictures and other items in your journal, keep your journal in a binder to which you can add pages. For example, in Step Two: Turning Out, you'll create a Design Guide, which can also be connected to your journal. I also suggest that you carry 3x5 or 5x8 index cards, or a small pad, to write on when you are away from your journal. That way, you can insert them into your Journal or Design Guide later.

Ideally, your vision of your future is dynamic. You imagine one kind of future today, and maybe a new kind of future tomorrow. Keep a record of these visions in your **LIFEDANCING JOURNAL**. Over time, you'll begin to discover themes and repeated visions. Visions are like clothes: You may have a lot, but there are probably some in which you feel most comfortable. These are the ones you'll explore first. They may be two-edged, comfortable and scary, or comfortable and confining. The best combination is comfortable and exciting. These are the visions and images that are the impetus for your dance of life. They are the clothes or costumes that motivate you to move and express who you are, who you're becoming, and help make your vision reality.

Some of you may already be comfortable with writing in a journal; some of you might still be wondering if you need to take the time. To inspire you, research[1] has shown that the mere act of writing down your innermost thoughts and feelings reduces stress and allows you to find personal solutions to your problems or questions.

Don't overthink this. Your **LIFEDANCING JOURNAL** is simply a good friend. It's a repository for your innermost thoughts, and it's easier than you think.

Write what you want.

Write when you want.

No one sees it.

Suspend judgment.

Remember, to get your copies of the **MASTER CLASS WORKBOOK** and the **LIFEDANCING JOURNAL**, go to www.lifedancing.com.

Have fun.

On with the dance!

"

Either write something worth reading or do something worth writing.

BENJAMIN FRANKLIN

THE STEPS

The Steps of the LifeDance
MASTERING LIFE'S MOVEMENT

I have chosen the metaphor of dance because it best fits the dynamic of life. Dance is movement and change, even in states of stillness.

When you watch a dancer who has mastered her art, her dance appears effortless. This state of self-mastery comes from a lot of practice, and the development of a strong center. She is always moving -- jumping, leaping or twirling. As she dances with others, there is harmony. Their moves are relational. They are individuals, complete, yet parts of a bigger whole.

Dance can be the movement of serene beauty or confidence in motion. Likewise, our own dance of life is a gradual unfolding. The skill of personal leadership does not come instantly; it grows over time. Paradoxically, the dancer who moves with greatest ease has also surrendered to the dance.

This book honors and meets you no matter where you are in life. It takes your hand and invites you to dance a life of your own design.

No more do you need to engage in a dance someone else has choreographed. You become the creator of your LifeDance in every moment. Come, harken to your inner music. Come join the dance.

> Dance, dance, wherever you may be
>
> I am the lord of the dance, said he
>
> And I lead you all, wherever you may be
>
> And I lead you all in the dance, said he
>
> - Lyrics from the *Celtic Lord of the Dance*

This book is organized in four steps, or sections:

Step One | THE AUTHENTIC DANCER: TURNING IN

Each dancer must know her center, the place from which she moves. In this section, you will meet and discover Your Authentic Dancer. You'll explore the Dance of Selves, roles, archetypes (underlying patterns), personal preferences, and discover your Motivations, Needs and Values.

Step Two | THE AUTHENTIC DANCER: TURNING OUT

As you move across the stages of your life, you best move with vision and passion. To do this you need to have your life purpose clearly defined.

In these chapters, we'll explore a purpose within a purpose.

Using Purpose as your compass, you'll turn your inner vision out to the world. You'll build a strong foundation using goal-setting, planning and time-management. Applying wholistic problem-solving you'll move through and around bumps in your dance. By creating your LifeDance Design Guide and visualizations you'll know you're honoring your unique dance of life every day.

Step Three | TAKING THE STAGE: THE DANCE ARENAS

We all live and move in many arenas of life.

Work. Relationships. Home.

Body. Mind. Emotions. Spirit.

These are the places where you perform your LifeDance. This section breaks down arenas of your life, one by one, showing you how to learn more about, and enhance and refine your dance in each arena.

Step Four | PERFORMING: MASTERING LIFE'S MOVEMENT

A solid, consistent performance results from practice, practice, practice.

In this section, you learn how to set up ways to be accountable to yourself, moving from your center. You'll deepen your definition of excellence, and you'll identify the ethics that guide you as you perform and integrate your Dance of Life. This section shows you how performing is not only about doing, but being and surrendering to the dance and joy of life.

Step One

TURNING IN

In each life, there is a unique cadence, an ebb and flow, as life flows from one
moment into the next. We each move to our own cadence. We become aware,
knowing who we are, and then we often wander into distraction.
Together, apart, together, apart. Our selves are the known and unknown at once.
We circle, returning to moments and memories that color our lives.
In this way, we dance eternally with the past, the present and the future.
We dance our lives as this mystery re-creates and unfolds within and around us.

THE DANCE OF SELF

We must embrace all parts of ourselves.
Understand your roles and deepen your understanding of your master patterns or
archetypes.

THE CENTER:
YOUR AUTHENTIC DANCER

Honor yourself as you are from moment to moment.

THE DANCE OF STORY

We are all unfolding stories.
Use the power of narrative to design your future story.
We all carry within us deep, sometimes unconscious stories. The more we know
about these stories, the more choices we have in each moment.

THE INNER DANCER & THE CONSCIOUS AUDIENCE

Turning inward is the dance of mindfulness, of knowing your inner dancer. We do this by attuning ourselves
to the present moment and acknowledging and honoring what emerges.

CHAPTER ONE

The Dance of Self

W ho are you? A provocative question with many answers. You get up in the morning. You stretch. You feed the cat or the dog. You make coffee or tea. You brush your teeth. You catch your eye in the mirror. You fuss with your hair. On this day, you may stay in your jammies for a quiet day, dress for work in business attire, or you may slip into sweats and go walking.

Who are you today? Are you the person with the strong voice, with the gleam of joy in her eye, and a smile on her face? Are you the young mother, the wise woman, the maiden; the father or heroine?

What voice calls to you, bids you to dance today? What sun warms your face? What light radiates from your being? The writer of this poem, which I heard years and years ago, conveys wonderfully the turning away from the shadows that dim our eyes to who we are, turning instead, inward, to the light that is within.

THE DANCER

The yonder calling is heard
Dance thee between thy shadows
Youthful folly has served thee well
Turn to the sun
For you are the light
Shining piercingly
Through thy own heart
Be true to yourself
Warm your soul
For you are your creator
Moving in majestic glory
Drinking from thy own cup
Deeply and joyously
As you leap into your profound future

-- anonymous or unknown

"

The first wealth

is health.

RALPH WALDO EMERSON

LIFE IS CONSTANT MOVEMENT

Imagine a surfer riding a large wave. She doesn't stop her movement on the wave to figure out how to manage it; she simply positions herself in the best place she can find to ride it as it unfolds. So it is in today's world where we experience much more change than previous generations. We may have more than one career, marry more than once and relocate more frequently. We may have times in our lives when we have children, but later, free from the obligations of child-rearing, there is a new life to live. Many of us create new careers and explore avenues that called to us earlier in life.

When I look back over my life, it seems as if I'm viewing frames of a movie, each from a previous lifetime. I was a child, a teen, then a teen mother. I was a hippie, living in the 1960s, who was very curious about life. I entered college, became a nurse and then a psychotherapist. Later, I was a business woman, author, teacher, coach and consultant. Now I'm a grandparent, friend and philosopher. My life work has changed over the years. Initially, as a nurse and clinical mental health professional, I focused on pathology – looking for disease via the DSM (Diagnostic and Statistical Manual). I looked for what wasn't working in people's lives applying insurance-mandated treatment protocols. Now, free of insurance and managed-care organizations, I've moved to a life-affirming wellness model. I explore how to counsel and teach others about living a life of quality and well-being, by discovering and honoring their own ability to heal and guide their lives toward happiness and peace of mind. Currently my passion is to help other professionals create practices that bridge the full spectrum – from working in the medical model treating illness, to offering services and products to promote wellness and optimal living. If you are a professional and find this intriguing, check out the Professional Practice Institute at www.ProfessionalPracticeInstitute.com. I no longer only look for what is wrong, but what is right with people, and build on that. Western medicine is the first place I turned when I broke my leg, but it no longer is where I look for prevention and optimal wellness.

This life dance has been a constant flow of external and internal change. It could not have happened 50 years ago. There is so much information available now that when there is an internal shift or desire to explore new ideas, it is easy to look outward and discover others who are asking the same questions and looking for new ways to be and move. To stay afloat in this sea of change, one must have a sturdy vessel, namely a sturdy sense of self, that can withstand the constancy and speed of the tides and winds of change.

THE OH SO CURIOUS SELF

The concept of "self," or individual dancer, is new in human history. In ancient societies, the concept of the individual existed only as necessary to serve the survival of the tribe. Tribal leaders suppressed any consciousness of one's self as separate from the tribe. This was still the case in hierarchal societies, in which a monarch or priest was deemed to be all-wise, and the individual yielded to the authority of the rulers who looked out for the whole of society.

Later, philosophers such as Aristotle began to espouse the concept of individualism. His ideas encouraged self-fulfillment, or entelechy, which means "having the end within itself." In some mystic traditions, this process is described as an essence actively working to know itself. Self-realization or self-actualization becomes the process of the "self" emerging.

In the 17th century, the French philosopher Descartes arrived at the concept of the self as an entity that thinks – "I think, therefore I am." English enlightenment philosopher John Locke carried that concept further, defining the self through a "continuity of consciousness." He believed that we are constantly creating the concept of the future self. In the 18th century, Scottish philosopher David Hume defined the self by its ability to perceive – to form impressions and ideas and interpretations. Without perception, Hume said, one ceased to exist. Because perception changes over time, the self changes over time. He saw the self as dynamic.

New age philosophers see the self as a continually re-creating dynamic, ideally in harmony with past, present and future. The Buddhist concept of self is one that is a process, not a static thing. The belief is that our bodies and minds change from moment to moment, that we do not exist separately from the multiple streams of causality that created the self who exists in this moment. Others relinquish the Self to spirit as it unfolds in the vehicle of Self. In any case, if you believe you are unique – that is, a unique human expression and experience, you are aware of your dynamic Self. Think of your Self as a tool

> "
>
> Develop an interest in life as you see it; the people, things, literature, music – the world is so rich, simply throbbing with rich treasures, beautiful souls and interesting people. Forget yourself.
>
> **HENRY MILLER**

you use as you dance through life. **Honor your Self and know that you are much more as well.**

THE DANCE OF SELVES

Who you are, ideally, is constant, yet diverse and dynamic. You have your inner sense of who you are. Then there is the outer YOU – the YOU that presents itself to the world or stage on which you are dancing (work, home, school). Then there may be an Ideal-Self, the vision of a future self that that motivates and calls to you. This vision may have begun when somebody asked you as a child, "What do you want to be when you grow up?" All of these selves can be present at the same time. For example, when I was a psychotherapist intern, I carried with me an internal sense of who I was, my self who played the role of intern and my vision of what I was becoming as I learned my craft.

When we are open to watching, learning from and allowing this dance of selves, we can observe, integrate, and be at peace with them all. We can watch the dances unfold and enjoy and appreciate their joy and creativity. When we are cut off from or critical of one or more of these selves, the dance becomes dissonant, or out of harmony.

It may be difficult to understand all of these parts of ourselves. It may be hard to embrace all of them. They may seem incongruent at times. They may seem disparate – identities that cannot be held together in any one dancer. The key to individuating – the process in psychology in which differentiated components tend toward becoming a more indivisible whole – is first awareness and acknowledgment, acceptance and then embracing and integrating the parts.

When you are willing to explore yourself, you begin to see a fluidity and thread of connection between the parts that connects them. This integral self is your Authentic Dancer. This is the part of you that is wiser than any one of the single pieces. This is the part of you that expresses who you are, creatively and joyfully in every moment.

Learn to trust the wisdom of your Authentic Dancer. Move with the fluidity of your life, and you can master your own sea of change.

MANY DANCERS

To become integrated and centered, we must explore the many inner selves and discover their commonalities. I think of them as different dancers:

THE INNER DANCER. This is our inner sense of self. This is the part of us that reflects on the world. It's the part of us that thinks, feels, remembers. The Inner Dancer gives meaning to our experiences, creating interpretations and stories about who we are.

THE PERFORMER. This is the social self, the dancer who performs in the world. This self is defined by the face we present to others. The Performer is defined by the roles we play in life. She is the way we interact on our many stages – home, work, family – and the way we identify ourselves through those many experiences.

THE IDEAL DANCER. This is the self we are becoming. This is our potentiality, the future self we become in every moment. The vision of the Ideal Dancer creates a dynamic tension that moves us forward.

To tap into Your Authentic Dancer, you must seek fluidity and congruence between these three dancers. As you achieve this, you'll discover an ease and flow to your LifeDance. Conflict and struggle are markers pointing to the places where these three dancers are not aware of, or congruent with, each other. Walk toward your cannons – meaning, don't avoid your inner fear, pain or confusion. Explore your inner dissonance. If there is something you are avoiding, do it the first thing each day. If you are confused, explore it in your meditation. If you feel pain, put your awareness on it and observe how it changes. Curiosity is what unpacks your inner mysteries.

Know that all parts seek resonance and harmony – all the time.

THE DANCE OF DISSONANCE: A DANCER WITH BRUISED KNEES

Like you, I have experienced dissonance in my life when my dancers were not congruent with one another. It's natural to want to shy away from dissonance. When we hear it in music, we want to cover our ears. Dissonance can cause a growing sense of confusion. What I eventually learned, through personal experience and reflection, was to relax and observe the dance of dissonance and allow the power of the dance to move it into harmony. Here is one story

> **"**
>
> Dancing is like dreaming with your feet.
>
> ## CONSTANZE

"

Do not rise so high you lose
touch with others.

I CHING

that may help you understand how this can happen.

I felt dissonance when I moved from Massachusetts to California for family reasons. In Massachusetts, I was a psychotherapist working in a private practice and teaching. That was my identity. I envisioned my life unfolding into roles in which I would write and teach, sharing my experience and insights with new and practicing therapists. When I moved back to California, I struggled to establish a consulting business, rather than a private practice, because my family needed me to be more available than a private practice allows. My Inner Dancer was still a healer or therapist, a teacher and consultant to other professionals, but in the general business community – on the new stage – my Performer was not congruent in the new role.

I experienced a period of professional dissonance, but I kept exploring it. I turned in. I reconnected with my values: love of learning, creativity, beauty, bravery, hope and optimism. I networked, taught, spoke of the benefits of wellness, used the skills I had developed to facilitate creativity in individuals and groups, and still found that people perceived me as a psychotherapist. As hard as I tried, the dancer of my past still was my public presence. I struggled with how to move into my next Dance of Self. My personal preference is to reach out using intuition and big-picture thinking, so I knew I needed to take some time to step back, look at the whole of my life and think of a new approach, or dance.

After a few days on retreat, the big "duh" hit me. I had been teaching professionals for years, guiding them in how to develop a practice or business developmentally, and all I had to do was follow my own teachings. I simply needed to specialize in an arena that was already well-researched and congruent with my values, personal preferences and beliefs. I was already a meditator, so I moved naturally to Mindfulness-Based Stress Reduction (MBSR), a program that integrates wellness and the skills I learned as a psychotherapist. I trained with Jon Kabat-Zinn, Saki Santorelli, Bob Stahl and others. I did what I believed was necessary for any teacher/healer: I walked the talk, enriching my own meditation practice. I shaped it to my own strengths and skills. The next step was simply presenting this new professional identity to the clinical and business community. Because I'm comfortable to go much deeper into a person or topic than most other consultants, coaches and teachers, the framework I describe is now Depth Coaching, Consulting, and Integrative Psychotherapy. The match seems to fit well, inside and out; now there is a congruence between who I am, what I do, and how I present myself.

Coming full circle, I, and you, will become both the dancer and the appreciative audience. As the Dance of Self unfolds, we watch the interplay, discover insights, adjust steps, send loving kindness to the bruised knees and confused minds, and enter the creativity and joy of the dance of life.

"

You know, if you hang around this earth long enough you really see how things come full circle.

PATTI DAVIS

CHAPTER TWO

Your Authentic Dancer

*A*gain: Who are you?

Have you ever wondered why some people are kind and gentle and others not so much? Why there are people you feel safe and comfortable with, and others who scare or repulse you? Yes, we're all very different. Each one of us functions, either consciously or not, from a set of values and beliefs we carry with us and act from, influencing how we ARE in the world.

When you are clear about your values and beliefs, they are like a handrail on a staircase; they are there to guide you, to touch as you take a step and sometimes reach out to for support. Your values and beliefs can also be your touchstones, helping you clearly express your Authentic Dancer.

Your values are the rhythm of your dance. What you value – what you hold to be true and worthy and base your beliefs on – they define the foundational rhythm of your movement through life.

ACTING FROM YOUR VALUES

When I walk into a room, I see shapes and colors. I notice where items are placed in relation to each other. In an instant, I sense whether there is harmony in the room. If the room is beautiful, I'm immediately and palpably aware of that.

On the other hand, when my husband walks into a room, being a "techie" he's looking for electrical outlets to power his computer. (He denies this).

I value harmony and beauty. My husband values functionality. We see things differently!

Values change over time and sometimes they are in conflict. When you're aware of them, they can be used differently in various areas of life – work, home, and leisure.

Do not let your ambition
diminish your integrity.

I CHING

Life is essentially
a question of values.

MEIR
KAHANE

THE SIX CORE PRINCIPLES OF VALUES

We use values to evaluate our actions and those of others. When we feel sorry about something we said or did, it's because we violated a personal value.

A few truths about values:

- **Values motivate us.** When we discover a new way to apply our values, it brings us happiness.

- **Values are hierarchical.** Some are more important than others.

- **Values can change over time.** As new aspects of life become more important, our values evolve.

- **Values can conflict.** When values are in conflict, we may follow one sometimes and another other times, creating conflicting results.

- **Values are the foundation of our beliefs.** We create and support our beliefs based on our values. If I value beauty, then I may believe that a home is not comfortable unless it is beautiful.

THE HEARTBEAT OF YOUR DANCE

Because your values color every aspect of how you live your life, it is foundationally important to know what your personal values are. To help you identify your values, I have used Marty Seligman and Chris Peterson's[2] extensive research on values and explain Values around the six Core Values that are believed to be universal.

MASTER CATEGORIES

Wisdom & Knowledge

Courage

Humanity

Justice

Temperance

Transcendence

Look at the expanded list below and ask yourself what your driving values are. Put a check mark next to the ones you believe are a constant in your life.

WISDOM AND KNOWLEDGE

Creativity

Curiosity

Open-mindedness

Critical Thinking

Love of Learning

Wisdom

COURAGE

Bravery

Persistence, Perseverance

Integrity

Authenticity

Enthusiasm

Vitality

HUMANITY

Love

Kindness

Generosity

Nurturing

Social Intelligence

Emotional Intelligence

JUSTICE

Citizenship

Loyalty

Teamwork

Fairness

Equality

Leadership

"

What you risk reveals
what you value.

JENETTE WINTERSON

"

Nothing endures but personal qualities.

WALT WHITMAN

TEMPERANCE

Forgiveness

Mercy

Humility

Modesty

Prudence

Self-Regulation

TRANSCENDENCE

Appreciation of Beauty & Excellence

Gratitude

Hope & Optimism

Future Orientation

Humor & Playfulness

Spirituality

To discover a deeper assessment of your Values, turn to your **MASTER CLASS WORKBOOK** and complete Assessment | 1.2a | **THE HEART-BEAT OF THE DANCE: YOUR VALUES**.

WHAT FOOT DO YOU PREFER TO START WITH?

Your personal preferences determine how you move to the beat of life, which hand you reach with or foot you start on when you leap into your dance. When you know your preferences, and the preferences of those people you are in relationship with, you know more about yourself and the differences and commonalities between you. Suddenly, instead of believing other people only do what they do so they can drive you crazy, it shifts to "she is different from me and how can we complement one another?" To determine what your preferences are, I suggest you take a simple self-assessment. Many personality preference tests are out there, but one that I have found to be the most reliable for revealing to people how they operate in life is the Myers Briggs Personality Type Indicator. The results are not good or bad, only how you are unique. The assessment was developed in the 1920s by Katherine Briggs and her daughter,

Isabel Myers, and is widely used today in many fields.

The Myers Briggs test helps you identify your preferences for:

• Determining your orientation

• Taking in information

• Using information

• Making decisions

The assessment is useful as a tool for self-knowledge, but it's also useful for understanding how we are different in fundamental ways.

DETERMINING YOUR ORIENTATION. Some people are extroverts, while some are introverts. Extroverts are oriented outwardly, seeking contact with people or things, and they are oriented on acting, rather than receiving or waiting. Introverts are oriented inward, to ideas, concepts and abstractions.

TAKING IN INFORMATION. Every individual has a preference for taking in information (perception) and a preference for reaching conclusions (judgment). We each have preferences for how much time we spend making decisions or judgments about the information we take in.

USING INFORMATION. Some of us like to rely on our five senses (the details) – taste, touch, sight, smell or hearing. Others glean information intuitively (big picture) – relying on gut feelings or hunches.

MAKING DECISIONS. When we make decisions, some of us emphasize our thinking ability, relying on analysis or logic. These people place a premium on fairness, one of the tenets of the core value of Justice. But other people make decisions based on their feelings. These people place a premium on harmony.

For a simple self-assessment, check off the statements below that best describe your preferences in a specific arena like home or work.

To quickly identify your preferences, select one of each of the two choices you are given. Make a check mark next to the answer you choose. You'll end up with a four letter acronym like ENTJ, which represents your personality preferences.

"

Every person's every action has an effect.

ROSANNE CASH

"

I'm always my own

person.

LITTLE RICHARD

Given the choice of what to do for an enjoyable evening I would prefer to:

1 - Go to a party. OR ...

2 - Stay home with a good book or movie.

When I'm speaking with a longtime friend on the telephone:

3 - I forget the time and talk until the friend has to go. OR...

4 - Usually I am the one who has to end the conversation.

If I were a decorator and was helping a friend decorate their home, the first question I would ask is:

5 - What is your budget? OR...

6 - What is your vision for this space?

You are serving lunch to five children around 8 years old. Lunch consists of macaroni and cheese with a glass of milk. When you serve, do you:

7 - Line up the plates and glasses and give each child the same portion. OR...

8 - Ask each child how much she wants.

Now, put a check mark by your choice for each pair:

1 - Extrovert E _____

2 - Introvert I _____

3 - Perceiving P _____

4 - Judging J _____

5 - Sensory S _____

6 - iNtuitive N _____

7 - Thinking T _____

8 - Feeling F _____

Myers-Briggs indicators

I am a (an) _____ _____ _____ _____.

For a more in-depth assessment go to http://www.capt.org/take-mbti-assessment/mbti.htm and pay for a personal assessment.

For another assessment of your Personality Preferences, turn to your **MASTER CLASS WORKBOOK** and complete Assessment | 1.2b | **YOUR PERSONALITY PREFERENCES**.

Can't make a selection between the choices? Or do you find the assessment here and in the **MASTER CLASS WORKBOOK** are different? Then I suggest you ask a professional to administer the Myers-Briggs Type Indicator.[3] It's important to be clear on your personality preferences; it's like a dancer who knows that she starts her leap from her left foot or her right foot. Knowing this is the way to begin your LifeDance on solid footing.

MOTIVATED SKILLS

I can make an excellent brownie, both vegan and not. In my lifetime, I've probably baked enough brownies, rum balls and chocolate chip cookies to sink a ship. This creation of delicious tidbits is a skill, but it is not one I choose to do. There are rules to be followed when nurturing a LifeDance, one of which is, "Don't do it if it doesn't feel right." Your spirit will be dancing elsewhere if you do.

Few of us have the luxury to do only what we want to do, or feel good about. Most of us are attached to where we live, the people we are in relationship with, the work we do and much, much more.

These external structures begin designing what we do, rather than our inner spirit and dancer. Unfortunately we may even begin to NOT notice what we like. I invite you to look with fresh eyes at what you're doing, and ask yourself if that is YOUR dance, or one you're caught up in. Most of us have many skills we are not even aware of, so step one is looking at what we do during the day and identify what we do well (or not), enjoy (or not) and also identify the times you aren't even aware of what you do, or did.

You'll also have to send your inner critic on vacation because competence can be in the eye of the beholder. Ask her to let you just be objective about activities and not place a good or bad value on it unless someone is getting hurt. Start with the assumption that over the years, you have developed many skills; they simply need to be clarified and identified. You also may have recent or new skills you are currently growing and exploring. If you are enjoying the learning process, these also need to be identified as emerging, motivated skills. To help you get started, here are some general skill categories.

1 FUNCTIONAL TRANSFERABLE SKILLS. These are natural tendencies you have, that can be applied to your life and work. They showed up early in life and may have been a constant in your self-expression. For example, as a child, I always took things apart to see how they worked or related to one another. I still do it, and I have learned that another important skill is putting

> I rate enthusiasm even above professional skill.
>
> ## EDWARD APPLETON

"

Skill and confidence are
an unconquered army.

GEORGE
HERBERT

things back together again. For example, my daughter was an animated story-teller, and still is today. It's an excellent match that she went into communications and owns a teleprompting business. What are your natural skills?

2 **SELF-MANAGEMENT SKILLS.** Self-management is your ability to manage yourself in different environments and situations. These days, brain researchers look at our brains in different situations and measure just how we "manage" ourselves. The brain's frontal lobes are the "executives" of the system, but when we are emotionally out of balance - in fight-or-flight mode – the part of the brain that's firing overloads, or floods, our management system; then we do deeds or say words we sometimes have to apologize for later. It's a good idea to be very honest with yourself about these skills. If you know you're uncomfortable in an environment where there might be a heated argument, then work on your management skills, but until you have some in place, stay away from those triggering situations (or dances) if you can. If you know you're very good at cooling down arguments and helping others find some resolution, then step up and step in. Your knowledge of your personality preferences can help here. If you know you work best alone or in a group, ask yourself what skills are coming into play in each situation.

3 **WORK-RELATED SKILLS.** I remember when I got a job as a book-keeper. This was possibly the worst possible job skill match. One, it did not allow me to work with people – only numbers. Two, I'm a big picture girl, not a "be in balance to the penny" kind of employee. I kept trying to be in balance to the penny and spent many evenings alone, at work finding that last penny, but, the skill just didn't develop. I've learned many great skills in work environments, and outside of that arena as well. For this skill category, think of work as just what you do to express who you are. This might be through a hobby, parenting, sailing, or whatever you consider "work" for yourself.

Turn to | 1.2c | **MOTIVATED SKILLS** in the **MASTER CLASS WORKBOOK** to brainstorm your motivated skills.

CHAPTER THREE

The Dance of Story
LIFE AS AN INSIDE JOB

*Y*our personal narrative, or inner story, has the power to free you to live your dreams. From time to time in this book, I'll ask you to tell your story. These stories, or personal explorations, are guides to discovering different aspects of your inner dancer. They guide you in establishing your natural choreography. To be authentic to who we are now, we must acknowledge the deep roots of our psyches. This chapter guides you in using an awareness of personal story, or myth, in shaping your LifeDance. Reclaiming the stories of your life, and tapping into the stories you have inherited, is a way of embracing an integrated, fully realized, solidly centered knowledge of self. Paradoxically, as you discover your inner narrative, you'll also realize how malleable it is, and how much more you are than your stories. The deeper you go into your stories, the more you learn about yourself. Sometimes we create stories about ourselves that help us survive difficult or traumatic events. Sometimes people need professionals to help them discover painful stories and heal and "retell" them in a way that makes them stronger.

Everyone carries around a story about who she is. Through this story, themes emerge. When you know these themes, you become your own story master.

Stories begin to form in us at an early age. We hear stories from our parents about who we are. Themes are imprinted early, such as "You are such a bad girl," or "You are a real prince." As a child, we take this in and believe it. It's a familiar refrain; it comes from someone we love and trust, someone who we believe cares for us, and we take it as truth.

You see the results of people's stories every day. Being bad was a common theme in the stories of teenagers I counseled at juvenile hall. One that women hear often as young girls is, "You are such a Princess. I'm sure one day you'll find your Prince Charming." (Unfortunately, not many young boys hear they are

"

"

future Prince Charmings – so there aren't a lot of them to go around!)

Take the time to write your stories: You may have them in your head, and you may tell pieces of them again and again when events bring up memories. Have you ever written your stories all down on paper? You'll find that when you do, small details emerge that trigger memories. These memories serve as markers, reminding you of how your story came to be. Through rendering your story, you'll see you have the power to create a new Ideal Story. Now, you can see how you created it in the first place and you have the power to create the best story possible for yourself.

YOUR STORY

Telling your life story may seem like a daunting task at first, but in the true LifeDancing style, you'll do it taking one step at a time. To get started, you'll need to set aside time, start with 30 minutes, and go to a place where you'll have some privacy.

You'll be reviewing your life from the earliest times you remember to today. You can do this using pictures of yourself, reminiscing with family or friends, or sitting in quiet contemplation walking yourself through the years of your life. If you're visual, start with pictures of yourself from different periods of your life. If you are a thinker, consider an interview with yourself about key events of your life. The tone of this interview is positive. If you were given negative messages from others, write them on a scrap piece of paper and burn them. You want the future steps of this LifeDance to be healthy and dynamic. If the negative messages are all that you have, simply reframe them to a positive perspective. For example, my mother used to call me a "brat" when I would ask why about something, and then why again about the answer to why. I've reframed that comment about being a "brat" to being "a relentlessly curious child." What's your reframed story? Fortunately, it's never too late to remember a happy childhood!

THE VISUAL STORY

It's a cliche that a picture is worth a thousand words, but there is truth in the power of photos and mementos to usher in a flood of memories. Visuals such as photos and souvenirs of your experiences can take you straight to the emotional aspect of a memory, bypassing your rational mind's attempt to interpret the event. You want all the pieces of your memories, the emotional and the rational. Together they create a rich picture.

Take a weekend afternoon to go through photos and record your memories. You can use your journal or if that is too awkward, use an audio recorder. There are also computer applications[4] that allow you to record your voice and write notes at the same time.[5] Put together a picture history of yourself. Get creative. Tell family members you'd like any photos that they might have of you and make copies for yourself to keep.

Your visual story can reveal a thread of continuity from childhood to the person you are today. To do a deeper assessment using Your Visual Story, turn to your **MASTER CLASS WORKBOOK** and complete | 1.3a | **YOUR VISUAL STORY**.

INTERVIEWS

If you're lucky enough to still have friends or family available that knew you during different periods of your life, now is the time to access their memories. One way to begin the conversation is to tell them you have been going through pictures and could they help you remember what you were like in the past. Keep in mind their memories and yours may be different. DON'T CORRECT THEM! Be an impartial interviewer and learn from them. They may remember things you have forgotten, or see things in a way you never thought of. Consider audio or video recording your conversations if everyone is comfortable with that.

THE INNER INTERVIEW

Interview yourself as well. To begin, take one time period, i.e., ages 13-17, and role-play a television news reporter interviewing you about yourself. Place pictures you have found for these time periods in front of you and describe, without editing, what you remember. You may remember, via any of your senses, smells, images, sounds, tastes, physical actions. Write them all down or speak into a handheld recorder. Allow the story to emerge on its own with NO editing. To do a deeper assessment using your Inner Interview, turn to your **MASTER CLASS WORKBOOK** and complete Exercise | 1.3b | **THE INNER INTERVIEW**.

"

Every doorway,

every intersection has a story.

KATHERINE DUNN

"

I am a part of all
that I have met.

ALFRED, LORD TENNYSON

FINDING THE PONY

I once heard a story, and I don't remember where originally, about two small children who wanted a horse. They were friends and they both loved ponies. A family friend of one of the children's parents had a horse farm and thought he would create a special day for the children and invited the families to bring their kids out to see his beloved ponies. The day came, and unfortunately it was the day they cleaned out the stables, and there was a large pile of horse droppings in front of the entrance to the stable. The first family arrived, got out of the car and walked toward the farmhouse. The child spotted the pile of horse dung, screamed and ran back to the car crying that the ponies must have left because they were cleaning everything out. The parents couldn't convince the child otherwise, so they left. The second family arrived and walked up to the same pile of horse dung. This child yelled in glee while jumping into the middle of the pile throwing horse dung in the air declaring, "With all this horse poo there must be a pony in here somewhere."

The teaching in this story is that everything is about perception. Nothing had changed at the farm. The only difference was how the child saw it. As you view your pictures, do your family-and-friend interviews and complete your inner interview, keep looking for the pony. What is the good news? What were your strengths? What brought you joy?

Now, reviewing your stories, select the four most significant events, ones that stand out in your memories, and record them in | 1.3c | **DEEPENING YOUR STORY** in **MASTER CLASS WORKBOOK**. Ask questions like:

Who influenced you?

What did you learn or enjoy most about this story?

Include at least one interview in each age group. Describe and elaborate on them in your journal and crystallize them in your **MASTER CLASS WORK-BOOK**.

THE HERE AND NOW

Now let's look at your present-day activities. What are you doing every day or week that you can build a happy life on? Answer the questions in Exercise | 1.3d | **THE HERE AND NOW** in **MASTER CLASS WORKBOOK**.

DEEPENING YOUR STORY:
ARCHETYPES AS
INNER CHOREOGRAPHERS

Underlying your stories may be a deeper story or pattern, one that has influenced you all of your life without you being aware of it. When I look back at pictures taken in kindergarten, I see a little girl with hair askew, fidgeting in her seat and not lined up properly like all the other children. My high school yearbook carried pictures of my cheerleading days, but no mention of the extended absence during my senior year because of my very pregnant condition. When I step back, I see a pattern emerge over and over again – the Jester, the Adventurer, the Explorer. I never followed the rules and always got myself out of scrapes with a sense of humor, adventure, curiosity and optimism.

Archetypes inform us about the life themes or dances we live out. They are like inner, unconscious stories. Bringing them to awareness can inform us of the influences that drive us from deep within. They are our silent, inner choreographers.

We know archetypes in everyday life: the Victim, the Healer, the Sage. Even the class clown, you might remember from your high school days, that's the archetype of the Jester. In our yearbooks, we played with the concept of archetypes, labeling photos: Most Likely to Succeed, Most Likely to Get Hit By a Speeding Truck, Most Likely to Be a Brain Surgeon. Take a moment and ask yourself, what archetypes may be underlying some of your actions.

WHAT ARCHETYPE BEST FITS YOUR LIFE?

Victim

Adventurer

Beauty Queen

Healer

Sage

Jester

Hero

Other

"

We live with
our archetypes,
but can we live in them?

POUL ANDERSON

> "
>
> Great dancers are not great because of their technique, they are great because of their passion.
>
> ## MARTHA GRAHAM

Archetypes appear early in our understanding because they are so elemental to our self-discovery. They appear in the earliest stories we are told – in fairy tales and myths. As a child, I remember "Heidi." She was a girl who emerged from a difficult setting and flourished in a new life. Heidi, like me, had been taken from her family and went to live with her grandfather. She sought friendship and helped another who was in need. This story touched my heart and gave me hope that life could be good.

What stories have touched your heart? Write about them in Exercise | 1.3e | **ARCHETYPES: YOUR CHOREOGRAPHERS** in your **MASTER CLASS WORKBOOK**. In the workbook, you'll find an Archetype Assessment tool available online for those who find this topic fascinating.[5]

THE WORLD DANCER

Dance brings people together. When people dance together they step across individual differences and become part of a larger dynamic.[6] An early teaching tool, the Tarot depicts The World or The Universal Dancer. This dancer is the final card in the Journey of Life, the point in the Journey of Life in which you are a fully integrated person. It's the card of attainment – attainment of the harmony that comes from embracing the whole of one's self. It's depicted as simply The World because in gaining wholeness, we also gain connection with the whole universe. This is the point on the Journey of Life when we are truly centered. We see our place in the universe. We see that we are not separate, compartmentalized from the others, and disconnected from parts of our selves but whole and dynamic. The dance of selves has become integrated.

Turning in, or self-reflection or contemplation, is a skill that is not often taught to us by our families or in school. If you have found the process of turning in difficult, you are not alone. Please trust that the payoff is enormous. I encourage you to make self-contemplation and awareness a life skill. It will serve you well.

Being a world dancer is about you, and about more than you. If you are called to connect with the world around you in a loving way, take the first step in bringing love and kindness to yourself and all living beings. Use the World Dancer Meditation that follows to bring warmth to your heart and grace to your dance.

THE WORLD DANCER MEDITATION

Begin by finding a place where you can sit undisturbed for at least 10 minutes. Close your eyes and begin breathing abdominally by placing your hands on your tummy and feel its rise and fall.

Now direct loving acceptance to yourself. If this is difficult for you, try pretending you are lovable, just for now and search your memory for someone you saw in a movie that was kind and loving.

A blessing I learned at a mindfulness retreat that I personalized so I would remember it is:

May all beings (or I) be safe

May all beings be peaceful

May all beings live lives of joy and ease

Feel free to personalize this to suit yourself so you'll remember it easily. If you still feel unworthy, no matter, you are embracing all that you are, good and bad, high and low, and sending unconditional positive regard and love to your own heart. Savor the feeling. Next you can expand your circle of loving kindness to:

- Your family and loved ones, remember your pets.
- Your friends and colleagues
- Your neighbors and community
- Your spiritual guides and teachers
- The planetary community

When your inner critic tells you that someone does not deserve your care, remind the critic that even your critic deserves love.

When you are through, return to your body, feel your breath and open your eyes. You have danced the dance of loving kindness.

"

Love isn't finding a perfect person. It's seeing an imperfect person perfectly.

SAM KEEN

CHAPTER FOUR

The Inner Dancer
& The Conscious Audience

When you watch beautiful dancers up on the stage, they appear to move effortlessly. They do not stop and think about where to go next. Their body, mind and spirit are congruent and their movements unfold naturally. As you watch their strength and ease of movement, you may wonder how they do that.

Those dancers are trained to dance; they are tuned into what is unfolding within their mind, body and spirit. Their outer expression, or stage performance, is their communication through their movements. You, too, can move through your life effortlessly, tapping into your inner rhythms and fine-tuning your LifeDance so that all parts of you move in concert making your LifeDance one of effortless movement and power!

Being able to peer inside yourself, behold and embrace your inner workings is simply a skill most all can learn. The key is to observe your inner dynamic with an accepting and loving attitude. To become aware of what you are thinking, feeling and experiencing in the moment, and then being noncritical, nonjudgmental, and compassionate with yourself, allows you to dance free of suffering and pain.

Almost everyone has some fear or suffering about their inner workings. Fear that there is some dark place no one can love and suffering from feelings of fear, hatred, anger or maybe of unresolved trauma. When those dark places are illuminated with the light of awareness, they can be explored with loving kindness, as you would help a young child explore and move through their fears of the monster in the closet. After many years of working with hundreds of clients both in state hospitals and private practice, I have heard many stories about dark secrets and fears. There has never been one that couldn't be explored and embraced. It was, and is usually, the individual holding the fear who has the most trouble looking at, forgiving, loving, and healing those fearful dark places.

> Every moment brings a choice; every choice has an impact.
>
> ## JULIA BUTTERFLY HILL

> The universe is transformation; our life is what our thoughts make it.
>
> ## MARCUS AURELIUS
> 121-180 A.D.

I encourage you to begin developing the skill of inner awareness. If you find that it is more than you can bear, I encourage you to look for a trusted person or professional to help you with this skill. Those places that are locked up inside of you can affect the quality of your everyday LifeDance and get in the way of a joyful expression of who you really are.

Mindfulness and intuition are two tools that can help you discover, and eventually, trust and love your inner dancer.

MINDFULNESS

Many of us live in the past, the future, or somewhere in between, but are not present observing the magical moment of NOW. No one else is as exquisitely aware of the dance of selves that unfolds within as you are, or could be. Harvard-trained psychiatrist and mindfulness expert Dan Siegel invites us to use mindfulness as a "journey into the heart of our lives." Being mindful means we are exquisitely aware of ourselves in the moment. If you learn no other skill offered in this book, please explore mindfulness.

Your relationship with your "selves" is your primary relationship, it's an intimacy with your own being. Ask yourself, "How can I be in relationship with anything, or anyone, if I don't know who I am?" Without a relationship or knowledge of yourself, it is impossible to be in a relationship, honestly, with others. Using mindful awareness, observing yourself like an audience watches a dancer, you can attune yourself to yourself, befriend yourself, and an added benefit is that you grow your brain in new and healthy ways while you do it.[7] A paradoxical outcome of mindfulness is you'll discover the beauty of who you are, and then find how to not take your Self too seriously.

Scientists call what happens when we observe our thoughts, feelings and body sensations, neural integration. This integration expands our ability to understand ourselves better, be more aware of others, feel more connected with the world and enhance our well-being. If you are looking for a fast track, a pioneer in the field of brain integration, Steve Harris of CenterPointe,[8] offers a meditation program using sound, that is purported to speed up the neural integration process.

INTO THE JUNGLE

The journey into mindfulness is like traveling into the jungle. First, you think you are completely prepared for the journey. Then you step in quicksand and begin to sink. Hmmm, you didn't read that part of the manual on extricating yourself from quicksand. You manage to get out and continue on with an added awareness that there may be some things about the journey for which you're not prepared. As you begin to see better in the jungle, and become aware of the geography, beasts and fauna, you begin to see for the first time things you never even knew existed. You grow more and more curious, then find that there is so much more to discover and that the journey itself is all there is to discover. My oh my, what an adventure. It may seem risky, but it certainly beats being oblivious to all that is within you, and being constantly at its mercy.

The journey into mindfulness is a life's work. It is not a place you get to, it is a skill you constantly embrace, expand and deepen. It also comes and goes much like a butterfly. One moment you are completely aware of yourself and your environment, and next you are bumped by someone in the line at the grocery store who has 20 items in a 15 item check-out line, you're in a hurry and you lose yourself in angry thought. Then, ideally, you take a breath, bring yourself back to the moment, and explore your thoughts and feelings with curiosity and loving kindness while you act or wait your turn. Once again, you are alert and aware in the jungle, ready to deal with whatever comes your way.

There are some excellent ways to learn mindfulness. Many books give good advice, but I have found the best way is to take instruction with someone who teaches mindfulness or a form of prayer or meditation practice. The instruction can be secular or grounded in spiritual philosophy. I began my exploration of mindfulness in the late '60s, using yoga as a focusing exercise. Then there were the Age of Aquarius ventures into hallucinogens that showed me altered states, some glorious, some frightening. Since then, I have learned from celebrated teachers, my clients, and my friends and family.

MINDFULNESS MEDITATION

To begin, here is a simple mindfulness meditation instruction drawn from my own experience and learnings. The teacher I have found that offers an excellent secular meditation training is Jon Kabat-Zinn. He has many books and audio recordings that easily guide you in your meditation adventure.[9] To get you

> "
>
> The bold adventurer succeeds the best.
>
> # OVID

"

Meditation is the soul's
perspective glass.

OWEN FELTHAM

started, you'll find below two approaches to meditation: Formal and Informal. I recommend both.

FORMAL MEDITATION

Find or create a space for yourself where you can sit comfortably, in a chair or on a meditation stool or pillow, with no interruptions. This means no telephone, interruption by someone else in the space, or any other type of distraction. This will be easier for some than others to accomplish, do the best you can. Find a timer that will let you know when the time you've allotted has passed. I suggest starting with 10 minutes and expanding to 30 to 45 minutes. Sit in a comfortable yet noble posture in a chair or on a meditation pillow or bench and begin to pay attention to your breath. Feel the sensations of the air entering and exiting your nose. You may also observe your chest or abdomen expanding and contracting with each breath. Maintain a natural breath, not a forced one. Simply be aware, do not think about breathing. Place your hands on your legs or in your lap, hand resting in hand or on your legs.

Now comes the adventure. Notice what happens as you try to keep your awareness on your breath. Your mind scoots elsewhere with thoughts, feelings bodily sensations and any environmental stimulation that occurs (What a beautiful bird-sound! What a loud car!). When this happens, and it will, gently bring your awareness back to your breath like you would take a child by the hand and lead her back to the path from which she's strayed. Soon you'll become the audience to the thoughts, feelings and sensations that dance through your mind. Be an open and generous audience, allowing a noncritical, positive regard attitude about the inner dance that unfolds.

I recommend a formal meditation time each and every day for 20-30 minutes. It seems so simple, yet it is tremendously rewarding and healing.

Your body is more a part of your mind than you realize. Your body and mind work together as a team. Bring this awareness to your everyday life using a Body Scan along with your meditation practice. Turn to **MASTER CLASS WORKBOOK** and follow the instructions for | 1.4a | **THE BODY SCAN**.

INFORMAL MEDITATION

Informal meditation happens as you live your life every day, every hour and every moment. Your inner audience or observer experiences it all. You are not in the moment when your mind is in the past, obsessed with what others are thinking, or wishing you were someplace else. You won't notice the beauty of a flower, an expression on the face of a loved one, or your dog's subtle cues to let you know she needs to go outside to pee. Of course we all "go away," and when you notice you are not in the moment, that noticing is simply a reminder to bring your attention to your breath, and to what is unfolding. When you're dancing with life, you'll discover an inner peace in the face of chaos and problems, a sense of balance in any situation, and clear observance of your LifeDance. When I'm especially busy and distracted, I wear a watch that chimes on the hour. I use this chime to bring me to the moment in case I've strayed.

Another informal mindfulness practice I find helps me with my health is Mindful Eating. There are so many ways to be mindless during the day, I find increasing my awareness when I'm eating brings me back to the moment and even helps me enjoy my food more. Being mindful, I'm actually able to savor tastes and eat only what I need. Mindful eating is a practice that involves bringing your full attention to the process of eating – first your hunger, then all of the tastes, smells, thoughts, and feelings that arise during a meal. Whether you are overweight, suffer from an eating disorder, have medical problems related to food, or just want to get more out of life, Mindful Eating may be for you.

Mindfulness helps focus our attention and awareness on the present moment, which in turn, helps us disengage from habitual, unsatisfying and unskillful habits, addictions, and other behaviors. Engaging in Mindful Eating on a regular basis helps you discover a far more satisfying relationship with food and eating than you've ever imagined or experienced before. Mindful Eating is about a lifestyle change, discovering healthy eating habits and using food to enhance wellness. There is an interesting process of formal and informal meditation blending into one another. The more formal meditation you do, the more informal meditation you'll find yourself doing.

INTUITION

Intuition is an inner knowing that grows as you begin to trust in yourself. Intuition allows you to trust your next movement, even in the face of everyone else telling you to move another way. Intuition is a non-rational knowing that comes from an integration of all your senses. Some sensations may be out of

"

The affairs of the world will go on forever.
Do not delay the practice of meditation.

MILAREPA

> If the doors of perception
> were cleansed,
> everything would appear
> as it is - infinite.
>
> ## WILLIAM BLAKE

your awareness at the moment but they can still create an "inner knowing" to move from.

The right brain[10] is popularly associated with the intuitive processes. Some attribute intuition to other forms of guidance such as angels or a collective intelligence. Albert Einstein said, "There is no logical way to the discovery of these elemental laws. There is only the way of intuition, which is helped by a feeling for the order, lying behind the appearance." The ancient Chinese philosopher Lao Tzu wrote, "The power of intuitive understanding will protect you from harm until the end of your days." Most people have had some kind of intuitive experience. If you haven't, I invite you to explore it with me.

Intuition builds on mindfulness. When you are being mindful and in the moment, you prepare an open stage for intuition to emerge. As you move, your inner guide helps you flow to the next step. A dialogue emerges between your inner wisdom, intuition, your movements, and your more critical rational mind. You'll move, then check in with your thinking and feeling, what's going on in your body and the environment, then begin again. You'll drop into your inner knowing and dance.

Getting rid of all the "noise" that's in the way of your intuitional emergence is the key. Your judgments, and criticisms, yours and other people's, simply clutter your stage and get in the way of your unfolding dance.

I have seen intuition emerge in people who said they weren't intuitive. During a weekend intuition retreat, we would talk, meditate and get back in touch with our inner dancer. In the last exercise of the day, participants would break up into pairs. One person would imagine a picture in her mind; the other person would try to get a sense of that image. People were so accurate so often, it was scary. After tuning themselves for days, their ability to intuit and communicate nonverbally was astounding.

WHAT IS INTUITION?

"The act or faculty of knowing directly, without the use of rational process."
AMERICAN HERITAGE DICTIONARY

Intuition is one of the many talents for which women were burned at the stake in the 17th century. Many of our so-called geniuses profess to using intuition to solve crucial problems in the development of new theories and inventions such as Einstein, Galileo, Newton and Carl Jung. Businessman Ray Kroc followed the advice of his "funny bone" and purchased the restaurant that would become the McDonalds franchise. You've probably eaten the results. Today, intuitional management is a highly valued skill in the corporate world.

Intuition is not taught in school yet. Everyone seems to agree that they have a way of knowing things that is not concrete and empirically provable. Unfortunately, often it is discouraged by others who want to know how you know something and when you have no answer but, "I don't know, I just KNOW it," you are belittled.

What do we know about intuition?

MORE ABOUT INTUITION

Have you ever been thinking of an old friend, and then heard from that friend an hour later? I often know when my daughter is going to call. This happens so often that when I say to my husband, "I wonder what's happening with Gretchen," sometimes he just hands me the phone.

Flashes of intuition are usually non-sequential. They are individual pieces of insight that relate to a larger complex or problem. They come to you when your mind is open, like when you meditate or do tasks that require no thought i.e., washing the dishes, gardening or walking. When I'm working with clients often I'll have an image flash through my mind that does not seem to relate to our conversation. When I tell my client about the image, it often has something to do with what is going on with them that they weren't aware of or didn't talk about.

A friend of mine recently completed a single-handed sail to Hawaii. He lost his mast 400 miles out of Oahu yet managed to create a small sail to keep the boat moving. All of his instruments were lost, and it was daytime so he was trying to figure out a way to know where to point the boat to reach land as soon as possible. While he was slowly making his way, two fish came up to the boat and started swimming alongside, he named them George and Gracie. What went through his head was, "Maybe I should just follow these fish." He had no other data or indicators that this was a good idea, but it was the best one that came to

> "
>
> Great spirits have always encountered violent opposition
> from mediocre minds.
>
> ## ALBERT EINSTEIN

"

'Healing,' Papa would tell me, 'is not a science, but the intuitive art of wooing nature.'

W.H. AUDEN

him. Sure enough, George and Gracie led him right to Oahu.

I'm sure you have stories of your own, or know of others who "followed their intuition," with a good outcome. There may be folks who've had disastrous consequences, but looking back, realize the right thing happened.

Unfortunately, many people stop listening to their intuition. Many times highly intuitive people know information and are unable to articulate their source of knowledge so when they are challenged for concrete proof they lack that. They are invalidated by others and stop trusting themselves. This can result in a personal lack of trust in intuitive abilities and intuitive awareness decreases. Over time, if this has been your experience, you may have stopped trusting in your intuitive abilities and stopped relying on them.

One of the goals of being a LifeDancer is to trust your inner wisdom and intuition. One of the tools that can help you dust off your intuitive skills is the MindMap, which we'll discuss in Chapter Eight: The Dance of Strategy. When you create and use a MindMap, you use the wholistic, nonlinear parts of your brain to capture ideas and information. As you create your MindMap, there is space for intuitive flashes to emerge. This nonlinear way of capturing information and shaping it into naturally related clusters of information can rewire your brain, enhancing the activity of the right side of your brain and increasing the connectivity between the two sides. The MindMap helps you discover and articulate how you know what you know. When you learn how to communicate intuitive information to others, you can use it more fluidly in problem solving and planning. In this way, the technique becomes integrative, drawing on both sides of the brain.

WAYS TO ACCESS INTUITION

Here are several ways to get in touch with your intuition.

MENTAL. Sometimes found in dreams and daydreams, a new order.

VISUAL. Images to which you gravitate or simply enjoy.

AUDITORY. Music, words that stand out.

KINESTHETIC. Movement that facilitates intuitional awareness.

EMOTIONAL SYSTEMS. Feelings that come without relationship to external events or a sense of "I've felt this way before."

SPIRITUAL. A global rightness, a oneness with life, a piece of the cosmic puzzle.

GUT LEVEL. A gut level feeling that things just are not right, often called first impressions. Usually an overview of a situation or personality.

DREAMS. Nighttime revelations that bring insights to us.

Intuition can reveal itself in your dreams. While you sleep, the mind has time to roam, make connections and create meaning. For example, during the day you may be with a friend or family member you know well. You're busy and don't think much about your visit. Then, at night, your mind begins to piece together subtle body language information you gathered, sometimes this is called meta-communication -- like a slight hesitancy or tremor in the voice that went on, or the tone of her complexion. That night you have a dream about your friend feeling ill So the next morning, you call and ask them how they are. Your friend reveals she is feeling slightly "off," and asks how you knew. Your unconscious may have observed telltale signs of an illness — the tone of the complexion, a imperceptible odor, a slight quiver in the voice — all these subtle signals may be unconsciously observed and then brought to your attention during sleep when your intuition is allowed to function. You tell them you just had a sense of them feeling off and move on.

Because of the personal nature of dreams, the dreamer is the best person to interpret their dreams.

To assist you in developing your dream intuition, here are some guidelines and tips:

1. Explore your dreams in the Dream Diary section of your **LIFEDANCING JOURNAL**.

2. The more you attend to your dreams by writing, talking and looking for possible meanings, the more information you'll gather.

3. Keep your journal by your bedside and try to write in it while you are still lying in the same position you were in when you awoke. This maintains your kinesthetic memory and helps you recall your dream. To catch your dream, have pen, paper and a small flashlight or light, or an audio recorder by your bed. Write or talk as soon as you wake up.

4. Communicate as if you were a reporter at the scene of a breaking news

"

Intuition becomes increasingly valuable in the new information society precisely because there is so much data.

JOHN NAISBITT

"

Dreams are true while
they last, and do we not live
in dreams?

ALFRED, LORD TENNYSON

event. Gather all the information you can without editing or criticizing. Use a MindMap, as described in Chapter 8, to gather disparate information.

5. Dreams are oblique. That means an image or scenario may be metaphoric of a waking reality. Your subconscious mind tends to use symbols and imagery in ways you may not think of during your waking state. After you have recorded your dream, it will be time to uncover its larger meaning/s.

6. Dreams fall into general categories:

DAY RESIDUE/DAY RESOLUTION. This is a dream that completes a situation that was going on during the day. You may have an argument with your boss and your dream that evening could be you overcoming someone who you thought was stronger than you.

BIG PICTURE RESOLUTIONS. A dream that pulls together a lot of pieces of your life into one story. You may have been trying to solve a large problem for some time, kind of like my trying to figure out how to move to California on a low budget and coming up with the solution to buy a boat to live and work on. Be open to solutions that are outside of your box.

FRAGMENTARY DREAMS. These are dreams with a lot of disconnected images, situations and more. You may need to simply record this dream and keep coming back to it for insight.

As you learn to trust your intuition, your dream interpretations will go more quickly. Hang in there and watch your skills develop.

To deepen your dream work, I recommend |1.4b| **INCUBATING A DREAM** in the **MASTER CLASS WORKBOOK**.

TOOLS TO ACCESS INTUITION

There are many intuitive tools such as Tarot Cards, Pendulums and Runes. I believe the insights gained by using these systems come not from the tools but from within the reader. Try a few tools and see if any are helpful for you. I use Tarot Cards personally and only read them for myself, never anybody else. If you're interested in understanding more about the Tarot, I recommend the home study course given by the Builders of the Adytum (BOTA) in Pasadena, California.

Use the | 1.4c | **INTUITION ASSESSMENT** tool in your **MASTER CLASS WORKBOOK** to help you understand how easily intuition works for you.

INTUITION DAILY PRACTICE

To increase access to intuition more frequently in small ways, play intuition games with yourself. For instance, guess the best route home in rush hour or the best corner to catch a cab. When you find yourself in a large parking lot, follow your intuition to the closest parking space to your destination. When waiting at an elevator bank, move toward the one that will get to your floor first. Sometimes when I'm driving somewhere with many routes and can't make a rational decision about which one to choose, I relax and wait until I get to the last turning point and let my intuitive body decide which route to take.

When you begin to feel you have more access to your intuition, explore how it works for you. Do you:

- Get a feeling from some part of your body,
- See a mental image in your mind's eye,
- Hear a voice

Does it wake you up at night or come to you first thing when you wake up?

Also, become aware of what disrupts your intuitive thinking, i.e., stress, pain, exhaustion, emotional crisis. When you notice you are "disconnected," use relaxation exercises, physical exercise, or biofeedback to get yourself back "on-line."

When you feel yourself stuck, draw a line with numbers from 1 to 10, one being total calm and 10 maximum stress. Identify where you stand on that line. Now find a way that works for you to bring your score down at least 1-2 notches. Think of the problem you are solving or the decision you are struggling with as a mystery play or giant puzzle. The pieces may come to you in various forms that are not clearly marked as pieces to your puzzle. Learn to trust the process!

WHEN YOU'RE UNDER PRESSURE

You may use this daily or when under fire of a deadline. Take 10 to 20 minutes to do the following:

Find or create a place where you will have no interruptions. Put your phone

"

It is through science that we prove, but through intuition that we discover.

HENRI POINCARE

"

The power of intuitive
understanding will protect
you from harm until the end
of your days.

LAO TZU

on "do not disturb," tell your spouse, children, housemate or administrative assistant not to disturb you unless the building is burning down. Sit or lie down, make yourself comfortable. If possible, put on headphones and listen to classical baroque music, tune into your breathing, breathe in time to the music from your belly. Exhale twice as long as you inhale: Inhale 1, 2, 3, 4; pause; exhale 1, 2 / inhale 1, 2, 3, 4, 5, 6, 7, 8; pause; exhale 1, 2, 3, 4. Expand your breathing pattern comfortably.

When you believe you have reduced your anxiety and stress, use whatever tools or exercises you have found that help you access your inner wisdom.

WHAT TO WATCH OUT FOR

Be on the lookout for ego attachment to your decisions, personal agendas,° fears, upper limits issues (fear of success) or personal "buttons." You may be on the right track to the perfect decision for yourself but you stumble over individual obstacles that keep you from proceeding down the optimal path. Watch for your first few reactions after you think/feel you have made the "right" decision. Then ask yourself where those reactions came from. Try to be as honest with yourself as possible. Look for habitual responses that get in your way. Most importantly, have fun. Play with alternatives, explore absurdities, laugh at your mistakes and move on.

Intuition is something we all have. The more you use it and believe in yourself, the easier it becomes!

Expand and grow your inner awareness and wisdom using the tools I've offered and make your LifeDance effortless.

GETTING UP OFF THE FLOOR:
THE PROCESS OF EMPOWERMENT

All this talk of dancing, using your intuition and creating a new life for yourself may seem rather daunting. Not to worry, you can just lay there on the dance floor of life and not move a muscle. Unfortunately, inaction is the same as action, because things change around you as you ponder the floor. There is no magic to finding the power and the will to get up off the floor and dance. The process of self-empowerment has been studied for years. Because self-empowerment is central to the work of helping people improve their lives, psychologists have researched this concept in many contexts. What they have found is that most people have a natural inclination to seek positive change.[13]

Self-empowerment is a process, not a destination. Some days are better than others, some settings bring out our strengths and other's don't. Self-empowerment works from the inside out. You define or discover important goals for yourself that are in alignment with your personal values, life mission and what you want in life. As the environment or others respond to what you do, you observe and reflect on what happens, and if necessary redefine your goals, and keep on acting and moving. Your personal sense of power comes from the process that unfolds and how you define it.

When you feel empowered, you believe your voice needs to be heard, you stand strong behind your values and beliefs, and you don't let anyone or anything take away your power. There's a wonderful life story that personifies this process, the story of Secretariat the race horse. Secretariat's owner, trainer, jockey and groomer believed in Secretariat from the beginning. In the face of personal and financial struggles, she persevered and championed her horse. Secretariat became a legend and many of his records stand to this day. Secretariat's owner faced pressure from her brother, husband, children, colleagues, financiers and many others to quit and sell him to someone else. But she believed that she and her horse could be great, and she powered through to the realization of her dream. Many famous people have done the same. In the face of tremendous challenges and pressures, they persevere. So here's the **SELF-EMPOWER-MENT FORMULA:**

1. Create personally meaningful self-empowerment goals. Goals that are congruent with and integrated with your self, core beliefs and values.

2. Believe you have the power to reach your goals. Act from the inside out and learn from others, and don't give away your power to them.

3. Create a course of action. There are many ways to accomplish individual goals, you simply need to shape your plan to your strengths.

4. Act boldly!

5. Observe what happens when you act and increase your knowledge about what you need to learn or do to be successful.

6. Revisit your goal/s to refine and/or expand them and move on.

As you can see, the empowerment process is circular. So, as you lie on the

> Power can be taken, but not given. The process of the taking is empowerment in itself.

GLORIA STEINEM

floor or slouch on the couch, know that there is power in moving. Take your time, and know that when you're ready to move, you have the opportunity to move with power.

"

Education remains the key to both economic and political empowerment.

BARBARA JORDAN

Step Two

THE AUTHENTIC DANCER: TURNING OUT

The LifeDancer takes her place in the spotlight on the stage of her creation, looks into the bright lights and turns her joyful face to the expectant audience. She feels her center of gravity and knows the place where she aligns into perfect equilibrium. She has looked within at her multiple selves, and she has created a vision for her life. She moves toward this vision. She knows joy and strength, and she expresses it through every movement as she glides through life.

Now that you've done the hard work of exploring your inner dancer, the time has come to greet the outer world. Shakespeare tells us that "All the world's a stage," and his words ring true to the dancer as she enters her environmental and relational LifeDance.

As you step onto your stages, you have choices to make. What face will you present to the audience? Will you show your Authentic Dancer or create a cover or false persona?

The false self or mask may feel safer, but it comes at a price. If you do not portray your authentic self to others, they will not know who you are. They will be in relationship to a false persona, a person who you are only pretending to be. It would be like a dancer wearing a mask on stage.

In Step Two: Turning Out, you'll use the power of your imagination to open the curtain to your stages of possibility. These visions of possibility emerge from YOU, and unfold over the course of a lifetime. As you realize your dreams, know that new dreams will take shape to follow them.

The stage of your life has unlimited possibility. You have a powerful opportunity to create any world, or any life, you choose. As exhilarating as that might be, it can be so heady that you struggle to choose. In these chapters, you'll not only start to see the possibilities, you'll work on the intentions that give your vision shape.

THE DANCE OF VISION AND PURPOSE

Having a vision and knowing your purpose brings you to the stage of possibility, where your dance of life unfolds.

THE LIFEDANCE DESIGN GUIDE

Create visualizations that open doors to your future. As a LifeDancer, begin by assembling an audio and visual compendium that represents what you gravitate toward and what resonates with you.

GOALS ARE VALUES IN MOTION

Armed with your vision and clear about your defining values, you are ready to set your course. In this chapter, we develop your BEST goals.

THE DANCE OF STRATEGY

The Dance of Strategy moves you successfully through your daily LifeDance.

THE DANCE OF SOLUTIONS: WHOLISTIC INTEGRATIVE PROBLEM SOLVING

Move through life's freeze-ups with Wholistic Integrative Problem Solving. This process creates integral solutions that enhance and optimize all areas of your life.

CHAPTER FIVE

The Dance of Vision and Purpose

If you live the life you love, you will receive shelter and blessings.

Sometimes the great famine of blessings in and around us derives from the fact that we are

not living the life we love; rather, we are living the life that is expected of us.

We have fallen out of rhythm with the secret signature and light of our own nature.

JOHN O'DONOHUE, AUTHOR OF ANAM CARA

THE STAGE OF POSSIBILITY

Do you remember yourself as a child dreaming or thinking about what you wanted to be or do when you grew up – a nurse, doctor, veterinarian or maybe just a hero with, or without, a red cape? The adults around you may have been supportive, or they may have laughed.

If knowing what you want to be when you "grow up" seems to be a daunting task, know that you aren't alone. Remember, you have a strong foundation of skills gained in the Turning In section of LifeDancing. If you are congruent (working from the inside out) and passionate about your vision, you'll find that others will come on board to join and help you.

When you find yourself limiting what is possible for yourself, as we all do, there may be more than one reason.

1. You have not been exposed to what is possible.

2. You suffered trauma when you told others what you wanted.

3. You do not believe you "deserve" to realize your dreams.

4. You grew up in an environment where people didn't believe that all things are possible.

5. You had a family member who always put you down.

6. _____ (Fill in your reason.)

"

Keep the channel open.

MARTHA GRAHAM

There are many reasons why people are not aware of or not able to believe they can create the life they dream of. They range from someone being completely unaware of the power of the mind and affective action to unconscious limitations and conscious and environmental restrictions. The reasons are as myriad as there are people. It does not matter your reason, you have a moral responsibility to yourself to be the best possible YOU. I find this magnificently expressed by Agnes DeMille quoting Martha Graham.

There is a vitality, a life force, an energy, a quickening that is translated through you into action, and because there is only one of you in all of time, this expression is unique. And if you block it, it will never exist through any other medium and it will be lost. The world will not have it. It is not your business to determine how good it is nor how valuable nor how it compares with other expressions.

It is your business to keep it yours clearly and directly, to keep the channel open.

MARTHA GRAHAM, QUOTED BY AGNES DEMILLE IN MARTHA: THE LIFE AND WORK OF MARTHA GRAHAM

Limitation may come from fear of failure or fear of success, from your past, or the way you relate to the future. The "impossible" may stem from attitudes you have toward yourself, or attitudes you have about others. Once you are aware of the limitations you have placed on yourself, the next step is to understand your style of meeting obstacles and taking risk. A full discussion of obstacles and risk taking is in Chapter Seven: Goals Are Values in Motion.

When you limit what you believe is possible for yourself, it's based on what you have experienced or been aware of in your life. When you step outside of these restrictions, your spirit soars You are able to visualize something new. You creatively design a future based on blue-sky visioning and new possibilities. Take the next step in your dance of creation.

A NEW VISION

What did you do as a child that made the hours pass like minutes?

Herein lies the keys to your earthly pursuits.

— **CARL JUNG**

Limiting oneself to only what has been possible in life is often the reason people can't imagine new possibilities for themselves. It's like a dancer who has only seen ballet all of her life and never seen or heard of tap dancing. How can she choose it if she doesn't know it exists?

The world holds so many choices that it would be impossible to know them all. Your dance must begin on the inside, emerging from the spark of self into your possibilities. When the Dance of Vision unfolds from this inner spark, you explore the outer world until you discover your resonances. You cultivate curiosity and discovery that leads to revelation. The Swiss psychologist Carl Jung believed that if individuals were aware of their inner paradigms, or structures, and sought lives congruent with that, they would discover the perfect match of skills, values and preferences while they engaged in an activity or experience that challenged and mobilized them. Modern positive psychologist Mihaly Csikszentmihalyi identified this unique match as an experience of "flow."[14] He describes being in the flow as when you are fully immersed in an activity, with an energized focus. In a flow state, you are focused and clear. Action merges with being. One must be fearless to walk this path. It is a dance into the unknown as your life emerges one step at a time.

If you already enjoy dancing, reflect on the experience of going to a dance and waiting for the music to start. Think of life as an opportunity to wait until the Dance of Self – your Authentic Dancer – feels, sees, thinks, or hears its musical cue, and begins.

Seeing more obstacles than possibilities is a way of being in relationship to the world. It's like a dancer who approaches a line of other dancers. She might see the line and turn away. She might see the line and engage with it. Or, she might go around it and see what's on the other side. So many choices. Each choice informs the dancer about how she deals with obstacles, how they become, or don't become, part of the dance.

So what limits us? I've equated limits with barriers to a new vision, but it's

> Great talents are the most lovely and often the most dangerous fruits on the tree of humanity. They hang upon the most slender twigs that are easily snapped off.

CARL JUNG

"

A man who limits his
interests, limits his life.

VINCENT PRICE

often true that limits can be because of issues with comfort zones. Limits come from messages you received from your parents and other adults who influenced your childhood, messages about being in the world. These form into beliefs – like "the world is hostile," – that become the basis of limitations. These beliefs limit our ability to see what's possible.

With limits, we don't need to expend a lot of energy acknowledging or combating them. This gives them power. The act of visioning is what I call the Disneyland step. Step away from your personal fears and limitations. **Allow magic to happen.** Let it be limited only by the stars. This approach opens the curtain to the stage of possibility.

When you were a small child, you just did what you loved to do. You didn't think about why. Considering what someone else would think of us comes later – between the ages of 8 to 11. By then the brain has developed enough abstract thinking to process those kind of thoughts. As we grow older, we learn to anticipate other people's reactions to our passions and pursuits because we have the ability to emphasize and bring subjective information to consciousness. If we are encouraged in our passions and pursuits, we invest more effort in these activities. If we are discouraged, or even shamed because of our pursuits, we may have dropped that activity from our lives. We may have even discounted the way we thought and felt about the activity, thinking that our effort wasn't that good, that it didn't measure up, that it wasn't all that pleasurable. We may have formed an identity around it: "I can't ice-skate" or "I'm not a good athlete."

This is an example of being outer-directed versus inner-directed. If as children, we are honored, we may be inner-directed. Or even if we are ignored and left to our own devices, we become inner-directed. In his book *The Lonely Crowd*, David Riesman identifies the "social character." This is how a person identifies themselves in relation to others. If all that exists is the social characterlogical identification, the personal "self" becomes lost. If our authenticity is not honored, we become outer-directed. If our Authentic Dancer needs to be nurtured from its seed self, it is your job, and no one else's, to breathe life into her!

You can create a new vision for yourself. There was a time before limiting thoughts came to you. Discover that place as you begin to liberate yourself from inner criticism and doubt. Go back to your source, the time when you were a child and the hours of your life were filled with joyful imaginings.

HONORING YOUR VISION

If you have hit many setbacks or obstacles in life, it can be difficult to create a future vision that you can confidently dance toward. The secret is, little by little, to re-vision or reframe the past and trust the process. You must build a vision from an inner supportive place. Reframe your beliefs. Say them out loud. Free yourself from the past or people who did not encourage you. They are "dream stealers" – people who stole your dreams. Don't be snared by your past, be drawn to your future! Create a vision of the future and dance toward it!

Take time to brainstorm a list of current beliefs, fears and limitations. These are statements that often begin with "I can't because ..." A useful way to eliminate these old beliefs is to write each one down on a slip of paper. Then, sitting before a fire, throw them into the flames to burn them away. Then, when these thoughts come into your mind, imagine them going up in flames, again. I remember as a little girl, I wanted to be a scientist. I had read about scientists in school and loved the idea of exploring and solving problems or conducting research. I told my mother and she laughed and said, "Girls don't become scientists. They get married and have children." I was disappointed, but my grandmother heard my dream and for Christmas she gave me a toy called The Science Lab. I had a wonderful time pricking people's fingers and looking at their blood with my new microscope. I enjoyed it so much, my mother's comments were forgotten. I've often thought that if I could respond to her today, my words would be, "I can do whatever I want." It's interesting to note these inner responses, because sometimes now, years later, we can say them out loud, and they can fuel our stick-to-itiveness to honor our vision.

A story told by a friend of mine goes: "When I was in sixth grade, I was writing a story that I was sharing with my friends each day. They loved it, and couldn't get enough of the next episode. At some point, they disapproved of the content (It was about a teenage girl who got pregnant), and they snubbed me. I didn't know why they weren't talking to me. One day, one of them came to me and said they would be friends with me again if I agreed to tear up the story." The belief that came out of that experience was: "If I want to have friends, I can't write anything that will shake people up." That belief can be "ReFramed." "I want to have friends who support my writing, even if it shakes them up." Reframing your beliefs gives you a new, solid foundation for creating a new vision

> The possible's slow fuse is lit by the imagination.
>
> ## EMILY DICKINSON

for your future.

To work with changing and optimizing your own beliefs, turn to | 2.5a |
ReFRAMING in your **MASTER CLASS WORKBOOK.**

THE VISION

Now that you have re-visioned, let's vision. A vision or mission is a blue sky, big and hairy idea. The following guided visualization takes you back to a time in your life when your vision for your life was crystallizing. It can help you remember when you had a solid vision for your life and remind you of a time when you dreamed more freely. It can also reveal to you when and how beliefs were formed. Examining both will awaken your ability to create a clear vision for your life.

EXERCISE
THE VISUALIZATION

When you experience a visualization, you are seeing that event, real or imagined, as if it is really happening. You are aware of it with all of your senses. If you are seeing a past event, you are back in your experience of that event. I DO NOT recommend going back to any traumatizing event unless you have already de-traumatized it or are working with a professional to guide you through it without further trauma. If you are visualizing a future event, you are living inside of it. This is one of the first steps to bringing your dream alive.

For this exercise, let's imagine that you are 8 years old, an age when your inner critic wasn't so well-formed. Take a moment to mentally journey back to this time in your life, if you can, and remember what you enjoyed doing or playing. See if you can remember what you enjoyed about pretending to be, a nurse, adventurer, or humorist.

What did you want to be when you grew up? Record these memories in your **LIFEDANCING JOURNAL** in Visioning. If you don't remember, use the | 2.5b | **REVISIONING THE PAST** exercise in your **MASTER CLASS WORKBOOK**.

> "
>
> Great minds have purposes; others have wishes.
>
> WASHINGTON IRVING

LINKED-IN VISION

Each one of us is a story unfolding. In every moment, our LifeDance is the culmination of the steps that came before. We have defined those experiences. They have been shaped by our experiences and choices. They are linked by memory and belief – what we remember, what we believed to be true in that moment, how we interpret them later.

In this unfolding dance of life, we are creating a vision every day. We are creating the re-vision, too. We can choose what we remember, what we believe to be true and resonate within this moment. Remember, we can always choose new stories.

After reflecting on your past, answer these questions in your

LIFEDANCING JOURNAL in Visioning:

- What does your past tell you about who you are today and where you are going?

- Examine your successful moments. What patterns do you see?

- Examine your obstacles and challenges. What patterns do you see?

- What themes do you see in all of these?

I'm sure you're beginning to see how an important event that took place 20 years ago can be as alive and present today as it was then. Take time to discover, explore and re-evaluate what you remember and believe about your past. Re-visioning is like tilling fresh soil, adding nutrients that feed the seeds you plant today for a new, joyful future.

ACKNOWLEDGING BEAUTY

In the fairy tale of Cinderella, she could not imagine going to the ball that her stepsisters were preparing for. She could not imagine where a beautiful dress might come from or how she might look if she had her hair in a "do-up." Those seemed far beyond her reach. But then her fairy godmother showed her the beauty that she was. Beauty she could not see or feel, yet it resided inside waiting to be revealed. She was transformed, went to the ball and charmed the prince.

Many of us need to wipe the thick layer of dust away that covers the beauty in our wise and wild souls. We cannot even imagine our potential. As you develop your vision story, keep looking to your past. Shine it up. Look in the

> "
>
> The most powerful weapon on earth is the human soul on fire.
>
> **FERDINAND FOCH**

mirror. See your beauty. Turn toward the light of your beauty.

THE VISIONARY DANCE
WHAT DO YOU WANT?

I've been asked this question many times in my life. Sometimes I have an answer, other times I don't. I'll share with you a time when what I wanted grabbed my Inner Dancer.

I never thought I would own a 41-foot sailboat. It all began when I first got the idea of moving back to California. My mother was ill in California, and I needed a place to live to be available to her. I wanted to live by the water but knew I couldn't afford to. One day I solved my problem by wondering if I could afford to live on a boat since it might be cheaper. I only allowed myself to dream of owning a 23-footer like a friend of mine owned. Mostly, I visualized not being able to afford even that. Then, I went to a boat show, and I saw the 41-foot sailboat LifeDancing. Something in me knew that was the boat I wanted. As I sat in the cockpit of that beautiful yacht, I felt my dream. Knowing there was no turning back, I took my dream one step at a time until I realized it.

In the beginning, the adventure of finally owning LifeDancing was not one I could have imagined. The day I saw her, I was healing from a broken leg, and my daughter had to help lift me aboard. As I entered the boat, I knew this was my dream. Then I looked at the price. My stomach dropped. I believed I could not afford it.

I returned home to Massachusetts, inspired and disappointed. My broken leg healed. Lamenting that I couldn't have what I knew I wanted, a few months later, I called the yacht broker and discovered that my boat was still for sale. Great, and I still couldn't afford her. I returned to California and asked the broker if the owner could reduce the price. After some serious horse trading, we (my husband and I) were only $600 apart from the asking price – a pittance compared to the overall cost. The broker wanted to move this boat and knew I deeply wanted to buy it. The broker decided to take the $600 difference out of her commission. The boat was mine. Yikes!

So there I was, the owner of a 41-foot sailboat with not the first clue about how to sail her or where I was going to put her. Taking this grand adventure one step at a time, and trusting that the right thing would happen, I worked daily

> Though we travel the world over to find the beautiful, we must carry it with us, or we find it not.
>
> RALPH WALDO EMERSON

to find a slip in the marina I had chosen to berth her in, and find a captain who could sail her to the site. This search continued until the broker told me the boat definitely had to be moved and gave me a deadline to move her. I gained a little time by taking her to a boat yard for some repairs. Then, the boat yard gave me a deadline. By the day before I had to move her, or pay high storage fees, I (with the help of friends) had found a captain and a slip to dock the boat in. The day we sailed her to the slip in Benicia, Calif., I was ecstatic. I invited 20 friends to join me on this momentous journey. We experienced high winds that day. We got to discover how my boat handled as she made it to her home port.

When we finally docked her, my captain turned the engine off. Much to my dismay, the very large diesel engine kept running. We tried everything we knew to turn her off – to no avail. Given that she had a 200-gallon diesel fuel tank, we figured she could run for days before running out of fuel. Friends disembarked. I waved goodbye, wondering how long I would have to stay aboard until she finally stopped running. Just then a friend of my daughter's, who was also a boat captain, walked by. We waved and told him of our predicament. He agreed to take a look. He discovered that a wire had come loose during the trip. The wire was the connection to the engine that turned it off. Voila, my boat finally rested in her new home, engine resting.

Today I use LifeDancing -- my boat -- as my office and retreat. Over the past seven years, I have restored her to her early elegance and spent many days sanding, cleaning, sailing and exploring the local waterways. She is my tribute to honoring my dreams. She's evidence of a universe that supports passionate dreams, and she continues to challenge me. There is always "When are you going to take her to sea?" "What about a world cruise?" All challenges are welcome.

This all came from one day, when I asked myself, "What do I want?"

By allowing myself to imagine it, I was allowing the possibility of a dream to come true.

If you look too closely at your dreams, you may not leap. You might get scared. You might not let yourself dream. Instead, take it slow and ask, "What's the next step?" and take those steps one at a time. When you find your passion, nothing will stand in your way!

"

Age wrinkles the body.
Quitting wrinkles the soul.

DOUGLAS MACARTHUR

"

Win as if you were used
to it, lose as if you enjoyed it
for a change.

ERIC
GOINIK

VISIONARY REALITIES

What makes you happy?

What do you want your life to look like in the future?

These are but two questions that point toward your own Visionary Reality, or vision of what you want your personal reality to be.

The act of discovering and creating this vision is powerful for your Authentic Dancer. Whenever you imagine something you want, or see something you are drawn to and wish you could have in your life, you are sending a message to your Authentic Dancer to "make it so."

Clearly this message should be conscious, considered carefully, and planned for, or else your inner "make it so" function receives a very long list of things to do and may become overwhelmed, confused or scattered. No clear dance emerges and you get swept up in others' designs.

THE VISION WITHIN A VISION

Some visions are more likely to become a reality than others. Researchers in the field of positive psychology[15] have found that what makes people the happiest are activities and interests that are internally driven and help others as well as yourself. When you work for something that is externally driven and only for your own benefit, you do not derive as much satisfaction. When your purpose has a benefit for others, when it doesn't only serve you, when others can get involved with it, your vision has a more broad support base. It has a solid foundation in your life. As you continue to develop your dance of the future, ponder this aspect of your vision.

MOBILIZING YOUR VISION:
LIFE AS YOUR MOVIE

Dancers move around the stage. They are not a one-dimensional picture. Your vision is more likely to become real if you put depth and movement to it. Imagine your life as a movie taking place in your future, i.e., one to two years from now. Your life is different. Your life has a renewed passion. Your dance is strong and congruent with who you are because you're tuned into your Authentic Dancer. You know who you are, and because you know who you are, you more clearly envision your LifeDance.

EXERCISE

THE BEAUTY OF YOUR DANCE:
A VISUALIZATION

You may want to read these instructions into an audio recorder so you can use them again and again. Allow 15 minutes for this exercise.

Close your eyes and picture yourself on a movie screen engaged in an activity that represents your vision, one that brings you joy and helps others. Use the first idea that comes to mind. If others arise, write them down and do them in a different session.

Slowly move forward in time enjoying the vision and beauty of your dance. Don't edit, judge or criticize. It's your life's dance, and it is what it is. You can go back and edit, or reframe, some other time.

- What day and time is it?

- What are you wearing?

- What are you doing?

- Who else, if anyone, is there?

- What are you thinking about this event?

- How does it feel?

- What about it do you enjoy the most?

- How does it affect others?

When you're ready, return to the moment, take a deep breath and thank yourself for allowing the time and space for this movie.

When you're ready, leave your inner movie and return to the present moment. Notice your breath, your body where it touches your chair or mat, the floor, and the sounds in the room.

Open your eyes.

Write notes about your movie in your **LIFEDANCING JOURNAL** in Guided Imagery. Once the movie is recorded, rewind, remember, play it again, and make it better each time. Write notes in your **LIFEDANCING JOURNAL** about how it changed.

"

My guiding principles in life are to be honest, genuine, thoughtful and caring.

PRINCE WILLIAM

> "
>
> I don't design clothes.
>
> I design dreams.
>
> ## RALPH LAUREN

RECORD YOUR LIFEDANCE VISION

Like success, your purpose in life is intangible. Your vision statement is a statement of your desires and lays the foundation for your goals and actions. The key to achieving your goals is for them to be congruent with your underlying values and life vision. This connection with your innermost needs and desires is the fuel that keeps the flame of personal motivation burning. Your inner passion is what carries you through the difficult and trying times we all experience when bringing new ideas and activities into our lives.

Record your Life Vision using the instructions in | 2.5c | **LIFE VISION** in the **MASTER CLASS WORKBOOK**.

GROWING YOUR VISION

What do you do if you don't get a clear, distinct image? How do you start? Your image may not be a full picture yet. It may be impressions. It may be bits and pieces, like the pieces of a collage. Brainstorm with trusted friends and colleagues. This is just a rehearsal. Collect the most vivid images, the ones that resonate, make the deepest impression. As the collage comes together, you are shaping a positive, new image that makes a deep impression on your mind. This image, as it comes together in bits and pieces, allows you to become comfortable with the vision before it becomes reality. It helps you gain "mental experience," rehearsing in your mind the actions and circumstances that make the vision come true. As the image takes hold, talk to people you trust about your vision. Ask them how they would imagine that experience. Record what you gather from the **MASTER CLASS WORKBOOK** or discover in your **LIFEDANCING JOURNAL**. To help you define this vision, and keep a record of how your vision grows and changes over the years, I've created a tool called The Design Guide, which we'll discuss in the next chapter and use through the rest of this book. The Design Guide is an important tool in creating your LifeDancing vision.

CHAPTER SIX

The LifeDance Design Guide

*Y*ou have created your LifeDance. To keep your vision alive and be open to and aware of the resources, you need to flesh out your dreams. Your Design Guide, which is part of your **LIFEDANCING JOURNAL**, is a tremendous tool. It helps you consciously create and integrate the stages and designs of your life. The Design Guide is like a pay-it-forward inspirational diary, it can be private or you can share it with people you trust.

In the previous chapter, we used The Dance of Vision and Purpose to fuse your intention together with the future you dream of. Visuals are powerful because they draw people to what they resonate with. Recording this in the Design Guide will help you bring to awareness what you are attracted to and intentionally help you grow your life.

Your Design Guide is a visual journal of what you are drawn to, what pleases you, what you would like your life to look like in every aspect. Once you develop the habit of using your Design Guide, you'll be able to look back over the years and see how you have grown and changed.

Your guide can be a binder that includes pages you write on with insert pages for pictures or a scrapbook. If you want to use your computer, there are many programs that integrate pictures and writing. When you have gathered enough pictures, you might want to create a collage board to put in your room or office. You might also choose an audio format for your collage.

Here is an exercise to set the foundation for your Design Guide:

EXERCISE

A VISUALIZATION: DOORS TO THE FUTURE

Allow 20 minutes for this exercise. You may want to record it first and play it back for yourself.

"

Design is not just what
it looks like and feels like.
Design is how it works.

STEVE
JOBS

"

Good design is making
something intelligible and
memorable. Great design
is making something
memorable and meaningful."

DIETER
RAMS

Sit in a comfortable chair, close your eyes, and take a series of long, deep breaths. Do a Body Scan (see **MASTER CLASS WORKBOOK** Exercise 1.4a) and release as much stress and tension as possible. As you inhale, imagine yourself igniting a warm, glowing ball of soothing energy in the center of your chest. As you exhale, imagine this energy flowing into your arms and legs and throughout all your muscles. Each time you take a breath and slowly let it out, allow yourself to feel each of your muscles releasing tension and gradually relaxing. As you begin feeling more relaxed, imagine the energy moving up through your shoulders and neck, into your head, and bringing calmness to your thoughts and feelings. Then, imagine the energy passing out through the top of your head and radiating a warm glow that envelopes your body.

- Imagine yourself walking into a building. You open the front door and before you is a long hallway with doors on each side. Each door has a number on it.

- Pick a door and put your hand on the doorknob. Turn it and walk into the life that lies beyond.

- As you look further, you see a dwelling, this is where your future self lives. Notice what it looks like. Glance around, walk in the front door and call out to who is home. You'll hear the voice of your future self. As she walks toward you, notice what she looks like, her attitude, what she is wearing. What questions do you have for her?

- What would be most helpful for you to get from where you are now to where she is?

Now you are going to follow her through her day.

1. What does she do?

2. Who is in her life and what are her relationships like?

3. How does she take care of herself?

4. What kind of work does she do?

5. What does she give to her community?

6. What does she do to nourish and expand her body and mind?

7. What does she enjoy?

8. In her day, what is the most important thing she does?

9. What movement best expresses this experience?

Ask her if there is anything you haven't asked she believes you should know.

Turn and walk out of the room. Close the door knowing that it is always there for you to enter for help and advice.

Reflect on your experience and ask yourself what surprised you.

When you're ready, leave and return to the present moment. Notice your breath, your body where it touches your chair, the floor, and the sounds in the room.

Open your eyes when you are ready and record this experience in your **LIFEDANCING JOURNAL** under Guided Imagery. When you repeat this exercise, you'll discover that what's behind the doors will change as you change.

SETTING THE STAGES

We all have many stages on which we LifeDance – home, family, work, play and many more. Each time we enter that stage, we take on a costume in order to play our role. The stage environment has a big impact on your dance. One of the most important functions of the Design Guide is to help you create environments that fit where and who you are and then, who you want to be – create environments that support your vision for a happy, successful life.

Remember, the Authentic Dancer designs herself from the inside – she is inner-directed. So she dances the Dance of Vision and Purpose on each stage of life.

We all know people who are one person at work, another at home and still another on other stages. They may or may not have a thread of continuity between these different stages. As an integral reality check, ask yourself:

- What do people think of me when they walk into my home?
- What do people think of me when they walk into my workspace?
- What do people view when they visit my social networking sites?
- How does what I wear express who I am?
- Can I wear the same thing on each stage?
- How does my car express who I am?
- How many cars do I have?

> "
>
> To succeed, you must have firm determination and adaptability to the environment.
>
> **I CHING**

"

Every exit is
an entry somewhere else.

TOM STOPPARD

DONNING THE COSTUME

Have you ever met someone who was "put together" – wearing the latest styles? More than likely, you've also met someone who appeared as if they dressed in the dark picking their clothes up off the floor. You probably know someone who creates her own style, one that's not based on the trendiest fashion, but rather inspired by a sense of self.

The first person probably copied her look. The second was metaphorically in the dark. And the third was unique and clear about who she was, pulling ideas from different sources that appealed to her and putting them together in her unique way.

Think about what kind of impression these different people leave with you. Then ask yourself, what kind of impression you believe you leave on others?

Now think about how comfortable you are in your costumes, internally and externally?

If you don't yet have a sense of your own style it's fine to copy others, trying on different designs until you find what feels right for you.

So where do you begin?

Start from where you are!

To discover that, take any day in the past and put yourself in the role of a news reporter describing the life of someone they haven't met yet. Walk into your home, workspace or wherever you spend work time. Describe the environment and what it reveals about the person who created it or uses it. Go to your home and look through your closet and see what the clothes say about their wearer. Look at all the designs of your life and ask yourself: What aspects will you keep or change? Record what comes to you about your individual style or design in your **LIFEDANCING JOURNAL** Design Guide.

EXITS AND ENTRANCES

Like Shakespearean actors, we can allow aspects of ourselves to exit and enter the stage. When we know from within who we are and where we are going, we can design our lives so that the aspects we want to emphasize take the stage, while other aspects slip behind the curtain.

To begin thinking about how you want to live and express yourself ask the following questions:

- What are my best features that need to be expressed?

- What are my weaker features that need to be supported?

- How is my inner attitude revealed in my "costumes"?

- Is my inner sense of myself congruent with my outer expression?

- Do my environments support what I want for my future?

Take a look at yourself and identify the first place you would like to change and/or upgrade and create a design for that Life-Stage. Pay attention to what you are drawn to. Cut pictures out of magazines and newspapers. Look at catalogues and identify the items you would buy for yourself, cut out the pictures. You may even be attracted to particular type styles, logos, disc covers, book jackets and business cards. Keep a copy of them all and put them into your Design Guide. Your Design Guide can also include music and video. What people have you seen in the media or know personally that personify what you want? Start by filing things by the arena you are working on. Start a folder on your computer for web sites and images you are attracted to.

THE PLAY'S THE THING

When you believe or feel that you have enough ideas to create a design, make a collage of the things you have gathered and pair it with sound. Give yourself a lot of border to add more things! This is where the stages and costumes come together within the dance. This process allows you to take your vision and put it all together in front of you.

Arrange the final selection of cut out pictures on a page or mat board. Leave it overnight. The next day, see if you still like the arrangement, if not, change it. Then coat the backs of the pictures with a glue stick and press them into place. If you are using a computer design program, set deadlines for when you'll create your collage and update it.

Create Design Guide sections for home and work or other arenas where you spend your time. Ideally what you'll find, or grow, is a thread of continuity in all the arenas of your life, namely you. If you don't know what you want in a particular arena, that's OK. Simply watch and listen to what you enjoy and to what you are attracted to.

You can use a two- to three-inch three-ring binder with plastic sheet pro-

> ❞
>
> Life must be lived as play.
>
> **PLATO**

"

Who loves, raves.

LORD BYRON

tectors or a scrapbook to collect your treasures. If you are facile with computers and the Internet, there are many software programs and online services that will help you create your own story. Carry your Design Guide or a copy of your online guide with you when you explore and shop. Look through your guide weekly or monthly to see how it is growing. Stop and look at how you live in comparison to what your Design Guide reflects. Are they similar or worlds apart? It may be time to create change. The most important factor in this process is integrating the inner and outer expressions of who you are so one flows easily into the other, always dynamic and ready to move with change.

To take this deeper, go to | 2.6 | **RAVE REVIEWS** in the **MASTER CLASS WORKBOOK**.

CHAPTER SEVEN

Goals Are Your Values in Motion

With your Values, Preferences, Skills, Stories, Vision and Design Guide in hand, it is now time to set congruent concrete goals for yourself. You'll create arena-specific goals later in this book. There are smart ways to set goals, and not-so-smart ways. For example, as I sit on my boat and ponder what it would be like to take her out to sea and never plot a course, part of me thinks, "Yes, I'll never have to plot a course, trim a sail, et cetera. Then my inner adult asks, "Okay smarty pants, when and where will you get fresh water; find food; avoid storms that might kill you; and if you can live at sea, connect with others?" Hmmm ... guess I need a few goals.

If I never plot a course – that is, have goals – I'll be driven by the currents and winds with no input from my inner guides. The goal of LifeDancing is to dance a dialogue between the two, inner and outer.

THE ROLE OF GOALS

Ideally, goals are an expression of individual or group values. Values provide the foundation for a vision. They inspire motivation and provide the direction and perseverance to attain a goal. So, the power to realize your dreams, achieve desires such as personal freedom, true success and lasting joy in your life, comes from being congruent from the inside out. The components are:

Need/Value + Vision/Mission + Plans + Actions

+ Reflection on Outcome + Change

= Your Life Dance

Armed with your values, skills, preferences, and personal mission, goals are the next step and are realized through the consequent plans you make and the actions you take. All of the pieces work together. For example, a dancer who knows her presence, orients herself on a stage and faces the audience; moving from her body's center of gravity she dances the story she is living.

ABOUT GOALS

You have probably heard someplace or know studies that prove the value of writing down your goals. A research study sponsored by the Ford Foundation[15] discovered that:

- 23 percent of the population has no idea what they want from life, and as a result, they do not have much.

- 67 percent of the population has a general idea of what they want, but they do not have any plans for how to get it.

- Only 10 percent of the population has specific, well-defined goals, but even then, seven out of the ten of those people reach their goals only half the time. The top 3 percent, however, achieved their goals 89 percent of the time.

That's a remarkable difference, isn't it? What's the difference between the 3 percent and the others? Those people **wrote down their goals**. You can reach 100 percent by creating your BEST possible goals.

Unfortunately setting goals sometimes is a setup for disappointment and frustration – much the way New Year resolutions can be if they are not well thought out. At a certain point, many people ask, "Why do it, because nothing happens?" When you follow the suggestions in this chapter, you'll be pleasantly surprised to find that you can actually set a goal – and reach it.

That is to say, not without a lot of hard work, but you will realize your goals when they are created wisely.

THE BEST GOALS

What is the difference between a wish and a goal? Ask 100 people if they want to be happier, have more money or have more leisure time, and of course they will say yes. It's like the classic line, "You can never be too rich or too thin." Your BEST Goals are much more likely to be realized. BEST Goals breathe life

---

> "
>
> A goal properly set is halfway reached.
>
> ### ZIG ZIGLAR

> "
>
> Think little goals and expect little achievements. Think big goals and win big success.
>
> ### DAVID JOSEPH SCHWARTZ

into your actions and fill in the vivid colors of your dreams. Your BEST Goals are:

B Bodacious

Your goals need to call to you. When they are courageous, spirited and remarkably enticing, you'll wake up each morning excited about what you are doing that day to realize your goals.

E Exist Now

Your goal needs to exist to you NOW. What does it look like, sound like, smell like, feel like? You'll need to work on this aspect because you don't yet know these things, yet, the more real you can make your goal, the more quickly it will come to fruition. Make your goal real by stating it in the present tense and setting a deadline. Give yourself a completion date: "My world cruise leaves San Francisco on Oct. 10 at 9 a.m."

The benefits of target dates for reaching goals are:

1. Dates alert your body chemistry to react to the timetable you've set.

2. Deadlines help you to think, act and react with urgency.

3. End dates create a personal challenge.

4. Deadlines keep you on schedule.

S Specific

This means taking "be happier" to the next level: "Feel more confident of myself," or "Share my life with someone." You can be even more specific than that: "Feel more confident of myself when I'm speaking to a group," or "Share my life with someone who loves the ocean the way I do." The more specific you are, the more you breathe life into your goal. It becomes real, something you can envision – and ultimately, something you can make happen.

T Timely

This means your goal is grounded in real time. Use deadlines to set a structure for your goal and keep it on track. Timely also refers to the hierarchy of needs, and if this goal is appropriate for the level of need you are at. (See Developmental Models, Hierarchy of Needs.) You wouldn't ask a drowning person what they want to be when they grow up; you would throw them a life preserver.

> A goal without a plan is just a wish.
>
> **LARRY ELDER**

"

Actions are visible,
though motives are secret.

SAMUEL JOHNSON

WORTHY GOALS

Now, let's explore your goal as a worthy goal, using the following five functions. Once you do, you'll find that your goals are easy to implement. It's easy to define action steps that are in line with your goal, and it's easy to maintain a focus on your goal.

A goal you are moving toward makes the world a better place, has intrinsic value to you, does not conflict with other goals and when it scares you, you are able to "walk toward the cannons." You are courageous when you are challenged.

MOTIVATION

Why do you want it? Is it about external success or internal happiness?

ORIENTATION

What is your focal point? Is this goal pulling you or pushing you?

VALUES

What conflicts might this goal have with other values?

ANXIETY

What scares you most – that you will fail, or that you will succeed?

NOBILITY

How does this goal make you a better person? How does this goal make the world better?

MOTIVATION

Your ability to manifest your goal often depends on why you want it. That's why it's valuable to take the time to examine what is motivating you. Success lies not necessarily on what we want, but why we want it.

Ask yourself if you are motivated internally or if you are gravitating toward a goal because of status or image – something external. Has this always been your dream, ever since you can remember? Why? Be honest. Ask yourself if you have something to prove.

Two people can have the same goal but have two different dominant motivating factors. While there is a little of each element in our motivations – we can desire a beautiful home because it makes us feel creative and connected to our loved ones. At the same time, we can still have a little part inside that likes the way others perceive us when they come to see our home. It's just a matter of understanding which motivation is in the driver's seat.

ORIENTATION

It's important to be conscious of whether we are moving toward a goal or away from a situation or emotion we don't like. This is the concept of approach or avoidance. Are you moving toward something you want to invite into your life? Or are you dancing away from something you don't want? Some goals have a "pull;" others are formed because of a "push" factor, something we want to get away from. Often, our orientation is a little bit of both.

I know of the story of Ruth, an older woman who lived alone and wanted to secure her future by living somewhere near people who cared for her and could help in times of need. Her orientation, though, was on aging, and her emotions about this were fear and insecurity. This influenced how she viewed the situation. She decided to move to the town where her brother and sister lived. It was far away from the town in which she had spent the past 20 years. She had many friends there. In this new town, she moved to a small house -- something that at the time she thought would be easier to maintain. But instead, she felt cooped up in the smaller quarters. She also found her family had little time for her. She spent most of her time alone, watching television, and she missed her friends terribly. She didn't have the security she sought, and her feelings turned bitter toward her family for not making more time to be with her. After a while, she noticed they would come see her when she was sick. So she found herself getting sick more often.

Ruth decided to face the fears that had influenced her orientation on her goal. She started to envision a different life in a place near the water, with a view, near her friends. In this new life, she would keep in touch with her family and make regular trips to see them. She would ask them to visit her when they had free weekends.

Everything changed for Ruth when she shifted her orientation. No longer was she moving away from something, but rather, she was moved toward a vision that called to her.

VALUES

If you have goals that are tied to your personal values, they can still sometimes be at odds with one another. The goal is not to prevent conflict, but to

> Continuity does not rule out fresh approaches to fresh situations.
>
> **DEAN RUSK**

> "
>
> Virtue is the
> truest nobility.
>
> ## CERVANTES

acknowledge it, dance with it and open the doors to creativity. Sometimes you need others to help, the key is knowing when, and being able to ask for help.

For instance, this can be seen in professional working women who value being a good mother and also value excelling in their profession. At times, both goals conflict, calling for creativity in aligning the goals. It's alright to have conflicting goals, as long as you are aware of them and allow them to move toward integration.

ANXIETY

"But what if I fail?" The degree of anxiety you feel around this question will tell you how much it matters to you. The more invested you are in reaching your goal; the more likely you are to succeed. You are also more likely to feel anxiety about failing.

You can work through anxiety by identifying short- and long-term goals. This way, you can enjoy the completion of small accomplishments as you take steps toward the "big hairy" goal of your dream.

"Big hairy" goals can be anxiety-inducing just by thinking about them. When I wanted to buy a boat, I didn't even want to think about the possibility of not being able to buy it or what I would do with it when I had it. I couldn't bear it. So I broke the goal down into smaller steps stepping away from the fears of the big hairy goal. First, I had to decide whether I'd like sleeping on a boat. Then, I needed to learn about types of boats in order to narrow down the choices. The next goal became finding a boat loan broker. This way I could focus on one goal at a time. "Buy a large boat" was too big. It freaked me out. Setting the smaller goals made it easier to execute because less anxiety was getting in the way.

NOBILITY

Not all goals are equal. Some are better than others. Goals oriented toward intimacy, spiritual development and generativity lead to more happiness, while goals related to only self and power do not. Research shows that trying to convince others that you are more powerful, smarter or better than others leads only to eventual dissatisfaction.

FEAR OF FAILURE, OR FEAR OF SUCCESS?

Ask yourself what frightens you more -- failure or success? If you succeeded, what would change about your life? What would you like about that change? What would you dislike? If you failed, what's the worst thing that could happen? Explore these questions. They will help you sort out the source of your anxiety. If your fear is of success, then go back to the previous sections and test the worthiness of your goal. Perhaps it's not on target with your values. Perhaps it needs to be more focused. Inject your vision with your values, and see if it shifts.

FEEL THE FEAR AND LET IT GO

Any major life change upsets the status quo. It may require letting go of something or someone and can bring up fears. If there is something you need to leave behind, you can either do it consciously and well ... or not. There are some who need to make the present so horrible they have to leave it. Examples are the teenager who has to get into some kind of terrible argument with her parents to leave home, the spouse or partner who makes the relationship so toxic she has to leave, or the partner leaves. You know the style. The healthiest choice is to feel the fear and do it anyway, taking small steps to create change.

ADVOCACY

Become your own best advocate by practicing positive thinking. Positive thinking is crucial when setting yourself on a course with your worthy goals. It's important to see the glass half full, rather than half empty. Sometimes I call positive thinking mental yoga. The goal is to increase your awareness of your inner dialogue and reframe negative thoughts to positive ones.

Your mind has a habit of jumping over negative declarations – when you think or say, "I will not eat chocolate," the statement becomes "I will eat chocolate." Whenever you avoid something, you are actually inviting it into your life.

Positive thinking reinforces your effort. As you work toward your goals, give yourself credit for your successes, relish your achievements. Go easy on yourself. Accept your imperfections. No one is perfect, and no one ventures into a new endeavor without mistakes. You're going to make mistakes. It's not about being

"

Action conquers fear.

PETER NIVIO ZARLENGA

"

Trust, but verify.

RONALD REAGAN

perfect and not making mistakes; it's about learning from your mistakes. It's more important to move forward than to do the right thing or what others expect of you. Don't wait for the perfect goals or the perfect circumstances. Don't wait to know the perfect next step. Instead, stay centered, stay in touch with your authenticity, and you'll know the steps to take. You may never know the entire dance all at once; you may only know the next steps. It's important simply to begin your dance and trust the process.

LIFE'S ARENAS

All of your life is unfolding on differing stages or settings, they are your body, mind, home, work and so on. Every goal in your life plays out on these stages in different ways. Take the time to map out how your goals will play out in different arenas of your life. This work is a bit like rehearsing. You can see how you will proceed, what might unfold, and how you can deal with obstacles you might face.

Let's take the example of my goal of buying a large boat to live on in California. This one goal generated goals in all the other arenas of my life.

BODY GOAL | Get back flexibility and strength in my broken leg so I can sail and walk around on a boat and not fall off.

MIND GOAL | Learn how to sail.

EMOTIONAL GOAL | Work on my fear of sailing.

SPIRIT GOAL | Allow myself to really enjoy sailing.

RELATIONSHIPS | Work with my husband, who doesn't like boats, to embrace the idea. Make new friends who sail.

WORK GOAL | Create a virtual office by getting a telephone and wireless service on the boat so I can do business there.

FINANCIAL GOAL | Figure out how to pay for it.

SERVICE | Offer boat cruises as raffle prizes for nonprofit organizations. Help others realize their impossible dreams.

DAILY GOAL PLANNING

Remember every day to keep an eye on the overall balance of your life, using your goals as a guide in prioritizing your time and attention. As you move into planning and scheduling your day, make certain you are acting congruently with your values and goals. Schedule the activities that support your body, mind, emotions and spirit as well as your home, professional and social life in accordance with your life plan. Then live your life in the present, free from worry about the future.

Like most things in life, you will get better at LifeDancing, with practice. You will begin to notice the knot in your stomach easing up and goals being met with more frequency.

THE UNEXPECTED
BUMPS & OBSTACLES

Another person's lack of planning often ends up being your emergency. The less tolerance you have for these interruptions, the fewer you will have in your life. You might want to begin to align yourself with people who value their lives as much as you do.

On the other hand, the unexpected happens. When researchers followed people who experienced natural disasters such as floods or earthquakes, they discovered that what made the difference between those who did or did not flourish in the face of disaster was that those who believed that they had some control or impact on outcomes did much better than those who framed themselves as victims. According to the International Critical Stress Foundation,[17] being at the mercy of events does not serve you as well as being the designer of your life. Using their model of Talk, Tears and Time, you sort out and take the trauma out of life's disasters.

Learn how to fall, jump and roll, it will serve you well, as you dance toward your goals.

SHARING YOUR GOALS

There is a time to share your goals with others and a time to guard them. If you're afraid of someone's criticism about any goal, be careful about sharing that goal -- just yet. Ideally, you will become so confident and certain of your goals that when you share them, your confidence is so high that other's criticism does

"

If it isn't good, let it die.
If it doesn't die,
make it good.

AJAHN CHAH

"

People in the zone are Relaxed, Confident, Focused, In Control and their efforts are Automatic, Effortless and Fun.

UNKNOWN

not phase you. You may need to dance for a while with your goals before that is true for you.

OBSTACLES & ReFRAMING

I remember telling someone about my live-aboard-boat goal and her response was, "Are you serious? Have you ever owned a boat before? Do you know how to go about buying a boat?" and much more. These questions could have fed into fears like not being taken seriously or having a really crazy idea, and my goal momentum could have been lost. Instead I took it as an opportunity to use some creativity, ReFrame my goal and explore the question she had asked. As a reframe, rather than thinking "she isn't taking me seriously," I thought "I've just surprised her with an idea that's outside the box." Then I started making lists of things to explore, such as how to purchase a boat, how to know what boat to buy and more. There is always a flip side to every coin or new way of looking at anything.

NEWS FLASH: "You can't make everyone happy" – and that's okay. In fact it's not your job to make everyone happy, it's each person's own job. Whenever you find yourself going tilt in the face of goal criticism, simply revisit your goal, check it out with the steps above, and if you emerge with a YES, I'm keeping this goal, the next time someone criticizes, you simply say," Thank you for your concern," and move on.

THE LAW OF FOCUSED INTEREST

Once you begin forming goals, you set in motion the function of focused interest, a force that draws resources to you seemingly from nowhere. This law works because you are receptive and open to anything that resonates with your goal. You are picking up information that was always there; you simply were not aware of it because your attention was not focused on it. Suddenly, you begin to see articles and books relating to your goals, you hear relevant conversations, meet new people and find new ways of doing the same activities. Once you focus on an area, you attune yourself in a way, like selecting a television station, so that you become fully receptive to information of concern to you and your goals.

SLIP SLIDIN' AWAY

Sometimes even with the best planning, we reach a point where we simply cannot take the next step toward our goal. I remember the lyrics from the song "Slip Slidin' Away" by Paul Simon that talks about when we are nearer our destination, the more we are slip slidin' away. Sometimes I don't notice that I'm near the realization of a goal that I've been working on for a very long time. One of the events that gives me a "head's up" is when I simply avoid doing something I know I must, and really want, to do. I noticed this when I needed to call and fire a property manager for my mother's home. I had worked for two years after her death to clean up her house; it was in very bad shape due to her decline and refusal to allow anybody to help her. Part of me was managing the estate, and part of me was making up for all that time she wouldn't let me help. All the work was done and the house sparkled. The last task was to hire a property manager. I had interviewed two property managers and one had jumped in and started acting in that role before we had signed a contract. I needed to call her, tell her to cease and desist so I could hire the firm I believed would be the best to manage the property. I would sit and stare at the telephone, telling myself it was only one phone call. I did this for three days in a row. Finally I accepted the fact that I simply would not do it. I called a friend and asked her if she would make the call for me. She thought I was being odd, because I'm not usually afraid of much, and made the call for me. As I figured, the person was angry and defensive. The call had been made and she was fired.

If you find yourself slip-slidin' away, get support, and help if you need it. Yes, when a goal is met you will need to move on. There is always a new goal, shimmering on the horizon.

BABY STEPS

That one phone call to the property manager was a small step in the termination of one phase and an opportunity for another to emerge. It also reminds me that the original goal seemed overwhelming: "To repair and upgrade the house so it could be rented." The first day I walked into the house, with my daughter, all I could do was stand there, totally immobilized, and stare with my mouth open.

> "
>
> Oh, how precious is time, and how it pains me to see it slide away, while I do so little to any good purpose.
>
> ## DAVID BRAINERD

"

Grief is a process,

not a state.

ANNE
GRANT

There was stuff everywhere! It hadn't been painted in 20 years. The yard needed work, the plumbing was clogged, and there were many spiders in residence in every room. My daughter took one look at me and knew I was in trouble. Being a good daughter, and a friend, she grabbed my shoulder and reminded me that we would simply take it one step at a time, and offered an idea that got me moving, "Mom, why don't you clean out this closet?"

My daughter's direction broke me out of my trance of overwhelm, and I got started on the closet. When we left and were chatting in the car about the magnitude of the goal that had grown into a project, we started to break it down into smaller goals:

1 - Go through the "stuff" room by room. Make three piles:

- Keep

- Toss or Donate

- I Can't Decide

2 - When all the rooms have been sorted, boxed to Keep, bagged to Toss or Donate, we would move on to the next phases:

- Repair

- Clean

- Paint or replace

- Redo the landscaping

- Interview property managers

- Hire a manager

If we got stuck at any stage, we would break that step down into even smaller steps :

REPAIR

- What needs to be repaired?

- Who would be the best person to do that?

- Us versus a contractor?

If a contractor, how do we find/choose one? Answer: Talk to the neighbors and see if they can recommend anyone.

We did that and found a great team to help us with the house. I also discovered that my daughter is a great plumber and she was the one to replace all the toilets. What a surprise!

So, when a simple goal expands into a major project, you can use the Project Worksheet in **APPENDIX B** and, as you'll see in **Chapter 8**, create a Mind-Map and break your goal down into Baby Steps.

PERSEVERANCE FURTHERS

The achievement of your goals and the acquisition of what you want rests on your willingness and ability to persist in your efforts. Daily practices such as meditation on your goals, informal meditation, keeping a Design Guide, and daily planning are the most productive and successful activities you have in your toolbox. Look past obstacles, or reframe them into opportunities, believe in yourself, cultivate your sense of humor, and remember to keep moving.

Acknowledge small successes in the attainment of your goals, each step is important and worthy of celebration. After each day working on my mother's house, my daughter and I would go out for dinner and relax.

Believe in yourself. Obstacles will arise. Learn from them and move on.

GOALS AND DREAMS

Use your Design Guide file to keep your dreams alive. The goals you create will be dynamic; as you get closer to them, they will become clearer and may even change. Create files for the following categories on your computer (Bookmarks in your browser) and in your filing cabinet. You'll have a place to put resources in that you come across.

Body

Mind

Emotions

Spirituality

Relationships

Work

Home

Service

Add others that are part of your life.

You'll be setting specific goals as you read about your life's arenas and assess your satisfaction in those areas. Let's get started by learning how to state your

"

Perseverance, secret of all triumphs.

VICTOR HUGO

> A goal is a dream
> with a deadline.
>
> **NAPOLEON HILL**

goals. You'll find it interesting to set some goals now before you assess yourself more deeply to see if you already know what you need.

Remember to state your goals positively and in the present tense, with a deadline. Here are examples of properly stated goals in each category to get you started.

BODY. By _____ I have a physical fitness program that I stick to and enjoy.

MIND. By _____ I meditate every day for 30 minutes.

EMOTIONS. By _____ I will have learned how to notice when my feelings begin to overwhelm me and have a coping skill to intervene, such as deep breathing.

SPIRITUALITY. I have scheduled a personal retreat to reconnect with my spirituality every quarter by _____.

RELATIONSHIPS. My relationship with my significant other is healthy, dynamic and loving by _____.

WORK. I have work I enjoy and am fairly paid for by _____.

HOME. I have a vegetable garden planted by _____.

SERVICE. I have committed to _____ to volunteer my services for specific days and times by _____.

Remember, a vision or purpose is not measurable; it is intangible, ongoing and constantly evolving. It dances with you. A purpose is an ideal toward which you strive, a vision or concept you hold to be of value. You begin to bring purpose into reality as you create and act on your goals. Use the following worksheet to ensure that your Goals are congruent with your Values and Vision.

Use the **PROJECT WORKSHEET** | 2.7 | in the **MASTER CLASS WORKBOOK** to practice organizing projects.

You will be setting goals for yourself as you read and work through the areas that follow. Refer back to this section on Goals as you create goals that work for you.

Your Goals must make you smile and help you enjoy your Dance of Life!

CHAPTER EIGHT

The Dance of Strategy

THE LEADER YOU'RE LOOKING FOR
IS INSIDE OF YOU
CREATING A LIFE PLAN

I know, you're already thinking about skipping this chapter, words like "I don't need a Life Plan," "Planning = Boring," and more flit through your head. I HIGHLY recommend setting those thoughts aside and bearing with me for a few pages to consider a Life Plan for your own benefit. I'm guessing those homeless folks you see on the streets didn't create a plan for their current lifestyle, life just happened and unfortunately, there they are today.

Setting objectives and reaching desired goals are essential to your Life-Dance. It is important that the most direct route to any desired outcome be plotted and reviewed as you live day to day. It is also important that you have a plan so that when you hit a bump or obstacle, take a side trip and wander off your path, you can alter or change the plan to bring you back to "Center."

Imagine watching a dancer trip and fall. Does she lie on the stage and wait for someone to save her? No, not unless it had been planned ahead of time. Usually, if a dancer bobbles, the audience doesn't even see it because the dancer uses the dynamics of her body to restore her equilibrium and continue her dance. She brings herself back to center because she's practiced coming back into balance many, many times. Falling and recovering from it, is part of the dance.

We all have "tripping and falling" stories. Relax, and enjoy reading one of mine that may make you smile. My story begins aboard my boat LifeDancing when a fellow sailor asked me if my family and I would like to join him and his wife to take our two boats up the delta and anchor out for a few days. It sounded like fun, so I checked with my family, which includes my husband, my daughter and son-in-law and their 6-month-old baby. They all agreed, including the dogs. I knew I didn't have enough dog food aboard, it looked like we needed a PLAN to get supplies and prepare the boat, before we could head up-river. Clearly it was

time to create a plan!

PLANNING CAN BE FUN

Planning is a process that ranges from the very simple – planning your day – to more complex – planning your life. Strategic planning is a way of getting from here to there as gloriously as you want. If you want a trip where you wander anywhere you like, you have a different kind of plan, one in which time is of the essence, yet both are plans. The planning process includes a:

- MindMap
- List of all essential steps, tasks, events
- Diagram that serves as a visual aid to planning
- Method for monitoring and evaluating the plan

Let's begin with what I consider the fun part of the process, MindMapping.

MINDMAPPING

I discovered MindMapping, or some call it Brain Mapping, in my last year of graduate school. When I discovered what a great tool it was, I was disappointed that I hadn't known about it before. MindMapping (as I'll refer to it) is the singular best way to gather disparate information and then organize it. I use it with clients and for myself whenever I approach something that needs to be sorted out or planned. I have a 100 percent success rate using MindMaps to demystify any problem. I used it to plan our boat adventure and my daughter and I made a MindMap of my mother's house project.

So let's get you started with a MindMap. Choose one of the Goals you identified in the previous chapter to create your first plan. Write your goal down on your | 2.8a | **MIND MAPPING WORKSHEET** or **PROJECT WORKSHEET** in your **MASTER CLASS WORKBOOK**. You've probably already started thinking about your first goal and many things have come to mind. Let's say I started a list of what to take on the boat trip, i.e., baby diapers and dog food and I have a thought of "check the rigging." Your MindMap allows both sides of your brain, the linear and wholistic, to work interactively so NO information is lost. While I'm thinking of diapers and kibble, I can start another track of boat preparation and not lose that important information. I consider the first MindMap to be a big information gathering process giving me the overview of the plan.

To create your own MindMap, begin by drawing a circle or other shape in the middle of the page and put the name of the plan or project in the middle along with the date. Draw lines, tracks or spokes, for any topic that comes to mind. I've started with Preparing the Boat, Stocking the Boat, Plotting the Course. Later, a track may become its own MindMap if it begins to get loaded with information. Draw tracks off the lines as new ideas come to you. As you explore the main idea, you can also write down feelings and intuitions as they emerge. Don't push yourself to make vague items clear at this stage, this is the big information-gathering event. When you believe or feel you've explored your goal as much as you can for now, put the MindMap in a project binder and save it for later.

Here's an example of the beginning Boat Adventure MindMap.

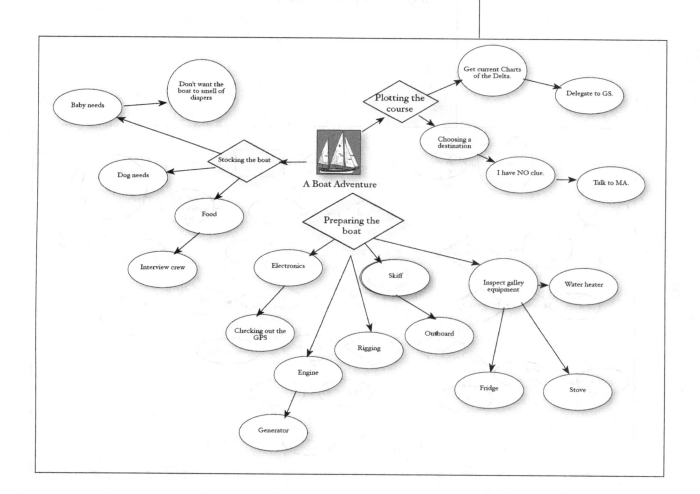

You see the name of the plan is at the center in a box "A Boat Adventure." Then there are lines, or tracks, pointing to diamonds that are separate tracks to be worked on. As I'm naming a diamond, ideas come to mind, so I draw more lines off of the appropriate diamonds. While I'm thinking of Baby Needs, in an oval, I think "What if the boat sinks, what about the baby that can't swim, we need a skiff with a good engine," so Skiff goes on the Boat Preparation track immediately and then I can return to thinking about baby food.

The only rule in creating a MindMap is that there are NO bad ideas, EVERYTHING gets written down somewhere. If you have an idea and some part of you edits it out, create a track which is entitled, "Edited Ideas," you really don't want to miss ALL of your ideas that pop up now, and may be important later.

Back to planning for the Boat Adventure: I've decided that Preparing the Boat is the most important place to start. I refuse to help drown my new grandson so I want the boat to be as prepared and safe as possible. A new MindMap is begun for Preparing the Boat.

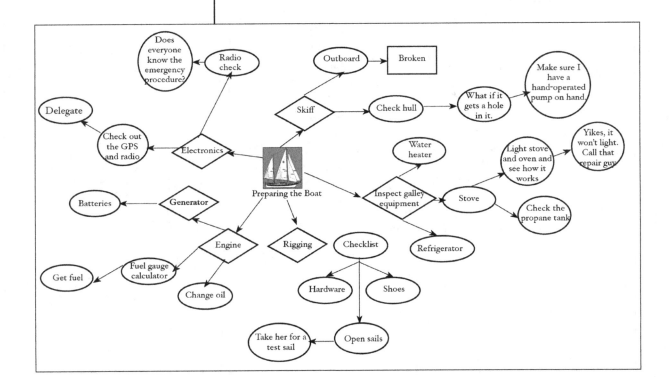

Let's say I want to start acting on my Project of the Great Boat Adventure, now what? Yippee is in order for you list lovers; it's list time. Look at the spokes on your center figure and put them in an outline form.

Wow, that's a lot of things to do! The question becomes, what path will get me to my Goal as quickly as possible. This plan is called a |2.8b| **CRITICAL PATH FLOW CHART** in the **MASTER CLASS WORKBOOK**. This path is concerned primarily with the completion of your project on time and within the limits of the human and other resources available. The technique includes the development of a timeline that shows the sequence and timing of the steps. It is the choreography of a path, or dance, such as the Great Boat Adventure, Cleaning the Garage, or Planning My Career that makes this plan Strategic.

The timeline diagram shows each event that must be accomplished before proceeding from one step to the next. Notice there are start and end dates.

Take a good look at your timeline and add any new tasks that come to mind. If you don't have computer software that helps you move from a Mind Map, to a list, to a timeline, you can complete the same process by using small stickies and a large sheet of paper to move them around on. The software I use is called Inspiration[18] and is used in schools and personal and business arenas.

This is clearly a first draft. The plan grew much larger as I progressed on my journey, but it gave me a place to start. Sometimes people have difficulty starting at the beginning and moving forward. If this is your case, start at the end point

PREPARING THE BOAT

1 RIGGING
  a Checklist
    1 Sheets
    2 Hardware
    3 Open Sails
  b Take her for a test sail

2 ENGINE
  a Generator
  b Batteries
  c Change oil
  d Get Fuel
    1 Fuel Gauge Calibration

3 ELECTRONICS
  a Checking out the GPS
    1 Delegate to GS
  b Radio Check
    1 Does Everyone Know the Emergency Procedure?

4 SKIFF
  a Check Inflation
    1 What if it Gets a Hole in It?
    a Make sure I have a hand-operated air pump onboard
    b Outboard

5 INSPECT GALLEY EQUIPMENT
  a Stove
    1 Check the propane tank level
    2 Light stove & oven to see they work
      a Yikes, it won't light. Call boat repair guy
  b Refrigerator
  c Water Heater

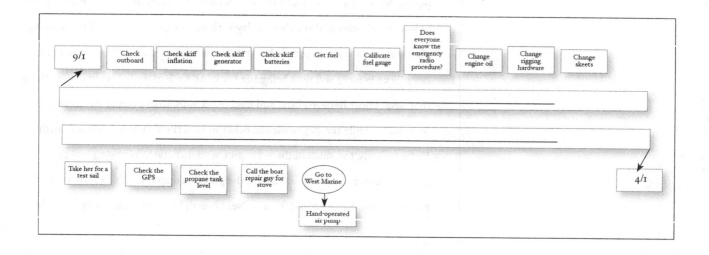

BACKOUT SCHEDULE

7 Go to West Marine for supplies on list

6 Call boat repair guy to check/repair stove

5 Check propane tank level so repair guy has fuel to test the stove

4 Check out GPS while afloat

3 Take her out for test sail

2 Check out sheets (lines)

1 Check out rigging hardware

Remember, number one is at the bottom.

and work backwards. This is sometimes called a Backout Schedule. Using this approach my last task of "Go to West Marine" becomes the point from which I work backward.

If you have difficulty deciding what priority or importance one step has over the other, refer to the "Step by Step" solution in the Wholistic Problem Solving chapter (Chapter 9).

LAUNCHING THE ADVENTURE

So, back to the adventure. I delegated the engine and rigging repair, told my daughter SHE had to plan for the baby. I prioritized the other tasks and put them on my calendar. When launch day came, I felt like we had accomplished a Herculean task. We left port with two boats, six adults, one baby and two dogs. We had enough food for weeks, water toys to keep us entertained and board games for the evenings. The one thing that completely changed our trip was a problem no one thought about or planned for.

The older dog decided she would NOT go poop on the boat. It had never occurred to us that one of the dogs wouldn't pee and poo on the boat. I thought I was a friggin' genius when I read about wrapping up a rope coil for them to relieve themselves on, and rinsing it in the sea. The boat was big enough that during a calm sea, they could walk forward or aft and have some privacy to do their business, but OH NO. The 55-pound Australian Cattle Dog would NOT. Of course the Yorkie would pee and poo anywhere, including the Salon. We tried everything to encourage Shaman, but NOPE, she was not going potty on the boat. It looked like we would have to take her to land.

This was one major bump we had not planned for. How does one get a 55 pound dog off a 45 foot boat that rides high in the water and needs at least 5 feet of bottom clearance, three times a day with no one getting hurt? The beginning plan was that we would paddle her over to the closest dike, take her ashore, let her relieve herself, and then bring her back. All we had to do was find something that would float between boat and land, with more than one person aboard so one could handle the dog while the other moved the floatable back and forth. Unfortunately, the small outboard engine wouldn't start, so rowing was the engine of the day. Luckily, someone in the group had an inflatable canoe that two people and a dog could fit into. Next bump, how does one lower a terrified

55-pound dog into a small canoe safely (three times a day)? After a lot of group head scratching and "adult" conversations with the dog, someone had an idea. They suggested we rig up a winch on one of the booms to lower her safely. Next problem, how do we hook up the dog to the end of the boom/winch arrangement. Right, more head scratching. Of course one of the women, being aware of wardrobe, remembered we had a lifejacket for each dog aboard and maybe it would act as a "dog holder." It worked! So, the daily drill looked something this: For four days, the dog and 5 people executed their plan. Two people would get into the canoe. Then we would "suit up" the dog and someone would hold her still while someone else hooked her lifejacket to the hook on the boom winch cable. Then, the two people onboard LifeDancing slowly released the cable and lowered the dog into the waiting arms of the two people in the canoe. Then two people, one paddling and the other holding the dog, paddled the dog to the dike. One person took her ashore while the other kept the canoe safely at the shore rocks. Then the drill went into reverse. It turned out that we used about four hours a day, taking the dog to go pee and poo. Who'd have thought? Clearly, our daily schedule changed dramatically. Planning for four days of relaxation changed to four days of relaxation, interspersed with taking a dog to go poo. Once we realized what we were looking at, it became yet another adventure on our trip. Then there was the day my friend slipped and fell out of the canoe.

SCHEDULING FOR RESULTS

When did each of these activities happen? It was easy with a plan once we knew what had to be done. After scheduling, people knew what shift and job they needed to participate in for things to go smoothly. Planning your time needs is a habit you will develop as part of your daily routine, just like brushing your teeth. Planning and scheduling are simply organizing and creating your future in a mindful way. I know this sounds REALLY boring, especially for a dancer, AND every dancer is tightly scheduled so that she can eat, sleep, practice, perform and celebrate.

I always start with the big schedule, Yearly or Monthly and move to "What am I going to do today?" So to plan and schedule for the Great and Wonderful Boat Adventure (yes, it's growing) I needed to look at the seven months between September 1, and April 1 At first it looked like plenty of time, so I ask why plan?

"

Time makes what is potential, actual.

I CHING

"

You will never win if you never begin.

HELEN ROWLAND

> The key is not to prioritize what's on your schedule, but to schedule your priorities.
>
> ## STEVEN COVEY

Answer - Because I know that I'll wait until the last minute or let life get in the way and be scurrying days before launch. Personally, I'd rather have more time than I need rather than cut corners because I don't have enough time and I'm rushing.

For your goals, start with your timeline, like the one above. I knew I'd be busy during Thanksgiving, the Christmas holidays and New Years and others would as well, so I knew I'd best get as much done during September and October as possible and leave the smaller (picking up supplies) until later. Using the master schedule as a template, I make the monthly plans. From there, I move into weekly and daily plans. There are many online or software calendar solutions. I'm on a Macintosh platform and use iCal. It lets me set up individual calendars and view them Monthly, Weekly and Daily. If you're a paper and pencil person, use the forms in this book (See Appendix B) or other planner forms you can find at any office supply store.

THE SCHEDULING PROCESS

As you enter activities into your working schedules, be certain to estimate how much time each activity might take. Also remember to schedule in some slide time. A good rule of thumb is to leave 25 percent of each day unscheduled. On the other hand, plan your day so the time is not eaten up by trivialities. This kind of planning gives you an idea of how much you plan to accomplish in the following week. Better to know ahead of time what you are facing, rather than at the end of the week when all your time and energy is exhausted, and there is no room for accomplishing your high priorities. When you are facing more to do that you have time to spend, you have some tools you can bring into play.

Start your scheduling by asking yourself, can I delegate any of these tasks to someone I can count on? Suddenly, my timeline has changed because I have more time. I also need to follow up and make sure those I delegated to are on time. I have found great joy in reaching a goal, on time. There is a real sense of accomplishment and empowerment to be savored at these moments.

Yikes, now the pedal is hitting the metal on the Great Boat Adventure, the engine starts and we motor out of our slip into the river to the delta area. The wind comes up and sails are unfurled. The dancer is on the stage of the adventure, leaping into the future.

So how did this all unfold? Here's the success process beginning with your MindMap and creating your List or Strategic Plan: (If you like, use the Strategic Plan form, which you'll find in Appendix B and the forms section of the **MASTER CLASS WORKBOOK**, section 2.8d.)

FIRST – DELEGATE

Are there any activities in your plan you can delegate to another person?

SECOND – PRIORITIZE

Ask yourself: How will this new project fit into my current plan? How high a priority is it, and do I need to move other things to a later date? Now is the time to let your family and friends know you will be busier than usual, also let them know how they can help and support you.

THIRD - PARE IT DOWN

Which one of those things can you say "no" to, eliminate or put off? OK, so I don't need that many cans of tuna.

FOURTH – MAKE IT HAPPEN

Fit the remaining tasks into your life. Here are some ideas to streamline each day:

- Start your day earlier.
- Don't answer the phone; gather your messages to call back later.
- Close your door and only allow visits during a scheduled hour if you're at work.
- Do all your correspondence at one sitting.
- Make all your telephone calls at once.
- Cluster activities such as errands or meetings.
- Don't stop until you've completed as much as your energy allows.

Depending on how busy you are, you may need to create a weekly and/or daily schedule. Each one gets more and more complete.

Each day, review your list of activities and decide which ones you can get done today. Depending on how complex your life is, you may have a simple list of things to do or a complete database to choose from. Being the Type A, creative overachiever that I am, I have set up a database in a software program with all my project tasks, prioritized and categorized. Once a week I check off the tasks that are completed and schedule this week's items. I usually create my daily schedule the night before or first thing in the morning. The night before is

> You got to be careful if you don't know where you're going, because you might not get there.
>
> **YOGI BERRA**

"

Wonder is from surprise,
and surprise stops
with experience.

ROBERT
SOUTH

best in case you need to get an early start and need to prepare things for the next day.

Time estimates are very critical when planning your day. Put your higher priority items first and include room for activities to expand. Don't forget to include time for meals, meditation, exercise, spirit and relationships. Remember: **You are a whole person with more needs than just getting the work done.**

This planning should take 20 to 30 minutes for your weekly plan on Saturday or Sunday and 10 to 15 minutes for each daily plan, preferably done the night before.

Knowing how you operate now, how much time can you realistically schedule each day to get the work done the way you want it done? As you proceed through the day and unscheduled events eat up your time, be sure to ask yourself if this unscheduled item is more important than the activity you originally scheduled for this time period. If the answer is yes, do what you must. If it is no, find a way to put it off until another time. Ask yourself if the item that comes up could have been planned. The more in control you are of your time, the more effective you will feel.

As you proceed through the day, find a way of indicating on your activities list which items were accomplished and which were not. At the end of each day, review the items left undone. Now, ask yourself if you begin to see patterns of the tasks you regularly do not begin or finish.

TRACKING A DAY

If you find yourself often wondering where all of your time goes, use the Time Log that follows.

These daily records create a portrait of your day. I like to do this periodically just to bring into my awareness what my current "rut" is. For example, I got up the other morning, fed the dogs, made coffee and hopped in the shower. My mind was caught up in a business issue and I found myself standing in the shower wondering if I'd washed my hair. My body was in the shower and my mind was at work. I prefer that my body and mind be in the same place, especially in a slippery shower.

In the Time Log, the section that lists thoughts and feelings, I could enter

"Took a shower," I would list that my mind was already at work while my body got washed. How did I feel about that? I felt robbed of one of my favorite activities – standing in a wonderful shower and taking in all the sensory experiences, including my overpriced body wash that smells like a sea of lavender. When you complete your daily log, look at the tasks and ask yourself:

- Were these items generated by me or somebody else?
- Were they interruptions?

More information about the Time Portrait process can be found in | 2.8c | **TIME PORTRAIT** in the **MASTER CLASS WORKBOOK**.

UNEXPECTED LIFE EVENTS: CRISES, INTERRUPTIONS & EMERGENCIES

Another person's lack of planning often ends up being your emergency or distraction. Now here's the good news, the less tolerance you have of interruptions by others, the fewer you will have in your life. If setting limits with others is a new skill for you, you'll have to be doubly emphatic about your need for privacy or personal space. Looking forward, you might want to begin to align yourself with people who value their time and their lives as much as you do by planning and reducing unexpected problems.

A few new habits could be to schedule time for phone calls, cluster appointments and travel time, and tell people when you will be available. Start meetings on time; don't wait for the late arrivals. I know I don't like it when I'm on time and then have to wait for the late folks. Manage unexpected drop-ins by creating meetings for them that are scheduled on future dates. Once they get used to it, family, friends and colleagues will appreciate planning quality time with you.

If you find that time disappears (flies or runs out the window) or you believe that you often are not spending your time fruitfully, you may need to examine your beliefs about how you manage your time before you can set boundaries like this. That's where your | 2.8c | **TIME PORTRAIT** form in the **MASTER CLASS WORKBOOK** comes in.

When you schedule your day, you need to know how much time you can plan and how much time you can leave available for unscheduled items. If you don't have a good sense of this, a Time Portrait will give you the information you need.

"

Each small task of every day is part of the total harmony of the universe.
ST. THERESE OF LISIEUX

"

All great achievements

require time.

MAYA ANGELOU

You'll be surprised how much time you use simply not being focused.

The Time Portrait helps you understand yourself as you bring your awareness to how you shape your time – it may be the vehicle for understanding that yes, you DO shape your time, not that time shapes you. To do this exercise, use a memory of a recent day, or choose a day within the next week to record a typical day.

EXERCISE

SCHEDULE DAILY FROM MEMORY

1. Using the Time Log like the one in this book or any day planner, picture yourself yesterday or during a typical weekday. Imagine yourself at work, home or any other place you regularly spend time. Experience the sights, sounds and details of the day. In the space for each hour, write what you did.

2. Circle the time period when you think you functioned best and were the most present and focused.

Draw a square around the time period/s in which you were least energetic and the most distracted.

LifeDancing TIME LOG

TIME ASSESSMENT	Keep track of each 30-minute increment of your day to see how you really spend your time.							

Reason for assessment								

TIME	ACTIVITY	THOUGHTS & FEELINGS	ARENAS					

"

Life should be great
rather than long.

B.R.
AMBEDKAR

SHOULDS VS. WANTS

We all have "shoulds" in our lives, of course – our family's needs, the demands of a job, housework, grocery shopping, paying bills. But wouldn't it be grand if all of our activities could be tasks we really enjoy or want to do. Too many "shoulds" make you feel out of control.

Review your Time Log. Put an "S" next to an activity for each Should and a "W" for each Want. Now, stop to think who is responsible for creating all the entries on your daily list of activities. YOU may be calling particular items "Shoulds," but after an honest moment of reflection you will probably agree that you really have chosen certain activities, for various reasons. On the surface, they may seem less than desirable, but you may not be willing to pay the consequences of eliminating the activity from your life.

It's also possible that you have not taken the time and energy to think of or create options that are more desirable. Maybe you believe that if your entire day was filled with "Wants," you would be enjoying life too much and that there was something wrong with that. Some people call it hedonism. I choose to call it "following what feels right;" others suggest "following your bliss." However you choose to feel about the things you are doing in your life is totally up to you. Even if you're doing something you committed to and don't believe you enjoy, you can look into it more deeply and find something you enjoy until you've arranged to ethically stop doing it.

ALONE & WITH OTHERS

Review your Time Log one more time and note how many activities you do Alone and how many with Other people. You may find your work keeps you isolated, that you don't have as much human contact as you would like. Or you may find you never have a moment to yourself.

Now, look back at your Myers Briggs Personality Type Indicator score from **Assessment | 1.2b | YOUR PERSONALITY PREFERENCES**. Does it mesh? Introverts may find they need more alone time, while extroverts may need more time engaged with others. Write a statement in your journal about ways you can alter your time to reflect your personality preferences.

TIME EATERS

We all waste a certain amount of time – even the most productive among us. The trick is to keep it to a minimum and use time to your advantage.

Keep remembering that you want to make life simple. While we may say events disrupt our intentions, we know that we are often our own biggest obstacle. These three big time eaters can make your life very complex: interruptions, waiting and procrastination.

Of course, there are times when resting is more beneficial than plugging away through the interruptions. Notice when you reach overload, and give yourself a break – literally! Enjoy the break you take rather than obsessing about the time your wasting. Many studies suggest that nappers and those who take power 10-20 minute breaks to do nothing or meditate, actually get more done than those who push through to the end.

What are your favorite methods of wasting time?

INTERRUPTIONS. In many ways interruptions and distractions are the hardest to control, especially if you have difficulty setting boundaries. I still feel guilty sometimes when I firmly say "NO, not now, can we schedule another time?"

This is an even greater problem if you work from home. The other day I was using streaming video with a new consulting client and suddenly my husband appeared in my office asking what he thought was an important question. I firmly waved him away, locked the door, and when I was done reminded him (probably a little loudly, OK, very loudly) "Never interrupt me when I'm with a client. The only acceptable reasons are life and death situations."

Work on your ability to say "NO." Remember, NO is a complete sentence that needs no explanation or justification. "Because I said so" is good enough when you are under pressure. Ask people to see you later to discuss it.

In this category, telephone calls and emails deserve special mention. Ask friends not to call during certain hours so you can reserve the time for work or forward your calls to an answering system. These days people seem to believe that they must answer calls or text messages immediately. Help others learn the skill of patience. Unless you're waiting for an important or emergency message,

> **"**
>
> Circumstances may cause interruptions and delays, but never lose sight of your goal.
>
> ## MARIO ANDRETTI

"

Procrastination is the
thief of time.

EDWARD YOUNG

put your mobile phone on airplane mode, mute, or turn it off. Looking for emails constantly is deadly. It is impossible to be fully in "flow" (the time when you do your best work) when you're scrolling through emails, Just don't do it!

Perhaps changing your routine will help. Move to a quieter place to work or meditate, even if you have to use the library or borrow someone else's space. One young writer confessed to working in the bathroom late at night because it was the only time her family wasn't hovering and it was the only room with a lock. You can put locks on other doors, as needed. They have these nifty little doodads at the hardware store with a lever that folds over the door. You don't even have to change the doorknob on your door and it only locks when someone is inside the room.

WAITING. Waiting can be frustrating. Ask yourself if you're realistic about it? Do you understand that there is a certain inevitable amount of it in every day? Just work to minimize it. If friends are always late, tell them that doesn't work for you anymore and that your time is as valuable as theirs. Tell the dentist the same thing. Perhaps you can go to the bank at a different hour to avoid the lines or bank by mail or digitally. Try putting waiting time to good use: always have something with you to do. With today's technology you can surf the web, read a book, play a game and check your e-mail (or not!). I find the most nourishing thing to do is an informal meditation. While standing in the line at the grocery store, center your body, take a deep breath, and take in all the visuals, sounds and smells. Watch other's dramas unfold around you and send each person loving kindness. Waiting can be creative and nourishing.

PROCRASTINATION. Procrastination is tough, no doubt about it. But here, as in nearly every area of your life, taking a good long look at it will make a difference.

Putting off or delaying starting something is often caused by that old tyrant perfection, or just not knowing where to start. Sometimes we set such high standards for a given task that it cannot ever be completed. If fear of failing sets in, we'll begin finding ways to avoid the task. Eventually, we begin name-calling, labeling ourselves lazy-good-for-nothing-fools, which only cements the cycle. If not knowing where to begin is an issue, this is a perfect time to start a **MINDMAP** (| 2.8a | in **MASTER CLASS WORKBOOK**). You don't have to find a solution, only gather data. One of my mottos is "When in doubt, gather more data." That can be internal or external information. Once you've gathered enough, something will emerge that you can do.

As soon as you notice yourself putting something off "as soon as I finish...," ask yourself if you really could do it now. If the task is too large to complete immediately, then try to finish at least one small step toward your larger objective. This is where having your goals broken down into objectives and your objectives analyzed into small tasks, saves you the time of having to figure out where to start.

Remember to give yourself small rewards after completing each task. The rewards do not have to be elaborate; even five minutes of relaxation can be enormously appreciated in a busy day.

Whatever your method of dealing with procrastination, keep remembering that the most important thing is to simply begin. You will never get anywhere if you do not act. Even if you are not right on target, at least you will know where you stand now and what you need to do to get closer to your mark.

When thinking about Time Wasters, you must have a sense of your objectives so you can set priorities.

To get started, look at the Time Eaters exercise that follows and identify your ten biggest Time Eaters. Decide whether each was caused by someone or something else, or your own creation. Write E or I (External or Internal) next to each Time Eater.

Next, think of a possible solution to each item on the list. It could be as simple as re-scheduling your morning tea or coffee so that it's a reward for completing certain tasks instead of a way to put off starting them.

Don't try to change all your habits at once. But do tackle the biggest or most annoying one first. If one solution does not work, try another. One of the biggest rewards you can get is to look back over the day and see how much more productive, creative and engaged in your LifeDance you have become.

"

We are time's subjects,
and time bids be gone.

SHAKESPEARE

"

Lost time is

never found again.

BENJAMIN FRANKLIN

EXERCISE
TIME EATERS

	Externally Caused	Internally Caused
1.		
2.		
3.		
4.		
5.		
6.		
7.		
8.		
9.		
10.		

One last strategy we all use to limit ourselves comes from something a teacher often called "Upper Limits Problems" or ULP. We all, consciously or unconsciously, have limits we have placed on how happy and/or successful we can be. When we begin to reach the top of that preconceived limitation we will begin to find ways to back off from moving forward (slip-slide-away). When you find yourself mysteriously unable to put the cherry on the proverbial cake and moving on, stop and ask yourself: "What is the implication in my life if I accomplish my goal? Will I be overqualified for my job and have to re-enter the job market? What will happen to my relationships in which I lack power and direction when I become more directed?" Some of this introspection can be done alone and some of it you may want to dialogue about issues with a close friend, coach or a counselor.

Remember, time is YOUR MOST PRECIOUS RESOURCE, use it wisely so you can keep on dancing!

MASTER CALENDAR

You may want to create a Master Calendar for yourself. Depending on how busy you are, this can be Monthly, Weekly or Daily. A Master Calendar is an Ideal Month, Week or Day. When you have a Master Calendar in place, and enter new tasks from your projects, you are taking into consideration the time you've committed to regular activities like meditation, exercise, working, shopping, meal preparation, phone calls, playtime, etc. Before making any new time commitments you need to honor what's already on your dance ticket. You might also write areas of focus at the top of the day's page and/or block out specific times you want to use for important purposes in the future. At the beginning of each week, review your purpose, goals and projects. Decide which action items you want to accomplish for the week and place these, with their priorities, on your Action sheet. When you plan your week, place these items on your schedule along with your regularly scheduled activities and new items from your monthly or weekly calendar pages. In the **MASTER CLASS WORKBOOK** | 2.8d | **CALENDARS** you will find examples of Calendar forms. You can photocopy these or find similar forms in most office supply stores.

A Master Calendar is a way of bringing together the key elements of planning your time. Think of it as the backbone of your calendar. By distilling your Values summary statement, your Life Vision and LifeDance goals into your organizer, you are giving yourself the gift of structuring your LifeDance by choreographing your time around your Values, Vision and Goals.

If you're using a paper planner, put your section dividers in the following order:

1 Values
2 Mission
3 Projects (each with a Foundations page)
4 Plans
5 Tasks
6 Calendars
7 Contacts
8 Other Information

> Until you value yourself, you won't value your time. Until you value your time, you will not do anything with it.
>
> **M. SCOTT PECK**

> Time is what we want most, but what we use worst.
>
> ## WILLIAM PENN

It is important that before you schedule ANYTHING, you look through your Values, Mission and Current Projects before you bring anything new into your LifeDance.

THE PROCESS SUMMARY

Here's how to use your Master Calendar.

Each day, or the night before, review your Values, Vision/Mission, Projects and Goals and identify the action items that you want to complete that day. Always ask yourself:

1. Is this activity congruent with my values and vision?

2. Is this the best match with my personal preferences and skills and strengths or can I delegate it?

3. Does this need to be completed now, or ever? Can I eliminate it or give it to someone else?

4. Look at your calendar/s and cluster similar items, like phone calls, errands and travel. Can you pick up your prescriptions while you grocery shop? Clear up your emails while you're on hold on the phone?

5. Create your Weekly Schedule when your Monthly becomes too full, your Daily Schedule sheets when your Weekly Schedule is too full.

Every day, review your progress, update data, visualize your goals and/or look at your Design Guide, repeat your affirmations and plan the next day of your life for success and happiness.

YOUR CHECKOFF LIST

Each day can be a new beginning for your LifeDance. Each morning, or evening before, remember to:

- Visualize your LifeDance
- Revisit your driving Values
- Remind yourself of your preferences, strengths and motivated skills Review your Goals, Projects, and Plans
- Put priority items on your task sheet.
- Schedule

Visualize the day's results and repeat any affirmations you have, and revisit your Design Guide. GO FOR IT!

AT THE END OF THE DAY

- Review your day and check off what you've completed.
- Transfer uncompleted actions back to your Task List.
- Acknowledge results produced and reward yourself.
- Plan the next day's dance.

PULLING IT ALL TOGETHER

SHAZAMM – You have done it. You are almost ready to begin the journey of the day. The final step is to allow yourself to live your day with your schedule and lists available, while always allowing yourself the freedom of choice and spontaneity that makes life fun, creative and worth the trouble. Enjoy your accomplishments and re-evaluate the areas you slip-slide away from. Maybe they just don't belong in your life any longer.

MAKING IT WORK

Become accountable to a friend, coworker, counselor, coach, spouse or support group. Each week review your objectives together to make sure they are specific, and check to see if you are sticking to setting objectives and eliminating time wasters. Most important of all, make it fun, and be proud of who you are and what you can accomplish with a little determination and help from your friends. There are great tools on the internet that allow you to put your calendar online for others to see and to integrate your calendar with others like Google Calendars and iCal.

So there you are. You're all set. You know each day how your dance is designed. You know when to start, stop, and plan for the next daily dance.

STAYING ALIVE
(OR UPDATES & UNPLANNING)

UPDATES - Do them as regularly as you need to keep projects current.

> Time is the coin of your life. It is the only coin you have, and only you can determine how it will be spent. Be careful lest you let other people spend it for you.

CARL SANDBURG

> The time you enjoy wasting is not wasted time.
>
> ## BERTRAND RUSSELL

Your goal sheet needs updating every six months. Your Master Schedule worksheets should be changed as your life changes. It helps to update them monthly just to make sure you're not spinning your wheels. You will find that sometimes you miss, forget and don't follow your daily schedule. Be firm but gentle with yourself and remember if you are serious about managing your time and your life, figure out why you are undermining your progress. Is it fear of change or success?

RETREATS - Sometimes it's way too much to even think about scheduling another thing in your life. This could be a sign you need a personal retreat. A personal retreat is not a typical vacation where you need more vacation after you get home because your time was so packed with activities. A personal retreat is time spent NOT doing anything except contemplating or meditating, eating, sleeping and general renewal. There are many wonderful retreat centers where you can simply get away and rediscover who the dancer is underneath all those daily activities. As an example, there is Spirit Rock in California, OMEGA in New York and Kripalu in Massachusetts. Consider these times to "unplan."

CHAPTER NINE

The Dance of Solutions
WHOLISTIC INTEGRATIVE
PROBLEM SOLVING

*A*t some point during this book you may have thrown up your hands, decided your life was "good enough," heaved the book at the dog or cat, eaten a quart of Haagen Dazs and decided you were too overwhelmed to go on. When people are faced with big life challenges, quite often, they become immobilized by the magnitude of the issue. The main questions become, where do I start to change my life and how do I start? When life throws you an obstacle, you may react by attempting random, unsuccessful solutions, lose your sense of power over your life or become frozen into inactivity accepting whatever happens. Personally, when I'm totally overwhelmed and in that frozen state, I lie on the floor and stare at the ceiling waiting for inspiration. It doesn't take long for me to get up because people have to step over me. Soon, I regain my sense of humor and curiosity, get up and move on.

Life problems are usually more ambiguous and complex than those we had on school tests, so, using wholistic problem solving is crucial to today's complex issues. Luckily, we face not only problems, but also opportunities. For example, consider my leaky boat. As you know, water moves quickly toward the lowest possible point. But on a boat, water may be coming from the top and settling on the bottom or rising up from the bottom. If the problem is not addressed completely, the leak does not go away. Unless an emergency arises and the water floods in from the bottom, the leak requires a complete solution to go away. As I learn more about where and when the water comes into the boat, and explore what I need to stem the flow, the solution emerges.

> "

We cannot solve life's problems except by solving them.

M. SCOTT PECK

> "

Being stuck is a position few of us like. We want something new but cannot let go of the old - old ideas, beliefs, habits, even thoughts. We are out of contact with our own genius. Sometimes we know we are stuck; sometimes we don't. In both cases we have to DO something.

RUSH LIMBAUGH

WHEN THE DANCER FALLS: THE FROZEN STATE

Know that lying-on-the-floor or the frozen state is normal given our biology as humans. We're much like that terrified bunny or deer who encounters a predator. We, too, have the fight-or-flight option, neither of which is usually a good choice unless we meet someone scary in an alley. All of these reactions can take place physically, mentally, emotionally or all at once. I can freeze physically on the floor, mentally by not being able to think clearly, or emotionally by not being able to feel anything about the problem or feeling flooded with emotion. Because freezing when faced with a problem is a real problem and must be addressed before any problem solving can take place, let's address it first. To help you understand why you may have seized up, here are some things that may be going on:

1 - MENTAL FLOODING. When the emotional part of the brain "floods," it overrides our frontal lobes, which govern higher-level thinking. That's why it is never a good idea to make decisions when you are highly emotional. You aren't using all your wisdom. If you take time to step away, calm down or go for a walk, you will be able to re-engage the part of your brain that does your best thinking. Flooding can be triggered by past and present issues. If this is a common occurrence for you, consider consulting with a professional.

2 - TOO MUCH INFORMATION. Today, the average person takes in more information in a day than people living in previous eras digested in a lifetime. Without filters – such as knowing your values, preferences, and creating your best and most worthy goals – it is difficult to decide what to pay attention to and what choices to make.

3 - OUTSIDE YOUR COMFORT ZONE. You have been pushed or are being asked to step outside of an area of your life where you are comfortable to where you are uncomfortable. Something like a new swimmer being asked to dive into the deep end of the pool.

4 - A PARADIGM SHIFT. As you use the tools in this book and learn new ways of living, you shift to a new way of thinking and/or feeling about your life. As with any new skill, sometimes it's awkward at first and maybe a little scary. Practice makes perfect, and helps you become more comfortable with your new LifeDancing skills.

5 - UNRESOLVED TRAUMA. When our body and mind are triggered by an event that relates in any kind of way to a previous unresolved trauma, the old trauma needs to be addressed. If you find you just don't seem to be able to deal with a particular situation no matter what you try, I highly recommend consulting with a counselor who specializes in trauma, such as a Sensorimotor Psychotherapy professional.

These are but a few reasons you may have shut down. Whatever the reason, the key to real life change is simply one step at a time and perseverance. Hang on until you thaw and are able to begin to act. Not to worry, the inner seas will calm, the body will go through its process, and your frontal lobes will eventually come back online. The tempo of movement will settle into an easy pace as you hang in there and move on to Wholistic Integrative Problem Solving.

WHOLISTIC INTEGRATIVE PROBLEM SOLVING

Wholistic problem solving is a way to get those bruised knees up from the floor and into action. Life is certainly more complex in this information age and most of today's complex problems require that we engage with them, discover our curiosity, and look for creative solutions. You'll discover that the motivator that moves you toward successful solutions is simply having a place to start (your center), things to do (strategic action), and a sense that even though you cannot solve a problem today, you are actively dealing with it and making a difference (one step at a time).

LifeDancing's Wholistic Integrative Problem Solving is easily done by anybody who makes the time, and follows the instructions outlined below. I have yet to find a problem that cannot be solved, or better yet turned into an opportunity using this model.

The Wholistic Integrative Problem Solving process looks at the person's WHOLE life, and using all the tools she has at hand, creates an integral solution that enhances and optimizes all of the parts of her life that are impacted. Here are the steps:

STEP 1 – GATHER INFORMATION

This process allows people who are overwhelmed or flooded to simply and

> *Intellectuals solve problems, geniuses prevent them.*
>
> ## ALBERT EINSTEIN

easily talk about what is going on and at the same time gather the information that will be part of the solution. In the beginning phase there is no need to choose, decide, edit, or criticize – only to gather information. This is best done by setting up a filing system to put information into. This can be on your computer or in filing cabinets. When you're ready to start, create a MindMap.

STEP 2 – CLUSTER

When this initial phase feels complete or simply comes to a stop, it is time to step back and look for patterns. Look at your MindMap and see if there are clusters of issues and information.

STEP 3 – CLARIFY

What do these clusters tell you? Do you see areas that can be addressed more easily that others? Do you need to focus on one cluster more than others?

STEP 4 – PRIORITIZE

Now that you have the issues more clarified, it is time to determine where to start. You'll find a VERY easy tool on the next page called Step by Step. You never have to choose between more than two items and if this is not possible, you simply move to another choice.

STEP 5 – FEEDBACK

This model is a dynamic problem solving process. As long as the problem or project is active, you will be coming back to add information and/or re-clarify and prioritize again.

STEP 6 - RETURN TO STEP I

When one area of the problem takes on more importance, it may be useful to approach it as its own problem.

THE OUTCOME

The problem solving process starts with the big picture and filters down to a single action step that is doable today; the power of action is returned to the system. Taking one step at a time you move toward a successful solution.

SUCCESSFUL SOLUTIONS

The successful solution to a problem creates a well-deserved moment of relief and satisfaction. Self-esteem increases, and space is opened for relaxation and the choice of another activity. The power of action, instead of reaction, releases you from the worry of the unknown and instills a sense of power. Learning to solve problems, not freezing, running or becoming aggressive, to make them go away, unleashes creativity into action.

The "solution" to a complex problem consists of an action plan that's flexible enough to change, yet holds direction for the future. Some of our teachers have encouraged us to believe there's only one correct solution to life's problems, only one correct way of reaching a solution, and there is no need to consider the problem again once the solution is found. This is a simplistic and false truth. Most problems have many more than one solution, and as you have probably found, as you solve one problem, others often arise.

LIFE IS A MATTER OF PRIORITIES
STEP BY STEP

Setting priorities or making a hierarchical list simply means you decide the order in which you want to accomplish certain tasks or choose options. You set priorities every day of your life, though you may not be calling them that. What most of us do is automatically act or when we are "thinking" about a choice, use random criteria to decide. Remember when I walked into my deceased mother's house and froze? My daughter, to simply get me moving, told me to clean out a closet. We hadn't made the time yet to MindMap the project and set priorities so she just chose randomly because the situation called for it. But, if we had done some preparation, she would have known what the next thing to do was on our project list and directed me there instead.

I'm a firm believer in a one-step-at-a-time approach to any large problem. When I decided to buy a boat to live on, the idea sent me directly to the floor. "How can I possibly do that?" was my first thought. Then came "Who do you think you are anyway, someone who could do this?" Once I had rolled through all my doubts and fears and had stood up and become functional again I started problem solving and took it one step at a time. When dealing with problems and deciding what to do first, the most important thing is to identify the action items you can and will actually do. In the previous chapter when we created a strategic path, that sequence of events were those that moved us toward a goal. They weren't necessarily problem oriented. Sometimes when we are facing an obstacle or problem, we find it more difficult to act. That's why it is so important to be a realist and make a list of things you will really do. An action plan is of no

"

Action expresses priorities.

GANDHI

"

Good things happen
when you get your priorities
straight.

SCOTT
CAAN

value, if you don't act.

After you've completed your MindMap and made your list of things that you need to do, if you are overwhelmed by the list, use this simple selection process that allows you to choose between two items at a time. Try to make your action items as simple as clear as possible. They need to be:

- Observable

- Measurable

- Specific

Here is an example of the MindMap I made when I discovered soon after I bought a boat that when it rained, the boat leaked inside the cabin. I had no clue what to do, so I started with a MindMap.

Here is the first list from an overwhelmed mind. First I thought I could solve it, then I wanted someone else to solve it, then I randomly had ideas:

1. Scrape off old caulk and replace with new

2. Hire someone to figure it out

3. Get bids

4. Find where the water is coming in

5. Catch the water before it ruins anything inside

6. Get a dehumidifier to stop the mold inside the cabinets

7. Dry out the inside of the boat

8. Come down when it rains and watch for leaks

9. Check the outer fittings for cracked caulking

Go over your list and see if any of the steps need to be broken down into smaller steps. You'll notice the step of "Find where the water is coming in," is a step that really includes many smaller steps to accomplish.

1 - I start by arbitrarily numbering the items on the list. The following grid sample is set up for five items. If you have more than 20, break your items into groups of 20. Cluster the winners from each group, and choose again.

We can usually decide between two choices. Remember non-action is an act, so when in doubt, make a choice anyway. You can always go back later and re-prioritize.

2 – Time to compare pairs of items, over and over again. Start with item number one and compare it to item number two. Next, compare item one to

three, then item one to four, one to five and onward. Put a check mark next to each choice you make, and work your way through the list. After you compare item one to two, three, four and five, move to item two. Compare two and three, two and four, and so on. When you are done, if you have items with the same number of check marks, simply compare them as you did in the beginning.

Compare the numbered items listed below and put an x next to the number that wins each time:

Items being compared	Item chosen	Number that got the most votes
1/2	——	——
1/3	——	——
1/4	——	——
1/5	——	——
2/3	——	——
2/4	——	——
2/5	——	——
3/4	——	——
3/5	——	——
4/5	——	——

Here is the Leaky Boat list after the 1 by 1 voting.

Each x is a vote for that item.

x	1. Scrape off old caulk and replace with new..
x	2. Hire someone to figure it out.
	3. Get bids.
xxxxxxxxx	4. Catch the water before it ruins anything inside.
xxxxxxxx	5. Get a dehumidifier to stop the mold inside the cabinets.
xxxxxx	6. Dry out the inside of the boat.
xxxxxxx	7. Come down when it rains and watch for leaks.
xxxx	8. Check the outer fittings for cracked caulking.

Here is the list prioritized after the one by one voting:

1. Catch the water before it ruins anything inside

2. Get a dehumidifier to stop mold from growing inside the cabinets

3. Come down when it rains and watch for leaks

> "
>
> There's no sense talking about priorities. Priorities reveal themselves. We're all transparent against the face of the clock.
>
> **ERIC ZORN**

4. Dry out the inside of the boat

5. Check the outer topside fittings for cracked caulking

6. Find where the water is coming in on top

7. Scrape off old caulk and replace with new

8. Hire someone to figure it out

9. Get bids

As you can see, the first list had no logic to it, it is a random listing of options. The second list is one made after some thought, it reflects the work of a calm, empowered mind. The inner experience moves from being freaked out to, "I'm in charge of this problem; it is not in charge of me."

Use the | **2.9a** | **WHOLISTIC INTEGRATED PROBLEM SOLVING WORKSHEET** in the **MASTER CLASS WORK-BOOK** for a problem you want to solve.

CHECKING IN: INNER OBSTACLES

Sometimes our greatest obstacles are ourselves. Some examples of inner obstacles to fixing the leaky boat could be:

INNER DIALOGUE

I should have never bought this boat. I am in way over my head.

I know nothing about boats, how can I solve this problem?

Once I solve this problem, another one will come along.

LISTENING TO OTHER PEOPLE'S OPINIONS

You should have never bought the boat so get out now.

You know nothing about boats and shouldn't be doing the work.

Boats always leak and can never be fixed.

RESISTANCE

Finding yourself resisting any solution other than your own and
    not having one of your own.

Being afraid to act because you might make a mistake.

Also called Fear of Failure.

FEAR OF SUCCESS

What if I really succeed? I'll be a different person, YIKES.

One or all of these inner messages can create the "freeze" response. Unless you're prepared to walk away from the leaky boat, the best way to deal with those inner saboteurs and outer critics is to acknowledge them, find them curious, and simply complete the next step on your plan. YES, you'll make mistakes, it's one of the best ways to learn something new. As you build on your successes, you'll gain a new sense of your inner strength and discover just how creative and powerful you actually are.

One method for identifying inner obstacles is to use guided imagery to open up blocks coming from your subconscious, using the process to solve them problem.

Turn to the | 2.9b | **YOUR INNER GUIDE** exercise in the **MASTER CLASS WORKBOOK** to work with this some more.

CLEARING OBSTACLES BEFORE THEY TURN INTO BIGGER ONES

Now that you have made some choices using Step-by-Step, ask yourself about them, one at a time. While you're pondering, if a word does not come to mind, pause a moment and check out how you're breathing. If your breaths are short and shallow, you may be angry or scared. If you are breathing deep in your chest and feel relaxed, your thoughts or feelings may be those of ease and safety. Here are some questions you can ask yourself about feelings that arise as you make your choices:

- Are my emotions limiting my choices or what I'm able to see?
- Am I afraid of losing someone or something I'm attached to by creating change?
- What effect will the changes I'm considering have on those around me?
- Am I willing to pay the price of going for what I really want if I am criticized?
- Do I have strong thoughts, feelings or body sensations I cannot identify?
- How am I going to figure out what they are or explore them more?

To clarify your decision to act, ask yourself these questions:

> "

Every solution breeds new problems.

ARTHUR BLOCH

"

The only difference between a problem and a solution is that people understand the solution.

CHARLES KETTERING

- What are the immediate effects, to decide, or not decide?

- What is my decision deadline?

- What are the short- and long-term consequences for each choice?

- What are the pros and cons of my choices?

- What resources do I have and what do I need?

- Which choices best fit into my Life Plan?

- How does this solution match my personal values and personality preferences?

- What skills do I have to solve this problem, and what do I need to learn?

- What areas need more data? How will I obtain that information?

- What Stage of Change am I in?

More problem-solving resources and techniques:

- Interview experts, counselors and people with experience in your situation. Research reliable, verifiable sources on the Internet, or visit your local library.

- Gather experience performing the job or task.

- Imagine the outcome of each decision. Use all your senses – sight, hearing, smell, taste, touch and movement.

NOW, JUST DO IT!

If, after all of the above, you still feel immobilized, do something, ANYTHING to move yourself forward. Whatever you do, you'll get more information – that it was not the right choice or a good idea. Many decisions, even those with extensive research, reach the coin-flipping or magic pendulum point. Facts are tools, but they aren't the same as your experience and inner wisdom; they won't make your decision for you. Learn to trust your inner wisdom, and don't allow yourself to be immobilized by indecision. Your response to the answer of the coin flip will tell you even more. When I reach this point, I use a hand-held pendulum, it is more elegant than flipping a coin, which always rolls under the couch before I can see it.

Finally, think of the problem you're solving, or the decision you're struggling with, as a mystery play or giant puzzle. The pieces may come to you in various forms but not as clearly marked as you would like them to be. Turning the pieces over and over will lend new light to their message. Fun, isn't it? Remember to not take your problems too seriously. That will only add to your frustration and get in the way of you seeing the light at the end of the tunnel.

WATCH OUT FOR ...

Personal agendas or fears, fear of success and personal "buttons." You may be on the right track to the perfect decision for yourself but may stumble over individual obstacles that keep you from LifeDancing. Watch for your first few reactions after you believe you've made the "right" choice. Ask yourself where those reactions come from. Try to be as honest with yourself as possible. Be aware of habitual responses like "I could never do that."

Most importantly, have fun and enjoy the dance. Play with choices, explore absurdities, laugh at your mistakes and for heaven's sakes, move on.

"

If you find a good solution and become attached to it, the solution may become your next problem.

ROBERT ANTHONY

Step Three
TURNING OUT

The first section of this book gave you tools to work with. The following sections explore the arenas of your life so you can use those tools by setting goals and using the other tools to realize your dreams. After you have read each of the following arenas, assessed and set goals for yourself, use your Project Worksheet and create one for each goal.

In each Arena you'll find information you may, or may not, be aware of. My goal is to spark your curiosity about this area of your life. I hope you will do your own explorations and learn more and more about what it means to be a joyful human. To stay current with new information in each arena visit www.lifedancing.com and discover new additions. You can also subscribe to our newsletter to bring current news and updates to you immediately..

Step Three
TAKING THE STAGE: THE DANCE ARENAS

The LifeDancer takes the stage. She twirls into each arena of her life with

a new vision and a new mastery of her art and skills.

BODY AWARENESS

The centered LifeDancer fully inhabits her body.

She's in harmony with her body and aware of her needs.

MIND

The authentic LifeDancer has deep knowledge of the inner landscape of her mind

that helps move through life with effortless fluidity.

EMOTIONS

The LifeDancer lives in awareness of her emotions and uses wisdom and movement to dance with them wisely.

SPIRITUALITY

As the LifeDancer becomes more integrated and congruent with her physical, mental and emotional world, the spirit that

is the soul of the LifeDance expands. Spirit-infused movement comes from the inside out, radiating through her authentic

Dance of Life.

RELATIONSHIPS

Live more fully and authentically in your relationships -- your relationship to yourself, and with others.

WORK

Creating work that is a true expression of who you are.

HOME

Designing a home that is safe, supportive, and inspirational.

WHOLENESS & INTEGRATION

Wholeness, integrity and authenticity are key to keeping the LifeDance arenas balanced and integrated.

CHAPTER TEN

The Dance Arenas: Body Awareness

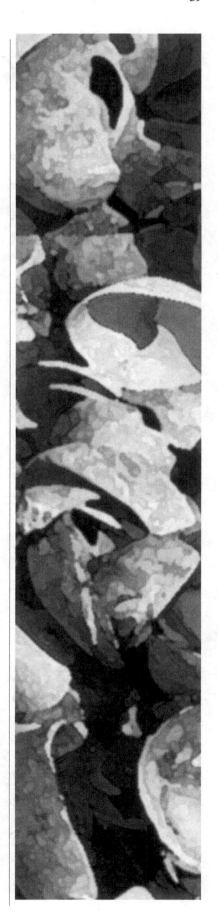

To fully inhabit your life, as an Authentic Dancer, you must fully inhabit your body. You may take your body for granted, most of us do. After all, you've been walking around in your body for years and it just does its thing usually without much attention, unless it breaks. Here's something most of us know, yet don't live, our body is NOT separate from our mind, thoughts, feelings and much more. Awareness of your body can help to bring all of these parts of yourself into alignment.

Sometimes body awareness is not fun -- the body brings pain as well as pleasure -- and we tend to shut off our awareness of the body when we experience pain or illness. This shutdown diminishes our awareness of ourselves and our dance of life. The key to a healthy, dynamic body is to walk toward our pain, be curious, explore what it has to tell us, be loving and nonjudgmental, and experience it as it changes.

So let's begin to explore the body. Ask yourself how well you know your body and how the way you feel, think and move with your body shapes your LifeDance.

In school, you may have learned about anatomy or physical health, but beyond the basics of nutrition and exercise, most don't usually get a course in how to be conscious of the body and keep it healthy. For the most part, the messages we receive early in life from our parents and other adults, is that the body is something that carries the mind around to think. Often major parts of it are off limits to touch or conversation. Having an awareness of, and a dialogue with, your body is central to living a healthy, congruent, authentic life – and to being an able mover in your LifeDance.

If you sit at a computer all day long, you may notice your neck and back get sore and stiff. You can choose to tune it out, maybe even take pain pills to numb it out, or you can honor your body's pain message – a message of a need for help -- explore a more ergonomically healthy sitting arrangement, and take stretch

Body experience... is the centre of creation.

BARBARA HEPWORTH

"

Wisdom comes alone through suffering.

AESCHYLUS

breaks throughout the day. The first solution will eventually break down, the second solution will support the health of your body and give you the ability to do what you want.

When we're young the body simply works, and we don't have to give it much attention. As we age, our bodies take more and more time and attention to continue working effectively. Western medicine, which is allopathic, tends to focus on illness and disease – eradicating the disease, illness or the symptoms, often with drugs or surgery. That model is tremendously valuable when you break a leg or your appendix bursts. Beyond the emergency, we also need a more personal, caring, prevention-oriented, and organic approach to keep our bodies healthy and dynamic. Before you numb or cut out or off parts of yourself, you might consider a more naturopathic approach.

PAIN & PLEASURE

Pain is the body's most frequently recognized signal and is often misunderstood. When most folks feel pain, the first thing they experience is fear or anger. Then they try to avoid feeling it by immobilizing the body part, taking pain medication, or numbing it out in some other way. Pain is the body's way of calling out for our attention, yet we respond by numbing out and ignoring it.

In his work with chronic pain, mindfulness expert and author Jon Kabat-Zinn has discovered what works to manage pain is quite the opposite – not to deny pain, but to be aware of it. With the awareness comes compassion. In his book, *Full Catastrophe Living*[20], Kabat-Zinn outlines a program for befriending your body, the pain and the pleasure in equal measure.

We may not run away from pleasure, but some cultures stigmatize the pleasure of the body – thus restricting our experiences to seldom or few. In the service of pleasure, health spas and wellness retreats that focus on healing and nourishing the body have created a billion dollar industry. To reduce the size of their bodies, according to the U. S. Food and Drug Administration (FDA), Americans spent an estimated 30 billion a year in 1992 (more recent figures are not available) on all types of diet programs and products, including diet foods and drinks.

It's important to open yourself to both of these experiences – pain and pleasure. Practice experiencing the pleasure of your body, building up your tolerance for, and acceptance of strength the pleasure of movement. When you begin to notice the "good news" about your body, you begin to build a new, healthier relationship with your body. You may begin by noticing pain, like a stiff back before you go to bed. Then, you do some stretching and relaxation exercises, working out some of the tightness. When you wake up the next morning and realize you slept better because of the stretching, it is the time to appreciate your body's ability to respond to care and give yourself a good night's sleep.

When you maintain a conscious focus on your body, you learn how to stay well and keep it finely tuned. Then, if or when something happens – like an imbalance, illness or accident -- you already have a good working relationship with your body and can do the things you need to do to help your body rediscover balance and healing.

SEEING YOUR BODY:
BEFRIENDING YOURSELF

The first step in befriending your body is to look at it from the outside. Try this exercise if you dare.

Lock your bathroom door, take off your clothes and look at yourself in the mirror. Record in the Body section of your **LIFEDANCING JOURNAL**:

Your thoughts

Your feelings

What parts you focus on

What parts you can't focus on

What you like

What you don't like

What parts need attention

Put your clothes on and sit down, close your eyes and envision your "ideal" body. Given the realities of your age and any physical challenges, what would you like your body to be like? Your body may have limitations, some of which you may not have explored or come to understand because you weren't willing to do the work, or took the limitation as your fate. I remember being a young girl in ballet class and not being able to balance like the other girls. I quit the class feeling like I was a failure. Later I learned that I had one leg that was shorter than

> "
>
> When befriended,
> remember it;
> when you befriend, forget it.
>
> ## BENJAMIN FRANKLIN

"

The body never lies.

MARTHA GRAHAM

the other throwing my hips out of alignment, making it almost impossible to balance like the others. Unfortunately no one explored why I couldn't balance easily and simply blamed me for not practicing enough. Is there any limitation you currently have that needs to be explored more deeply? Don't just accept any limitation you may have; instead, ask yourself if there is some way to challenge yourself or explore new ways to make things better.

Use | 3.10a | **BODY TOUR** in the **MASTER CLASS WORK-BOOK** to list all of the parts of your body that you don't like and create an action item for yourself about how you're going to create change. Take a picture of yourself in your undies and mark the parts of your body that you want to change. Keep this picture someplace safe so you can refer back to it periodically, not too often, to see how things have changed, or not.

KNOWING YOUR BODY: NARRATING THE STORY OF YOUR BODY

Now that you have faced your body and looked at it from the outside, you may have lots of scripts running through your head about it. Your body didn't get into the condition it is in today overnight. Let's explore how you got to this point with the body you saw in the mirror. One way to bring your complete awareness to your body is to write a story of your body's life.

If you interviewed your body about the story of your life, how would that story be told? Your body has its own memories and narrative, and you might be surprised to learn that exploring your life from the viewpoint of your body is a unique experience.

Writing your body's story is a good way to begin to familiarize yourself with her, and begin a more compassionate relationship with your physical being. Your body has been with you since birth, and responds to and delivers messages to you. Just like you might get to know a new friend by listening to their story, explore your body's story. Think of yourself as a journalist, and report what you hear as neutrally as possible. To get started, make a timeline of your life, birth to present, and begin to list all the memories and experiences that come to mind that your body was involved with, i.e., accidents, illnesses and other surprises. As you write, you may begin to get a new perspective of just how resilient and strong your body has been as it carried you through your life's challenges. You may realize, probably for the first time, that your body is a true friend and ally.

Map out your body's history starting with the stories you may have heard about your mother's pregnancy and your birth. Look at pictures of yourself during your life span, ask relatives and friends what they remember about your physicality. Here is an example of a body that belongs to Wendy.

In utero – I was two weeks late being born. My mother had to slip and fall on a wet floor to get me to come out.

Age 4 - Mom didn't like my straight hair and would give me permanents. I remember the pulling of my hair and the stink of the chemicals, yuck.

Age 5 – I loved to run and play with the boys. They seemed to have more fun climbing trees, playing in the dirt and exploring down by the river, than the girls.

Age 6 – Mom had me take tap dancing lessons. I liked the music and figuring out how to get my feet to dance the steps the teacher showed us. Unfortunately I often had bruised knees from climbing trees which made dancing sometimes hurt a bit. I also learned to ride a bike. That first ride downhill into a fence really hurt.

Age 7 – I had scarletina, a mild form of scarlet fever, which meant I was in bed a lot with people bringing me cold things to drink and keeping the lights low. It was a good rest but not much fun.

Age 8 – Ouch, how can anything hurt that much? I broke my arm swinging on the clothesline pole. It didn't hurt at first but after my grandma took me in to lay on the bed, boy did it hurt. Then there was the doctor's office where they put a mask over my face with yucky smelling stuff and put my arm in a cast. The cast itched but they wouldn't let me scratch it with a pencil. Then when it came off, it hurt stretching it out again.

Age 10- I got hit by a truck riding my bike across the street. They say I flew 40 feet but nothing broke except my bike.

Age 11 – It hurts to swallow. They call it strep throat. No, I don't want to eat anything. It hurts. Yea, ice cream!

Age 12 – I love being a cheerleader. It is so much fun to jump and yell with the band at school.

"

The body is a sacred garment.

MARTHA GRAHAM

"

Your body hears
everything your mind says.

NAOMI
JUDD

Age 13 – I also love going to the beach and lying in the sand and listening to the ocean.

Age 14 – I had a small car accident. Some friends and I "borrowed" their brother's car and tried to drive it. We hit a tree and it really scared us all. No more driving.

Age 15 – Back to cheerleading in high school. It is so much fun.

Age 16 – Well I discovered sex with a boy, and oops got pregnant. Maybe if I don't tell anyone it will go away.

Age 17 – It didn't go away and now I'm a mom. Boy, having a baby really changes your body.

Age 18 - Learned to ski this year. What fun – except for the tree I ran into.

I think you get the drift here. I bet you'll be surprised at how much your body remembers. She may still hold memories or scars of past experiences. There are many ways to access the body's memories. Please don't delve into any traumatic body experiences alone. Get professional help, ideally a professional trained in working with body trauma. Once you have written your body's story, put the story at the beginning of the Body section in your journal, where you can keep a running dialogue with your body.

Create your body's story in | 3.10b | **YOUR BODY'S STORY** in the **MASTER CLASS WORKBOOK**.

MOVING WITH YOUR BODY:
THE BODY'S DANCE

Moving the body is done mostly unconsciously. I stand and walk away from my desk to answer the door without any thought about my movement unless my back hurts or my leg is broken and I have to think about my movements.
The use of movement meditations, through yoga, walking meditation, authentic movement and more helps you become increasingly aware of how your body moves naturally. The practice of yoga brings the mind to an awareness of the body and the breath as you move and stretch, Authentic movement is a form of dance in which an inner, and sometimes outer, observer watches how your body moves in space; a walking meditation brings the mind to the automatic

act of walking and being with the body. What these all have in common is that they awaken us to the body we all take for granted, every day. Anytime you find yourself lost in thought or out of sorts, you can use the LifeDancing Body Break. Turn to | 3.10c | **BODY BREAK** in the **MASTER CLASS WORKBOOK**. Movement can clear the mind. Your mind and body often run on different tracks – parallel, but not intersecting, not necessarily dialoguing with one another. Conscious movement brings the two together and integrates who you are in the moment.

Practice your new body awareness. Go to a mall and watch people walk and move. While you are watching someone, ask yourself how much information you can gather by looking at their body and how they move. You may think about how healthy they are, how old they are, how smoothly or rigidly they move, maybe what they're wearing. Keep in mind that you were doing this before, but you were not as aware as you are now about how much information you get from simply watching how people move. You can't see inside their bodies, but you probably can tell if some body part feels pain because they will favor that area. You don't know what they are thinking but you can probably get a sense of their emotional state or if they are thinking about where they are going, by watching their movement. Have fun!

> Opportunity dances with those already on the dance floor.
>
> ## H. JACKSON BROWN JR.

BEING WITH YOUR BODY: CARING

It takes some work to pay attention to your body and how well it functions. There is a lot to know about how to manage and treat illness, aging, nutrition and creating optimal health. You'll need to discover regional resources for yourself so you can make body-intelligence part of your life. Here are some ideas to get you started:

- Join a gym or engage a trainer to help you learn how to exercise and increase your cardio, flexibility and strength.

- Subscribe to at least one periodical that keeps you up to date on the latest information on physical wellness.

- Use one or more of the exercises below on a regular basis to enhance your body awareness.

Your physical wellness and illness are your job to manage. You MUST be-

> "
> If you want others to be happy, practice compassion. If you want to be happy, practice compassion.
>
> ### DALAI LAMA

come an informed health consumer. Whenever your body requires attention or an intervention to maintain health, educate yourself! There's a lot of information and misinformation on the Web, so be careful.

It may be obvious that taking care of your body is critical to your Life-Dance, but many don't. The lithe, limber, quick body of my 20s is no longer. The older I get, the more responsibility I must take for staying physically well. As the body ages it requires more, and different kinds of exercise, movement and health measures. Create a wellness team for yourself. This team can include your:

Physician

Fitness trainer

Dentist

Yoga instructor

Chiropractor

Dietitian

Exercise partner

Massage therapist

Health club counselor

Always meet your body where it is. Acknowledge what she needs as soon as possible. There are many levels of need from needing to go to the bathroom when you get up to taking care of an illness. If you are afraid of knowing you have an illness, please step over your fear and get as much information as possible, do as many diagnostics as possible, then, after considering your mainstream and alternative healthcare options, begin to make decisions. Your path may not be another's. There are those who always follow the doctor's orders and do well, there are those who follow their inner guide and do fine and vice versa. In any case, never blindly follow what others tell you to do. Get as much information as you can, dialogue with your body, and make your own decisions. You will become more sensitive to your body's needs as you increase your body awareness. A great tool to enhance body awareness is the Body Scan.

PRACTICE: BODY SCAN

One that is used frequently in many awareness modalities is the Body Scan, which I introduced in Chapter Four: The Inner Dancer in the context of mindfulness. If this intrigued you or you felt lifted by the **Exercise** | 1.4a | in the **MASTER CLASS WORKBOOK**, I encourage you to use the Body Scan specifically to build awareness about your body. Return to the **Exercise** | 1.4a | in **MASTER CLASS WORKBOOK** with this intention.

Awareness is given to EVERY part of the body, as well as loving kindness. After a Body Scan, I feel much more connected to, and compassionate about my body. With regular practice, it can help you enter and explore deep states of relaxation, become much more intimate and accepting of your body as it is. It will help you learn how to work effectively with body sensations and feelings of discomfort and pain, and cultivate increasing powers of concentration (one-pointed attention) and mindfulness (a flexible, moment-to-moment, non-judging awareness).

PHYSICAL RELAXATION

Harvard cardiologist Herbert Benson, a pioneer in the field of body/mind medicine and founder of the Mind Body Medical Institute (BHI) near Boston, Mass., focuses on stress and the relaxation response. He believes the Mind-Body are one system, and emphasizes meditation as a tool to reduce stress. Eliciting the relaxation response:

- Your metabolism decreases.

- Your heart beats slower and your muscles relax.

- Your breathing becomes slower.

- Your blood pressure decreases.

If practiced regularly, it can have lasting effects. Accessing the relaxation response is at the heart of the BHI's research and clinical mind/body programs. A relaxed body is better able to deal with stress and life situations. The Body Scan is a good place to start identifying parts of your body that are chronically tight.

I highly recommend Benson's classic book, *The Relaxation Response*[21], for more information and exercises you can do at home. Choose the tools and practices that you resonate with and actually do. The bottom line is that you be aware of and care for this miracle of a body. It is the foundation of your life on this planet, treat it accordingly.

To begin the process of identifying your level of knowledge and satisfaction in this arena, complete the self-assessment in the **MASTER CLASS WORK-**

"

Realize that this very body, with its aches and its pleasures… is exactly what we need to be fully human, fully awake, fully alive.

PEMA CHODRON

> "
>
> Effective health care depends on self-care; this fact is currently heralded as if it were a discovery.

IVAN ILLICH

BOOK. Once completed, identify goals in this arena. Meet your body where you are, as you are now. Commit to learning more and increasing your awareness of your body. Continue building on your body awareness knowledge through movement, relaxation and mindful awareness of pain and pleasure, and the many ways the body talks to you. As your body becomes more fluid and able to move freely, your LifeDance will do the same.

Please turn to | 3.10d | BODY ASSESSMENT in the MASTER CLASS WORKBOOK.

CHAPTER ELEVEN

The Dance Arenas:
The Mind of the Dancer

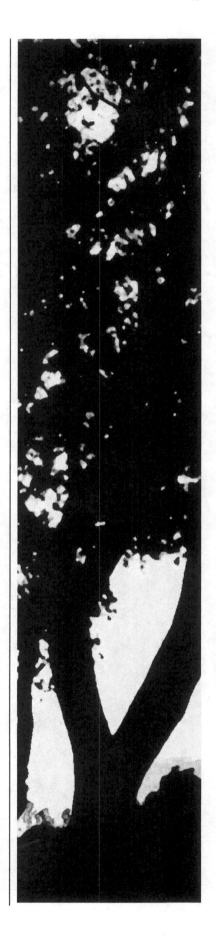

*W*hen you watch dancers perform, do you ever wonder how they make it look so effortless? An accomplished dancer moves fluidly because her body and mind are continuously engaged in a dialogue. Every movement has an expressive quality that reveals an integration of thought, feeling and movement. What comes across to the viewer is flow, fluidity, and patterns of meaning.

As a LifeDancer, how you feel, and what you think affects the fluidity of your life dance. The mind and emotions are hardwired into the body, yet able to grow and change. What you think and feel affects your whole being, whether you're tired or energetic, have a headache or your stomach is upset or at ease; conversely the vitality of your body affects how you think and feel. For example, when I was working in the state mental hospital (a difficult job), about an hour before it was time to go home, I would feel tremendously tired and I would wonder how I could finish my shift. Finally, quitting time arrived and I would go to the bathroom, wash my hands and imagine all my job stress flowing down the drain. I'd leave the hospital unit, walk to my car, start the engine and get on the road home. As I drove through the beautiful landscape of Napa, California, my spirit would renew and all vestiges of tiredness flew out the window. I'd arrive home revitalized and ready to spend the evening with my daughter. My mental attitude clearly affected the energy I felt in my body. You have probably had the experience of your body feeling under par because of overexertion or a virus. When my body is under the weather, I find I don't think as clearly and my attitude is not as chipper as it could be.

YOUR MIND

You probably know that how you think affects your sense of well-being, but your experience of this process can be much richer the more you understand it and implement a wellness practice to improve it.

> "
>
> Mental illness is nothing to be ashamed of, but stigma and bias shame us all.
>
> ## BILL CLINTON

Our culture promotes and rewards physical fitness but has lagged behind on providing practices and validation for healthy thinking. There are many reasons for that:

- Mental and emotional problems are less well understood and have historically carried a stigma.
- There has been a lack of hard science about how the mind and emotions operate.

Yes, these are both changing, but not quick enough for me.

STIGMA

Only recently insurance companies have been mandated to cover mental/emotional illness as thoroughly as physical illness. This caring for our minds has been a cultural and political issue since the pilgrims developed colonies in the United States. In the early communities "the distracted ones" would live at home and wander the community at will. People dealt with them as best they could but when there was a problem with someone, they, and their family had no support or help. The religious community stepped up and created places for these troubled people to live. Politicians got involved by promising a safer village life and better care for the troubled people. Mental hospitals, or asylums, were created to hide these problems from the rest of the community. Mental and emotional disturbance have been blamed on spirits, the devil, mothers, families, cultures and many other scapegoats. This culture of blaming and hiding the "insane" has created a stigma about mental/emotional problems. Today we still wave mental and emotional problems away with a drug or hope that anxiety or depression will go away on its own, and happily, sometimes it does. If someone breaks a leg, she doesn't hesitate to get it fixed by a doctor; yet when someone is depressed, she often does not seek treatment. This stigma is changing, yet slowly. I still find that when I'm talking to the public, it is much easier for people to tell me their brother-in-law fell off a ladder and had to go to the hospital to be put back together again than it is for them to speak of a friend or relative who was hospitalized for depression or post-traumatic stress symptoms. Ask yourself where your stigma indicator lies: Isn't it about time we stepped up and decided the brain deserves as much honor and attention as the rest of our body?

SCIENCE

As we create new technologies to map the mind and its relationship to, and impact on, the body, we are discovering, and hopefully addressing, mental/emotional wellness more strategically. As we understand more about how the brain processes information, identifies and manages emotions, we can create treatment approaches for imbalances that actually help the brain regulate and manage itself more effectively.

AWARENESS & MINDFULNESS

You've already been introduced to mindfulness and meditation earlier in this book. This skill will serve you well for the rest of your life. Meditation is the single best practice you can do for your mind. Commit now to increasing your awareness and understanding, one step at a time, at your own speed, about what you're feeling and how you are thinking. It is with this awareness that you become the choreographer of your own LifeDance. Mindful awareness gives you more choices about how to move at any given moment. Awareness leads to dialogue – the same dialogue in the dancer that presents fluidity to the audience's eye. You'll discover that when you engage in a dialogue in the moment of how you think, feel and act, you'll find a singular freedom – a liberation not available to many.

I mentioned earlier in this book when I first discovered this freedom. I was working in a job I hated and was in two difficult relationships. I went to see a Gestalt-oriented therapist, who showed me how much I was responsible for creating my own reality and how many more choices I had. In fact, the choices were infinite. The day I "got it," I walked out of his office and, to my eye, the world had changed. I could hear the birds in the trees, smell the fresh air and see the world with heightened senses. Mentally I was no longer a puppet of my past or imagined future. In that moment I could do anything I chose to do. I could feel like a victim or hero. I could continue to think in those same terms, or, I could act. I could get help. I could do anything I wanted. It was an amazing day. That's not to say there wasn't more work to do dealing with past issues, shame and regret, but, I now had the power to tackle how I thought and felt, rather than being a victim of thoughts, feelings and my inner stories.

How is this possible? The answer starts with understanding how the mind

> Between stimulus and response there is a space. In that space is our power to choose our response. In our response lies our growth and our freedom.
>
> ## VICTOR FRANKL

"

The experience of being in a collaborative healthy relationship can facilitate the creation of new neural connections and pathways in the brain that support an integrated sense of self and others.

LINDA LAWLESS

and emotions function for us. So yes, this is neuroscience, and I'm going to give you a quick tour.

CONSCIOUSNESS AND INTEGRATED PERCEPTION

The mind is often equated with consciousness, the feeling we each have of our own lives, or self-awareness (inward perception), and our perceptions of the world around us (outer perception). These two awarenesses appear to be different but are actually the convergence of two kinds of perception that the nervous system provides us.

Knowing how the brain grows and functions helps us understand ourselves better. As organisms began, the role of the nervous system was to protect the organism via an automatic and reflexive system. For example, I was walking down a path recently and found myself moving way to the right of the pathway. Wondering why, I turned and looked back and saw a small snake darting for cover. The view of the snake had been in my peripheral field of vision and I was completely unaware of it. My outer sensory system on the other hand, had an "unconscious" alertness that perceived "danger" and moved me out of harm's way. This is a function of the "old brain," the part of us that developed early.

There are other "old brain" components as well, like the reptilian brain or R-complex, which triggers the fight-or-flight response, helping us flee from danger, recover from trauma and perpetuate the species. The reptilian brain manages arousal, homeostasis and reproduction, while the next development, the "old-mammal" brain manages learning memory and emotion. Sitting on top of these two is the "new-mammal" brain, which we use for conscious thought and self-awareness.

It is important to understand this because the older parts of our brains direct a large part of our lives and seek dominance outside of our conscious awareness. By the time we believe we are making a conscious choice, information has been processed and reprocessed in the more primitive areas, exploring memories and triggering neural pathways that were created by past learning or trauma. Early experiences in life – the crucial first few years when our brains develop -- build intricate and foundational neural systems. **The way our brains develop in the early years of life affects us our whole life long, yet can**

also be changed.

Consciousness has no specific center or pathway. It relies on structures that trigger and regulate the nervous activity that uses the centers of perception and analysis. One of these functions is the Reticular Formation. I remember being taught about this function in my eighth-grade science class. We watched a movie that portrayed the focusing function of the mind as a small man in a control room with an array of video screens. As events took place, internally and externally, the little man was responsible for activating the needed parts of the brain, or body, to mobilize them into action. In my case during my walk, the small snake needed to be responded to. The motivator could also have been a memory of a traumatic event in relation to a snake, and I could have had a full-blown panic attack. As I attempted to avoid the snake, I could have fallen over a log and broken my leg, which would have called for chemical changes in my body to deal with pain. This little man (or woman) operating the video screens has a hierarchy of responses. If the event is life-threatening, it overrides lesser tasks like deciding what I'm going to have for dinner; saving my life takes the highest priority.

When any response is chosen, a neural pathway is created. If I were to repeatedly walk down paths with snakes, my brain would create a stronger neural pathway for snake detection. This is what happens in the case of repeated trauma victims in which we often see symptoms called post traumatic stress reactions. As neuropsychiatrist Dan Siegel, author of *The Mindful Brain*,[22] quotes, "Neurons that fire together wire together." So when you habitually do something good for your brain, you create new neural pathways to support your wellness.

Here's an example. Meet Carol, who was raised by a critical and unrelenting parent. Every time she failed at school or got a bad grade, she was slapped. After she grew up and left home, she knew she should attend college to further her career, but every time she walked into a school she would start to cry, and her ears would hurt. As you can probably imagine, she didn't stay long and would walk out. As she began to meditate and inquire into her mental and physical reactions, and ask herself "when have I felt this way before?" she was able to remember what had happened as a little girl. Given this information, she no longer felt "crazy," about school and was able to work with her feelings until she was able to begin taking some classes. If she had not personally been able to demystify her reactions, she could also have gone to see a professional to help her uncover these issues and

> "
>
> All forms of self-defeating behavior are unseen and unconscious, which is why their existence is denied.
>
> **VERNON HOWARD**

"

He is half of a
blessed man.
Left to be finished by such
as she; and she a fair divided
excellence, whose fullness of
perfection lies in him.

WILLIAM SHAKESPEARE

work through them.

Sometimes it's only an illusion that we have free will. Too often, we are simply the puppets of our unconscious processes. For you to begin to be the director of your own dance; you must bring these unconscious workings more and more into awareness, with a loving attitude, and make choices about changes you want to make.

ARE MEN & WOMEN'S BRAINS DIFFERENT?

Yes, women are different from men! The less than 1 percent difference between the genome of the sexes appears to be small, yet this difference affects every single cell in our bodies. Women's brains are more compact, and yet have the same number of brain cells. As a result of recent tools that are used for neuroscientific research, we're discovering an array of structural, chemical, genetic, hormonal and functional brain differences between women and men.[23] So, what does this mean in everyday life?

- Women's brains are more affected by hormonal changes throughout their lives.

- Women's brains have more circuits for communication, emotional reading and nurturing behavior in utero. This specialization is needed for them to respond to and care for future babies and help them survive. Unfortunately, having more relational "sensors" puts them at higher risk for emotional and relational abuse because they are more sensitive to this activity. Being more sensitive creates a greater impact on the entire neurological system. Females are hard-wired to prevent social conflict through relational solutions. Because they may have children to protect and have less muscle strength, they must stand and solve rather than run or attack. Given this way of operating, they may fear conflict and not deal effectively with direct aggression or competition. The female solution to a threat is communication and collaboration with others.

- Women's brains change when they become mothers. Besides becoming protective of the infant on all fronts, they also may have better spatial memory, be more flexible, adaptive and courageous. Because they must protect their offspring, they will go the extra mile to save them. On the down side, a nursing mother may have difficulty focusing outside of the mother/child dyad.

- Women have more connections between the two sides of the brain so they are better able to use both sides of the brain in symphony. The left side of the brain that is spatial, wholistic and nonlinear is able to coordinate with the right side of the brain where language and linear thinking take place. This allows a woman to enter a room of many different people, get a "sense" of where common interest or safety lies, and approach another and talk to them, creating a human link (safety) through dialogue. Because the wholistic perceptual part of the brain has an enhanced connection to the verbal sites in the brain, women can more easily articulate their relational perceptions and their thoughts and feelings.

Because the world's cultures are primarily patriarchal, hierarchical and male-dominated (left brain), women have had a layer of this left-brain dominant model superimposed on their natural feminine modalities – they may have lost touch with their "female" strengths, such as integrated collaborative solution techniques or access to nonverbal information, also sometimes referred to as intuition.

> ,,
>
> Brains aren't designed to get results; they go in directions. If you know how the brain works you can set your own directions. If you don't, then someone else will.
>
> **RICHARD BANDLER**

MENTAL FITNESS

What have YOU done for your mind lately? You probably take better care of your car than you do your mind. It has never made sense to me that the one thing about humans that sets us apart from other species, our minds, has been the last part of ourselves that we nourish and grow. We not only don't understand it; we actually put a stigma on people whose minds are broken as mentioned earlier. I propose we step back from our minds and treat them with the respect they're due, and keep our brains in good shape. To whom do we turn for help? Unfortunately many professionals in the mental health field do not know how the brain works and can't help you with that.

At a mental health professional education workshop recently, I heard Dan Siegel ask a room of mental health professionals, "How many of you have had a class on how the brain works?" A few people raised their hands in a room of more than 300 people. I was amazed to realize that for all these years in the

An intellectual
is someone whose mind
watches itself.

ALBERT CAMUS

mental health field, most of our theories are based on theorist's observations and their guesses at what works, rather than brain science. It would be like watching a turtle walk, eat, eliminate – and guessing about what systems are inside the shell. You could come up with a gross generalization but would not really know until the turtle died and you did an autopsy. Unfortunately, then the turtle would be dead and nothing would be moving, so you could see the structures but not the dynamics. The ideal would be to be able to see inside of the shell and watch the heart pumping, the elimination system processing food and so on. This is what we can do with the brain today; we can see how it is working in real time using functional MRIs (Magnetic Resonance Imaging). So how do we keep this miraculous part of our body in shape?

MENTAL FITNESS EXERCISES

Clinical neuroscientist and psychiatrist Dr. Daniel Amen suggests six ways to improve our brain function in his book, *Making A Good Brain Great: The Amen Clinic Program For Achieving And Sustaining Optimal Mental Performance*.

STRESS CAN MAKE YOU SICK. Amen says that stress hormones kill brain cells in the memory center and cause serious trouble for the body. Just realizing that and deciding to work on reducing stress is a good step.

GET ENOUGH SLEEP. Amen notes that since the invention of the light bulb, we've become sleep-deprived. "As a species, we have not evolved to need less sleep," he says. "Six hours isn't enough. We really need nine hours of sleep, and almost no one gets that much."

GET REGULAR EXERCISE. Amen says that regular exercise boosts hormones that keep your brain young. There are studies that show that exercise increases the circulation to the brain that promotes cell health. Amen calls table tennis the best brain sport. It improves hand-eye coordination. It's aerobic, uses both upper and lower body and causes you to use many different areas of the brain to function.

AVOID SUBSTANCES THAT STRESS THE BRAIN. Chief offenders in this category are caffeine, nicotine, drugs and alcohol. These substances actually decrease the blood flow in the brain, which is damaging and can cause premature aging.

TAKE SUPPLEMENTS. There are lots of things you could take, but

Amen wants to keep this simple. He says that there is research that shows that Omega 3 (fish oil) and a good multiple vitamin promotes brain health.

DEVELOP AN INTERNAL ANT-EATER. Amen calls ANTs (Automatic Negative Thoughts) stressors for the brain. These are the daily, automatic negative thoughts that go through your head through the day. "Whenever you feel sad, mad or nervous, you need to write out what you are thinking. Look at them," he says. "Are they reasonable or are they torturing you unnecessarily? And then you talk back to them. You don't have to believe every thought you have. They are only thoughts and thoughts can lie. Correcting them will go a long way to treating depression and anxiety."

THE HEALTHY MIND PLATTER[FT]

The term mental fitness has been around for some time, but here is a more current approach to a healthy mind. Dr. Dan Siegel and Dr. David Rock have created The Healthy Mind Platter for Optimal Brain Matter. Think about the food pyramid. The Healthy Mind Platter is the shape of a plate with portions for "seven daily essential mental activities to optimize brain matter and create well-being." They are:

- **FOCUS TIME**. Focusing on tasks, like goals, and dealing with all that comes to us in the pursuit of the goal.

- **PLAY TIME**. One of my favorites! Mental play is allowing ourselves to be creative and spontaneous, doing new things and creating new connections in the brain as we do them.

- **CONNECTING TIME**. Connecting with other people, ideally face to face, and connecting to the world around us. Spending time with Mother Nature is a great way to connect with the environment.

- **PHYSICAL TIME**. Moving our bodies, such as dance or other aerobic activity.

- **TIME IN**. Reflecting on our inner sensations, thoughts, images and emotions.

- **DOWN TIME**. Zone-out time with no focus. Daydreaming, mind wandering, resting and rejuvenating.

- **SLEEP TIME**. Giving your brain the rest it needs to repair and consolidate the day's experiences.

Just like you choose healthy food, you can choose a healthy inner dialogue. Some days it may be easier to find an apple than a positive word. You may need to be the healthy news for others. Say something kind and healthy every day.

LINDA LAWLESS

> "
>
> There is no enlightenment outside of daily life.
>
> ## THICH NHAT HANH

Since I learned about The Healthy Mind Platter, I carry around a 3x5 card with me and look at it during the day. When I want to sit in my favorite chair and read a mystery or stare out the window at a beautiful tree, I now do so with great glee, knowing I'm exercising my brain, not "wasting time."

REFRAMING

When you are mindful of the moment, you have access to another tool you can use called "ReFraming," as we did in Chapter Five. Just like you can reframe a painting, you can also reframe your memories, thoughts and current reality. As I mentioned earlier in this book, I experienced this recently just after my mother died. I'm an only child and having to deal with the home she had lived in for the past 25 years was overwhelming. Every time I walked into her house to begin cleaning it out, I became 12 years old again and completely immobilized by emotions. My mind would race to and get lost in the past; I'd relive the recent passing and hours spent in hospitals. Thank goodness my daughter was helping me out, and as soon as I would stop moving, she'd look me in the eye, jiggle my arm, and say, "Mom, there's a lot of work we need to do today, why don't you...." I'd return to the present moment, reframe my presence there as a loving daughter helping to clean up her house, make a mental note to self to write in my journal later, and move forward.

People also get lost in the future. I have a friend who is constantly wishing for what her parents told her she should have when she grew up. She was supposed to have a husband, two children, etc. ... you know the drill. She had opted for a career and had become moderately successful. What she discovered was that she was undermining herself at work because there was a part of her that believed that she should really be looking for the right man and having children. Once she became aware of this inner part of herself, she engaged in a dialogue with it and began to reframe her current life so she could truly embrace what SHE wanted from her life, and not what her parents wanted for her.

There are many more examples, and I'm sure you have some yourself. What this means is really awesome. It means that you are the designer of your life, past, present and future. You can reframe your past, make peace with people and events, support your current reality, reframe events in the moment to support your peace and well-being, and, envision a future that is the best it can be for you and those around you, maybe even the world. Use the section in your **MASTER CLASS WORKBOOK** 2.5a to apply Reframing.

FLOW STATES: WHEN ALL OF THE PIECES DANCE TOGETHER

Have you ever been doing something and lost all sense of time because you were so engrossed in it? I often find this happens when I'm writing. I take off with an idea and the next thing I know, I'm late for an appointment. This experience is called a flow-state. It is a state in which you are completely immersed in what you are doing and completely engaged with it. Some people call it being in the "zone." Any dancer, musician, athlete, even gambler, will tell you about his or her flow experiences. To experience flow, you must truly surrender to the moment. Use your journal to record those times during the day when you entered "flow." That way you will begin to see what activities elicit this state for you.

This concept was brought to popular awareness by positive psychologist Mihály Csíkszentmihályi in his book *Flow, the Psychology of Optimal Experience*.[24] He describes flow to include the following:

- **CLEAR GOALS.** Expectations and rules are discernible and goals are attainableand align appropriately with one's skill set and abilities.

- **CONCENTRATING AND FOCUSING**. A high degree of concentration is trained on a limited field of attention. A person engaged in the activity will have the opportunity to focus and to delve deeply into it.

- **A LOSS OF THE FEELING OF SELF-CONSCIOUSNESS.** This is the merging of action and awareness.

- **DISTORTED SENSE OF TIME.** One's subjective experience of time is altered.

- **FEEDBACK.** One experiences direct and immediate feedback – that is, successes and failures in the course of the activity are apparent, so that behavior can be adjusted as needed.

- **BALANCE BETWEEN CURRENT ABILITY LEVEL AND A CHALLENGE.** The activity is neither too easy nor too difficult.

- **CONTROL**. One has a sense of personal control over the situation or activity.

- **INTRINSIC REWARDS.** The activity is intrinsically (inner) reward-

"

The hallmark of flow is a feeling of spontaneous joy, even rapture, while performing a task.

MIHALY CSIKSZENTMIHALYI

"

It is possible to experience an awakening in this life through realising just how precious each moment, each mental process, and each breath truly is.

CHRISTY TURLINGTON

ing so there is an effortlessness of action.

- **ACTION AWARENESS MERGING**. People become absorbed in their activity, and focus of awareness is narrowed down to the activity itself.

Note: Not all of the above are needed for flow to be experienced.

There is so much to know about the mind, and more is discovered every day. I highly recommend that you stay abreast of what is being discovered. The Internet is an excellent tool to do research. Just be careful you are using dependable resources. To stay abreast of neuroscience, I recommend the MindSight Institute, online at www.drdansiegel.com. The popular magazine Psychology Today, is a good user-friendly periodical to keep you tuned in to what's in the popular focus. For more clinical information, WebMD (webmd.com), is a wonderful resource.

You are the keeper of your brain and mind. Treat it well and it will serve you well and be a co-creator of your LifeDance.

Please turn to | 3.11 | **MIND ASSESSMENT** in the **MASTER CLASS WORKBOOK** to complete your assessment.

CHAPTER TWELVE

The Dance Arenas: Emotions

W hat moves you – fear, love, lust, greed? Emotions are deeply intertwined with our bodies and thoughts. Because they have such power to move us, let's look at them closely.

Are your emotions felt in the moment, remembered from the past, or triggered by your thoughts of the future? Emotions ask to be identified, shape our thoughts, and move us to action. They are part of our everyday life. Emotional fitness is a skill that can be learned allowing you to work with them rather than react to them.

Emotions come in many names and colors and can be VERY confusing. Here are some real-life examples.

- Every time Sarah saw a Dalmatian, her adrenaline would kick in. Her heart would race, and she felt scared. But why?

- After a San Francisco earthquake, Chris felt terror when he crossed the bridge because he had been on the Bay Bridge when one of the roadways collapsed. He had a panic attack and pulled to the side of the road. But this was many months after the trauma. Why?

- Midge was devastated over her boyfriend's betrayal. For months and months afterward, she couldn't stop crying. With time, she was able to explore and understand where her sadness came from. How did she do this?

A question in the field of psychology has been, which happens first – the feeling or the thought? The panic attack on the bridge, or thoughts about the earthquake experience? The sadness about a breakup, or the crying that brings up the memory? Seeing a Dalmatian, or feeling scared around the dog? It turns out that both can happen first, the emotion or the memory of the experience. I told you they are confusing. Another belief is that emotions arise out of any sense of imbalance or transition in life.[25] Maybe your emotion is simply your

"

The key to change... is to

let go of fear.

ROSANNE CASH

body communicating with you and your job is to embrace it with loving kindness. Here are some examples.

SARAH

Sarah didn't often have the experience of crippling fear when she saw a Dalmatian, but when she did, she had no control over it. It was so intense she wondered what was wrong with her. It was so disconnected from her every day experience – from any belief she had or any situation she could remember. The event would unleash a torrent of inner personal criticism of how emotionally unstable she was.

Finally, one day she shared this curious experience with her older brother, who offhandedly said, "Don't you remember seeing a Dalmatian get hit by a car when we were at Uncle Jack's for Thanksgiving?" The answer, of course, was no, or she would have understood where the fear came from. Sarah was very young when the accident happened and she had no conscious memory of it. Now that she is aware of the event, when she has that same reaction, she knows where it comes from. This allows her to calm herself more easily by reminding herself that is only a memory, allowing her body to calm itself, and quieting her inner critic.

CHRIS

Chris regularly commuted into San Francisco over the Bay Bridge. The day the Loma Prieta earthquake rumbled, the bridge broke, the upper level falling on the level below. He was two cars behind a car that slipped from the upper level to the lower level. The experience was terrifying.

While the bridge was being repaired, Chris used the ferry to get to work, but that increased his commute time from one to two hours each way. Every time he thought about the earthquake he would feel afraid. He used distractions to stop thinking about his experience, and vowed to deal with it some other time. After the bridge re-opened, Chris decided to tough it out and drive over the bridge, thinking of the savings in commute time. But as he approached the bridge, he felt anxiety building. When he got to the same place where the bridge collapsed, his anxiety was intolerable. He was trembling and sweating. He had to pull to the side of the roadway. Chris made the choice to avoid dealing with his fears, so they remained raw and overwhelming simply waiting for a trigger, something that brought them to the surface, to set them all off again. If Chris had faced his fears, or as a friend of mine describes this, walking toward the cannons, he could have taken his terrifying experience and defused it to a memory of an experience that was simply part of his life, rather than a debilitating memory. He wouldn't forget it, he would simply take the emotional charge out of it and manage his "here and now" response to the memory. There are several ways to deal with trauma clinically, three that I have experienced as effective are EMDR (Eye Movement Desensitization and Reprocessing[26]), EFT (Emotional Freedom Technique), and SensoriMotor work.[27]

MIDGE

Midge was 20 when she fell hopelessly in love with a musician. She followed him around from gig to gig at different nightclubs until he finally asked her out. They dated for a year, and then moved in together. They had what she thought was the perfect relationship. After about five years, one day a male friend asked her out. She said, "No, I'm in a committed relationship with Joe." Her friend acted surprised, and she asked him why. He told her that he knew Joe dated other women so he thought she could date as well. Midge went home and confronted Joe, and to his credit, he admitted that he had been seeing other women for their entire five years together. Midge was heartbroken. Her fantasy of the perfect man and relationship was destroyed. She cried for days, told Joe he had to leave and eventually moved on to other relationships, but every time she thought of Joe, she would burst into tears. She thought she knew why, but for the life of her, she couldn't think or talk about him without crying. As she was able to distance herself from the experience, with time, whenever she thought about Joe, she would feel the urge to cry and then simply forgive herself for being naive and accept Joe and the loss of her "dream" relationship for what it was. The crying over time turned into a deep sadness over her loss of Joe and the myth she had created, then lost. Today, she is in a long-standing relationship and looking back, fondly remembers the good times she had with Joe and realizes that what she was crying about was the loss of the myth she had created about her perfect relationship.

UNDERSTANDING EMOTIONS

Many of us have long-buried emotions that have made us emotional cripples. They keep us from living fully in the moment, taking risks to create a more ful-

> Let's not forget that the little emotions are the great captains of our lives and we obey them without realizing it.

VINCENT VAN GOGH

> Being unwanted, unloved, uncared for, forgotten by everybody, I think that is a much greater hunger, a much greater poverty than the person who has nothing to eat.

MOTHER TERESA

> "
>
> A man who is master of
> himself can end
> a sorrow as easily as he can
> invent a pleasure. I don't want
> to be at the mercy
> of my emotions.
> I want to use them, to enjoy
> them, and to dominate them.
>
> OSCAR
> WILDE

filling life, and making good, if not difficult decisions. You may have experiences in your past that you avoid walking toward, or even experiences you have buried so deeply you don't even remember them. Understanding how emotions "work," and walking towards them, one step at a time, increasing your awareness, and learning new ways to be emotionally smarter will make you a stronger LifeDancer.

To understand emotions, we need to look at the area of the brain where they originate: the limbic system. The limbic system affects the release of chemicals to enable your body to survive in the face of a threat. Emotions are a chain of loosely connected events triggered by an internal or external stimulus. Physical changes occur, and concepts and actions follow. This can be the fight-or-flight response. When Chris had to go over the bridge, his fear got the best of him. He had a "flight" response, but he couldn't flee, so he froze, or shut down. Midge learned how to move the devastating sadness to a sadness over her loss. She was running from a normal grief response over the loss. If it was beyond normal it could have been a trigger for, or metaphor for a deeper loss, that is, loss of another loved one like an absent father.

Sarah, who had an early experience about which she didn't have a conscious memory, was swept away by her limbic system that responded to the image of the Dalmatian. The visual kicked in a fear response. To work with that, she could increase her awareness of her reaction, slowly, using new skills like reframing, journaling, asking herself what lessons she could learn from the experience, externalizing it through creative expression, talking to a professional, and turning it into a part of who she is rather than being immobilized by it.

BALANCING THE DANCE OF EMOTIONS

You are always going to have emotions. It's how you deal with and direct them that is the key to staying balanced and dynamic in your LifeDance. Some folks who have had strong emotional experiences try to shut down their feelings or go numb. Others avoid dealing with them through addictions or other destructive behaviors. Think of emotions as the water or music of life. If you crimp a hose that has water running through it, when you let it go it explodes for a while. If you dam a river, eventually it overflows. It is the same way with emotions, if they are not acknowledged, honored and managed they too will overflow out of control. After Chris had his panic attack going over the bridge he knew he had to deal with his fear or never drive over the bridge again. He joined a support group for earthquake survivors and gradually was able to desensitize himself to driving over the bridge. He also worked with a personal therapist using SensoriMotor techniques and allowed his body to complete the trauma reaction he had aborted during the event. His fears abated, his body regulated itself and his earthquake experience became a powerful memory, not a debilitating fear reaction.

Emotions can throw us off balance if we are not aware of their triggers or able to regulate them, like Sarah. They can create disequilibrium between ourselves and the event or other people associated with the event. Midge couldn't talk to Joe because she would cry so hard she couldn't talk. There are many ways these basic emotions might affect your life.

THE IMPORTANCE OF NARRATIVE

Many times, we create a story or narrative to explain an emotion or justify our response to it. That story can become a theme for our lives like always being a Victim, Jokester or Princess. But the story affects our dance – and we don't dance as passionately or freely as we possibly can. Sarah's story was that there was something wrong with her until she discovered what had triggered her responses. Her theme was "I'm broken." Do you have stories about how emotion affects you, i.e., I'm oversensitive, I'm an angry person or I'm a loving person? In this chapter, we're exploring how you can increase your emotional awareness to enhance your dance of life.

EMOTIONAL INTELLIGENCE

Emotional Intelligence is a concept introduced into the mainstream by Daniel Goleman[28]. He coined the term to define a person's aptitude for engaging with individual as well as other people's emotions. Educating yourself about emotions becomes a guide for personal thinking and acting. The arenas of emotional intelligence are:

> "
>
> You must have control of the authorship of your own destiny. The pen that writes your life story must be held in your own hand.
>
> ### IRENE KASSORIA

> It is very important to understand that emotional intelligence is not the opposite of intelligence, it is not the triumph of heart over head – it is the unique intersection of both.
>
> ## DAVID CARUSO

- **SELF-AWARENESS.** Recognizing an emotion when it comes up and giving it a name.
- **ABILITY TO HANDLE FEELINGS APPROPRIATELY.** Being able to choose how to express or manage emotions in a healthy way.
- **ABILITY TO USE EMOTIONS IN A CREATIVE WAY.** Rather than being "stuck" in emotion, to use it to move to the next step.
- **ABILITY TO RECOGNIZE EMOTIONS IN OTHERS.** Being aware of others as well as ourselves.
- **ABILITY TO MANAGE EMOTIONAL EXCHANGES WITH OTHERS.** Being open and willing to discuss feelings and manage our own in relationships.

Makes a lot of sense. But when you are flooded with anger, depression or even joy, sometimes it is impossible to act like an adult. How do you redirect a flood toward a quiet stream? Some of the tools are:

1. **SELF-CONTROL.** Learning how to manage disruptive emotions and impulses effectively;

2. **TRUSTWORTHINESS.** Displaying honesty and integrity with yourself and others;

3. **CONSCIENTIOUSNESS.** Dependability and responsibility in fulfilling obligations;

4. **ADAPTABILITY.** Flexibility in handling change and challenges; and

5. **INNOVATION.** Being open to novel ideas and approaches.

This is an arena that has been explored in depth and applied in personal and business settings. I highly recommend Goleman's[29] work if you want to explore it more deeply.

TRANSACTIONAL ANALYSIS

The field of Transactional Analysis (TA), also gives us a simple way to understand emotional intelligence. TA identifies three primary types, the Adult, Child and Parent. The Adult can step back and look at emotions and make rational decisions about how to act. The Child becomes lost in their emotions and may act out irrationally, potentially hurting themselves or others. The Parent is able to step back and at the same time, empathize with the emotional child guiding her in a healthy direction. All three approaches are important. We need to have the delicious experience of our emotions and allow spontaneity – the Child. But we also need the empathic nurturing Parent, who can guide, and the objective Adult, who can make decisions.

For instance, planning the holidays at our house is an exercise of many people and many roles working out a single event from many passions. We usually start talking like "Adults" about how the holiday event will unfold, who's invited and so on. Then we roll into "where's the magic" for the kids in the family; reminiscing about our own childhoods and what we enjoyed; then bartering for what's going to happen. Then, back to the adults who begin to vie for what they want until someone gets emotional and someone steps in, "Parents" them and lets them know they will get what they want, and finally we end up with a basic plan that we all know is simply a guideline, not a mandate.

TIPPING POINTS

As you increase your emotional awareness, you'll begin to get a sense of your personal range of feelings, and where your "tipping" points are. A tipping point is a place where you begin to slide out of control into an emotion, sometimes called "flooding." In terms of your LifeDance, imagine a dancer who hears a strong, dramatic piece of music and loses herself in it – delicious. It's what we all love to watch in a dancer. But what if the dancer cannot leave her frantic dance and begins to fall down from exhaustion? It is important for this dancer to be able to know when she is tired, take a break, and then decide just what parts of the music she wants to use in her personal dance.

Your tipping point is the place where anger, fear or even joy become so intense you can't stop the feelings. They take on a life of their own. The key is to stop the flood of emotion before it tips and races out of control, taking over your dance.

Dancing with your emotions wisely means befriending them. Often we are critical of how we are feeling because we have inner scripts that tell us we shouldn't feel negative emotions – anger, jealousy, or fear. It is all right to feel it, explore it, but not act on it if it would cause damage to self or others. If a particular feeling or emotion is affecting your life in a destructive way, it needs to be acknowledged, explored, and if you cannot understand and manage it, get help with

> "
>
> The tipping point is that magic moment when an idea, trend, or social behavior crosses a threshold, tips, and spreads like wildfire.
>
> MALCOLM GLADWELL

"

No one is in control of your happiness but you; therefore, you have the power to change anything about yourself or your life that you want to change.

BARBARA DE ANGELIS

it. This personal work you cannot understand and manage it, get help with it. This personal work needs to be done before you can be wise in relating to others emotions. If you feel uncomfortable with your own anger, then you will be that way with others. I know a woman who was not allowed to be happy as a child; she was told it was frivolous. Now, she feels guilty any time she feels the least bit happy. Her job is to allow her feeling of joy to simply be there and begin to befriend it. She's doing this personal work because she wants to be able to be comfortable with her children's happiness.

EMOTIONS & TRAUMA

As you learned in the chapter on the mind, neurons that fire together, wire together. So, if you experienced repeated emotional trauma, your mind and body will take longer to learn new ways of feeling and acting. If you find the suggestions in this chapter are not enough for you to manage your emotional state, i.e., a deep depression or mania, please consult with a mental health professional for support and guidance. There is a very large field of professionals who are doing research on trauma and healing and there are many excellent resources available to you. One I can personally recommend is the Sensory Motor Training Institute at sensorimotorpsychotherapy.org.

A dancer uses emotion to motivate and move her, provide her with feedback on the quality of her dance, and to express to others, the story of her dance. Emotions are a bit like wild animals, they are not to be beaten into submission, rather, they are to be ridden like a wild stallion. First you must get aboard, then experience the dynamic, and slowly, the two become one in their dance of life.

Please turn to | 3.12 | **EMOTIONS ASSESSMENT** in the **MASTER CLASS WORKBOOK** to complete your assessment.

CHAPTER THIRTEEN

The Dance Arenas:
Dancing with Spirit

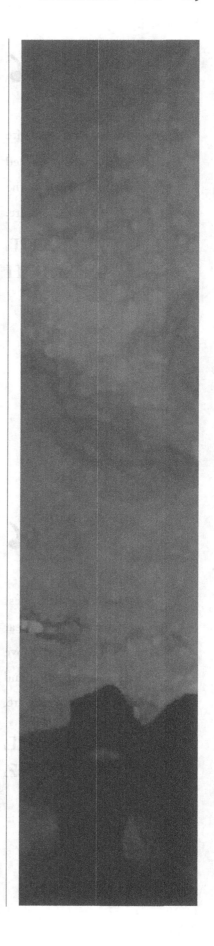

Spirit is the spark and soul of your LifeDance. There are some who believe our dance of life is only a vehicle for the expression of spirit. Imagine a dancer who had no connection to her inner spirit. The expression would lack passion and appear soulless, flat and robotic. Fortunately, as the dancer becomes more integrated and congruent with her inner needs, values and personal mission, the spirit of the dance grows. Spirit-infused movement comes from the inside out — not the outside in. Spirit radiates from an authentic LifeDance.

This chapter focuses on spirit with no religious theological identification, with room for you to define your deity and your faith as you choose. Here are a few approaches to the subjective or inner experience of spirituality:

In the English language the word "spirit" comes from the Latin spiritus, meaning "breath." Historically the power of spirituality has been given to shamans, earth-based representations, i.e., "The Green Man," mythologies, gods and goddesses.

Ralph Waldo Emerson (1803-1882) pioneered the idea of "spirituality" as a distinct field he called transcendentalism. This was a philosophy declaring a person's spiritual awareness transcended the logical, rational world. He believed that spirituality could be experienced through emotions and intuition, and believed in the power of individual and divine messages.

Friedrich Nietzsche's rationalism looked to the idea of spirituality as an alternative to materialism.

William James found commonalities in all religions, mainly man's search for meaning, in his book, *The Varieties of Religious Experience* (1902).

As you begin to open up to the spirit and connectedness of all life, you learn to trust your LifeDance more and more. You become more fully integrated in body, mind and spirit. Spiritual awareness grows out of your integration and access to your essence. As you perform your LifeDance, you come more authentically into your own experience. You are completely present in the moment. As you, the dancer of your own LifeDance, become a clearer channel for personal spirit, creativity flows into expression. You allow your inner spirit to manifest through your dance. Then, as you begin to see spirit in everything, you see how we are all connected. Love of self and others becomes a response that helps spirit grow and manifest all around you. As you become more loving of your own Life-Dance, you naturally express love via your dance.

MY STORY, OUR STORIES

I asked myself, "Who are you to write a chapter on spirituality?" The answer, I'm just another person who wonders in awe at the complexity of life and its mysteries and has experienced their own spiritual quest. My introduction to spirituality started as an infant. Because I had a Midwestern Protestant mother and a Catholic father, I was christened Catholic and baptized Protestant, "just in case." Then as a small child, after years of Bible school (Protestant because my mother raised me), I became curious about all those other churches my friends went to and asked if I could go along with them. At that young age, it seemed to me that everyone was saying the same thing, just in different ways. That same thing was that there was a benevolent power greater than we could imagine all around us and that we should live our lives caring for each other. Years later, I haven't moved very far from the last part, and have come to the place of creating my own spiritual way.

Human beings appear to be hard-wired for spirituality. We appear to be able to experience an all-pervading loving presence and inspiration and recognize a meaning to existence that transcends our immediate LifeDance. I believe spiritual practice is not confined to any one specific form of belief or practice. It can be embraced and personalized in whatever form is relevant and effective in keeping you in dialogue with that which touches your inner spirit.

My own spiritual way is inclusive and curious. As a psychotherapist, I have learned to explore, without judgment, my clients' beliefs about spirit. What I've discovered is that each person has a unique twist on spirit, even if she or he belongs to a particular church or belief system. I make no pretense to identify a "right" path or church for anyone. I do believe we all need to be conscious about our individual spirituality and the ways it improves or degrades our quality of life.

THE DANCE OF SPIRIT

As a LifeDancer, I find I must bring spirit to every moment by increasing my awareness and being present and available in the moment to divine inspiration. Being present allows me to experience spirit unfolding, supported with an attitude of loving kindness. I do this for many reasons, some of which are self-serving. I have noticed that when I am calm, centered, noncritical and present, people are more open and less defensive with me. When I am up in my head, out of touch with my body, moving ahead into the future and away from the moment, people withdraw, defend, and just try to get out of my way. I also can be VERY critical of others and find that very stressful, for myself and others. When I open my heart to myself and others, and don the mantle of loving kindness, life becomes much more peaceful. This practice serves me, as well as others, in many ways, here's but one experience.

Recently I went to interview a new chiropractor. I was prepared to fend off a sales job and hear a lot of what I already knew. As we drew to the close of our interview he looked at me and said, "You're a tough cookie aren't you?" I surrendered to the moment yet was defensive, and said I was whatever he experienced and watched him get out of the room as quickly as possible.

Then, noticing I was a BIT EDGY, I stopped at the video rental store where they had lost a video I knew I had returned. I stopped in and went to the counter, VERY EDGY, and asked them to look for it again because I was certain THEY had lost it., Once again, I was told it wasn't there. Hmmm, time for another approach. I slowed down and stopped by again later in the day. This time I waited patiently in line focusing on my breath and preparing myself to accept whatever answer I received, graciously. When my turn came I stepped up and explained my problem. I asked the woman behind the counter if the video had somehow shown up or been misplaced in the store. She took her time to explore all the nooks and crannies of the store and yes, she found it. I thanked her for her excellent customer service and left.

The difference in these events in the video rental store was my spirit. In the first one I was closed, critical, judgmental and not open to what was being offered. The result may have been the same, but the "feeling" could have been much kinder. The second event unfolded so much better. A difficult customer service problem was solved successfully this time because she wanted to do a

> Be kind whenever possible.
> It is always possible.
>
> # DALAI LAMA

"

A man's errors are his portals of discovery.

JAMES JOYCE

good job. I was in need and appreciative of her efforts. Comparing the two, the "spirit" of the moments were different.

Beyond the daily moments, there can be those times when everything is crashing down around your ears, and there is really nothing to support or save you except the spirit you hold within. If nothing resides within, you truly are at the mercy of the events that unfold around you. One of my favorite stories about the spirit of optimism is the one about two boys and the pony. I told it earlier, but here's a quick reminder. One boy arrives at a castle to pick up his pony. The doors of the castle open and he faces a very large pile of pony poop. He screams and runs and demands that the pony be brought to him, no pony arrives. The second boy arrives, the doors open, he too is faced with the large pile of horse poop. He screams in excitement and jumps into the pile and flings pony dung everywhere, convinced that under that pile a pony must be waiting for him, and it stands just on the other side of the pile.

So, whenever life gives me poop, I think of this story, and begin to dig for the spirit of the pony. I know it is there somewhere, I simply can't find it, yet.

PRACTICES: THE DANCE OF SPIRIT

I find three essential practices can create the dance of spirit – meditating, being in an inner or outer sacred space, and being in a spiritual community. Use these tools as the foundation for a spiritual practice in your life. You may set up or find support groups around these practices to help establish them in your life. A key to spirituality is to bring it to daily life. Yes, practice makes perfect. If I practice loving kindness every day – in the line at the grocery store with the person who brought 15 items to the 10-item line, in traffic with the person who cuts me off, or at home with a loved one who "gets in my way" – it gets easier and easier to do it when I'm under pressure.

Make it a point to schedule your practices. If you schedule them, they are more likely to happen. Give yourself reminders, put a reminder on your calendar, a sticky on the bathroom mirror, a bracelet or ring you never take off, a picture in your home or office that reminds you, and – brings you back to your practice. At a networking meeting I attend weekly, I always begin my introduction with something that is inspirational for me that day.

SILENCE, MEDITATION & CONTEMPLATION

More than ever before, people today feel the need for silence, meditation and contemplation. We live in a busy and noisy time. We are not usually offered time for silence or centering so we must make the time for it ourselves. I use the practice of meditation to find my inner peace. Meditation forces me to take time for my spirit. Sitting with myself forces me to be present with my body, mind, spirit, and emotions. It allows spirit to be present in all of these. I've tried many methods of meditation, including Sufi, concentrative meditation using a mantra and mindfulness meditation. The benefits of all are enormous – reduced blood pressure, increased focus, increased ability to manage pain, reduced stress and so on.

Meditation is a practice that is embraced in many spiritual traditions. It can be a nondenominational practice such as that used in Mindfulness-Based Stress Reduction or a spiritual practice as in Centering Prayer. However you want to approach it, the core is the practice of being in silence with oneself and listening to, but not being attached to, the chatter of the mind, the sensations of the body, the emotional dramas, and opening to spirit. Explore the chapter on meditation in this book to create your own practice if it appeals to you.

SACRED SPACE

There are inner and outer sacred spaces. The outer space can be a church, temple, synagogue or a place communing with Mother Nature. The inner space is a subjective or inner awareness of the sacredness of self and the connection to spirit everywhere. Earlier humans created places in the outer world like Stonehenge and other altars and sacred sites. As masonry and building skills developed we enclosed those spaces and gave them identifications, usually connected to a church or religion. The inner sanctuary is a natural progression and has been named by some spiritual leaders as the inner temple of God. Ask yourself where you feel at peace and at one with the world both in the outer world and the inner world.

OUTER SPACE

Usually there are few places immediately available in most lives where you

> "
>
> You can go on changing the outer for lives and you will never be satisfied; something or other will remain to be changed. Unless the inner changes, the outer can never be perfect.
>
> **OSHO**

> What lies behind us and what lies ahead of us are tiny matters to what lies within us.

RALPH WALDO EMERSON

can feel distanced from the chaos of daily life, and uplifted to another, more compassionate and healing plane. I personally find Mother Nature to be a slam-dunk, but to get away from the neighbors loud music, sirens and much more, it takes time to make a retreat to pure Mother Nature. In lieu of sitting beneath a magnificent redwood tree in Big Sur or wandering the seashore on Cape Cod, I have created my own Sacred Space at home.

This was no easy task. First, I had to claim a space, which we were already short on, then prepare it and finally, defend it from invasion and clutter. I claimed a corner of my home office, put a lock on the door, and now I make certain it is always clean, inviting and ready for me when I need it. I have my aromatherapy machine, meditation pillows, a humidifier, a yoga mat, journal, inspirational books and favorite mandala with me there. Trust me, unless you live alone, someone will be attracted to the peace and calm of your space and will attempt to either pollute it or use it without your approval. My dog and cat discovered my meditation pillows were the best place in the house to snooze, so I had to place a towel over them to ward off dog and cat hair or worse. My husband decided the best place to put his outdoor workbench was just outside the window and I had to defend the immediate outside environment. Whatever it takes, I highly recommend you create your own Sacred Space for personal retreat, meditation and renewal. Oh, and remember a place for that cup of tea.

INNER SPACE

You probably already have a way of retreating inside to protect yourself. Some people do this by getting angry and repelling people away or withdrawing inside. Others get down or depressed and withdraw from the world. I suggest you create a healthy, healing inner place where you can withdraw anywhere you are. You can prepare this place during your formal meditation period designing an inner world that brings you peace.

EXERCISE

FORMAL PRACTICE

Find a place where you won't be interrupted and lock the door. Set a timer so you don't have to worry what time it is while you sit in silence. The following fourfold process can help you tune into your inner spiritual, silent space:

1 - Begin by settling into your breath and the silence between your

thoughts, the gaps where there is no thought. Over and over again bring your awareness to your breath and allow your body to enjoy a state of relaxation.

2 - As you enjoy the peace and relaxation notice how the mind allows thoughts and desires to arise and how more or less attached you become to them. They may take the form of thoughts like:

My back hurts, I need to move to another place.

I've been sitting here too long, I should ... instead.

I lit the wrong incense scent. I should light another one.

Allow those thoughts to come and go, like a butterfly lighting on a leaf and then flying away. You are creating a silent space for spirit to gently arise.

3 - Having moved beyond attachment to thought, allow yourself to reside in the inner light of silent awareness.

4 - Finally, residing in the state of non-desire, disengaged from external needs, you are free to simply witness the natural stream of subtle, non-directed thought and feeling flow within. This state can open the gates to an inner flow of creativity, beauty and insight into your own LifeDance.

After any Formal Meditation use your **LIFEDANCING JOURNAL** in Spirit or Meditative Moments to chronicle your experience.

You can, and you must, create your own sacred space, it's central to being more authentic, and centered within yourself. Spirituality invites an ally and supporter into your LifeDance and helps you see more clearly. Also, this practice gives you hope because you sense and commune with a power greater than yourself. It helps you tap into an awareness of the natural order of things and the blessing spirit of the universe.

SPIRITUAL COMMUNITY

The term "spiritual community" can mean many things. To some it is a residential community that has spiritual seeking at its center. Everyone there lives and walks the same path. Then there are spiritual centers or churches that people attend weekly, more or less, that fill the members spiritual needs, provides inspiration, support and affirmation for their beliefs. For others spiritual community is a center or place where those with similar beliefs or searchings go for retreat, study, or community events such as Spirit Rock in California or Kripalu in Massachusetts. Or, as Thich Nhat Hanh describes his community Plum

"

When you find peace within yourself, you become the kind of person who can live at peace with others.

PEACE PILGRIM

"

A friend is a present you give yourself.

R.L. STEVENSON

Village Monastery in the Dordogne region in the South of France to Oprah Winfrey in an interview, it is simply a group of people, on the same wavelength who meditate together and support one another in their dance of life.

Looking at these solutions, as appealing as leaving behind my life's struggles is some days, I'm not ready to leave my life, family, friends and work behind to join a residential community. I've been an eclectic explorer of religion since my teens and haven't yet found an organized religion or church that works for me. There isn't a local church or center for Mindfulness Meditation and the bringing of spirituality to everyday experiences. The retreat center I enjoy most is an hour drive away making it difficult to visit daily, or even weekly. Yet, I would like to be able to connect with others in my local community who feel the same and practice similar meditation approaches.

I notice I need a community when I sit in meetings with peers who are talking about the last episode of "Survivor" or listen to them discussing Oprah's most recent spiritual personality interview. It may be interesting, but I soon long to get home to meditate, alone. On the other hand, I, like other human beings, am a social being. It's not just that we like community, it's that community and interdependence are hardwired into the structures of our brains. We need community. We can't help longing for community.

To support my spiritual growth, I believe I need to be with others for inspiration, learning and support. To accomplish this, I need to consciously create my own community to support my daily practice and help me grow in my spirituality. Because there are no groups in my area that have a regular meditation group, I've made a plan to create my own "community," which I'll share and hope that it may help others in the same predicament create one for themselves. Here's my plan:

1 - Check out all the local spiritual centers and make sure there isn't already a meditation group I just don't know about. If not, ask them if I could start one at their facility.

2 - Make a media list about other people's meditation experiences that will help me understand my own experiences.

3 - Create a beautiful sitting space in my home where I can listen to soothing and spiritual music and meditate in peace.

4 - Find an online community I can write to in the dark night of my prac-

tice to stay on the path and stay true to my inner dancer.

5 - Start a spiritual journal where I can chronicle my journey.

6 - Finally, I'll continue to reach out to others. As I am better able to articulate my own spiritual path, the better I'll be able to describe it to others. With this clarity, I just might find others to join me. It only takes two to create community.

Just creating my plan to create spiritual community makes me feel hopeful it will come to pass. For those of you who also long for spiritual community, I wish you well, and please know you are not alone.

Please turn to | 3.13 | **SPIRITUALITY ASSESSMENT** in the **MAS-TER CLASS WORKBOOK** to complete your assessment.

"

If we learn to open our hearts, anyone, including the people who drive us crazy can be our teacher.

PEMA CHODRON

CHAPTER FOURTEEN

The Dance Arenas: Relationships

*H*umans appear to be created to be in relationship. Our brain, the limbic portion, produces emotions that facilitate and are generated by relationships. The brains of mammals – that's us – are hardwired for parenting because our young are dependent on us longer than most other animals, meaning human relationships are critical for our survival.

There are many ways to dance in this life – alone, with a partner and with a troupe. If you choose to dance alone, you are still in relationship with yourself. Relationships occur on a spectrum from, outer (as in people and other living, breathing folks, i.e., Yorkies and Cats, other outer, i.e., environments, media, mother nature and the culture) to inner (a sense of SELF, self-esteem and the inner dialogues). Let's start with your relationship to your SELF because this is the one that colors your relationship with all the others.

INNER RELATIONSHIP
YOUR SELF

The relationship you have with yourself builds a foundation for all others you have in your life. In order for your other relationships to be healthy and successful, you must understand the SELF you imagine yourself to be, and feel love and acceptance for your SELF. For example, if I believe that I'm unworthy of another's love and attention, I won't be able to be in a reciprocal healthy relationship with anyone else. If you have no empathy for yourself, you won't be able to have those feelings for others. Sometimes people stay in abusive relationships because they do not believe, or know how, to be loved in a healthier way.

If you find you're not clear about who YOU are, use the exercises provided earlier in LifeDancing to create an inner sense of your own uniqueness. Keep in mind we are ALL a dance that is unfolding.

> "
>
> You, as much as anybody
> in the entire
> universe, deserve your love
> and affection.
>
> ## BUDDHA

> "
>
> When you face the
> demons in the deep
> dark forest, they tend
> to become your friends.
>
> ## TARA

YOUR RELATIONSHIP WITH YOUR SELF, OR YOUR SELF-ESTEEM

The term self-esteem has been in our vocabulary since 1657 when John Milton (the author of Paradise Lost) coined the term. It describes how you hold yourself in esteem, or value yourself. There is a global sense of yourself, and you may also value yourself in particular roles or arenas, i.e., I'm a good parent or teacher. Your ability to be intimate with others is also affected by your valuation of yourself. If you don't feel good about yourself, you'll put up barriers so they will not be able to know about that part of you that you feel shameful about. In order to value yourself, you first need to clarify who you are. That is the initial work you've done in the LifeDancing process. You may never have thought about this, but, it turns out that our beliefs about ourselves are stories we have been told, or ones we have created (sometimes called narratives), and they ALL are subject to change. Your job is to clarify who you are by exploring your values, views and judgments about your SELF.

THE SHADOW: DISCOVERING YOUR SELF THROUGH OTHERS

We also see negative facets of ourselves in others, though sometimes this process is out of our conscious awareness so it is called "the shadow." In Jungian psychology, the shadow or "shadow aspect" is a part of the unconscious mind, consisting of repressed weaknesses, shortcomings, and instincts. "Everyone carries a shadow," Jung wrote[30], and the less it is embodied in the individual's conscious life, the blacker and denser it is. An example might be someone looking at a friend whose office or home is messy and judging them to be incompetent. That person may have had a critical parent who was always demeaning them about their messy room and implying they were wrong or bad to live that way. So, when they see their friend's mess they immediately jump to "they're wrong or bad" without realizing that it is an internalized belief about themselves that they are imposing on another. This function can be a wonderful teacher about SELF. When I find myself judging others, the next thing I do is ask myself "what about them has to do with me, or what part of me is being revealed through them?" There are many very competent people who live with messy offices or homes. The personal work would be to value myself even though sometimes, I'm messy.

THE DANCE OF LOVE:
ROMANTIC RELATIONSHIPS

What comes to mind when you hear the words "Valentine's Day?" Maybe you experience feelings of love for another, notice a sadness about a lost love, or worse yet, remember a unrequited love. The theme running through all these is Greek "eros" love, the love of lust, attraction and attachment.

Love can be confusing, but science helps us understand the differences in different kinds of love by what happens in the body and mind as we step into the dance of love.

• **STEP ONE** - Lust, generally begins with hormonal releases of estrogen and testosterone driving us to gain the favors of our love target.

• **STEP TWO** - The attraction continues and our bodies release a set of chemicals, including pheromones, dopamine, norepinephrine and serotonin, which act in a way similar to amphetamines, stimulating the brain's pleasure center. This is when you notice an increased heart rate, loss of appetite and sleep, and an intense feeling of excitement and euphoria. The good news is this step in love generally lasts from one and a half to three years.

• **STEP THREE** - Lucky for the kids, the bonding and attachment phase sets in. New chemicals are linked to this phase such as higher levels of oxytocin and vasopressin. These chemicals give us a sense of peace and contentment. Most of us have experienced one or more of these steps or phases, sometimes getting stuck somewhere. Reflect on high school and the guy or girl that caught your eye. You may have loved them from afar leaving step one unresolved. The best cure for this is to go to your 40th high school reunion and see what became of that football star or homecoming queen. Then there's the disillusionment of the fading of step two when no electricity sparks when your loved one walks into the room. Phase three is the least dramatic, but most long term rewarding of the phases. The long term, in spite of the midlife crisis, relationships. Many people in today's culture haven't experienced step three yet, or one walks into the room. Step three is the least dramatic, but most long term rewarding of the phases. The long term, in spite of the midlife crisis, relationships. Many people in today's culture haven't experienced Phase 3 yet, or were never able to navigate this phase.

You can simply think of this love dance as attraction and attachment. The attraction phase resembles hunger, thirst, or craving for chocolate or drugs.

> "
>
> We can live without religion and meditation, but we cannot survive without human affection.
>
> ## DALAI LAMA

"

People become attached to their burdens sometimes more than the burdens are attached to them.

GEORGE BERNARD SHAW

These events all take place in the same part of the brain. The attachment phase follows, which is very different. A researcher, John Bowlby, was one of the first to identify "attachment theory." The types of attachment are:

- **SECURE ATTACHMENT** - This means you had a caregiver who responded to your needs promptly,

- **AVOIDANT ATTACHMENT** - Your caregiver was inconsistent and you never really knew if you were loved.

- **CONFLICTED ATTACHMENT** - Your caregiver gave you little or no loving response.

- **DISORGANIZED ATTACHMENT** - Your caregiver was frightening or totally withdrawn and unavailable.

The primary attachment phase takes place during the first two to three years of life and much of it is pre-verbal, or remembered somatically (in your body). As you grow, you have new "love" experiences and create behaviors, beliefs and styles of relationship that are particular to you. If you or the people you choose are not able to move to longer term relationships, attachment issues could be at play.

What's clear in all of this is that "love" is a complex experience played out in our bodies and minds. Given all this complexity you may ask:

Question 1 - Can a person change how her mind experiences "love?"
Answer - The simple answer is YES! There are a whole range or resources from professional counseling to personal self-reflection and inner change.[1]

Question 2 - While change is taking place, is there a kind of love that is simple, good for you, and for most, easily attained.
 Answer - Yes, this is the love of compassion and kindness. The Greeks called this love "agape."

In a study of 37 cultures around the world, 16,000 subjects were asked about their most desired traits in a mate. For both sexes, the first preference was kindness (the second was intelligence). Lovingkindness releases oxytocin (called the cuddle hormone), which evokes contentment, reduces anxiety, and creates feelings of equanimity and security. The object of your lovingkindness can also be non-human. You can experience this secure equanimity when you are petting your dog, cuddling your cat, or even helping a trapped bird free itself. We humans are able to love and care for others who are young and innocent and vulnerable (puppies and hummingbirds). As a psychotherapist, I have discovered that often the most difficult being to love is ourselves.

Make this Valentine's Day, the day you wake, look at yourself in the mirror, and send loving kindness to your inner spirit. Take your spirit of love and sense of peace and share it with everyone you meet. All of this is free of expenses, calories, and memories of lost love. Your new Valentine's Day can be an opportunity to give love in new and larger ways.

OUTER RELATIONSHIPS:
LEVELS OF KNOWING IN RELATIONSHIP

The Johari Window is a tool created by Joseph Luft and Harry Ingham in 1955.[31] It is used to help people understand their interpersonal communications

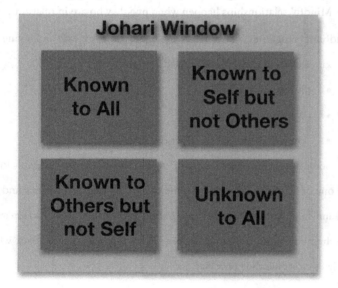

and relationships. The window has four quadrants. Each is a different aspect of information that is known about YOU.

In the Johari Window, the squares show a combination of what you know and what you don't know about your SELF, also what others know about you, and what they don't know. It describes how at any given moment in a relationship, there are four possible situations. For example, let's say that Sue was sexually molested as a young child but currently has no memory of the experience. When she is in relationship:

99

Once we accept our limits, we go beyond them.

ALBERT EINSTEIN

99

How do I love thee? Let me count the ways.

ELIZABETH BARRETT BROWNING

"

If conversation was the lyrics, laughter was the music, make time spent together a melody that could be replayed over and over without getting stale.

NICHOLAS SPARKS

1. She avoids sexual relationships and wonders why. (*Not known to anybody*), OR Sue discovers in therapy that she was molested but doesn't want to tell anyone (*Known to her but not to others*), OR

2. You talk to Sue's mother who tells you Sue was molested as a young child but asks you to not tell her (*Known by others but not by you*), OR Sue and I talk to her mother about the molestation and wonder how it is affecting her today (*Known to all*).

This tool is helpful when you find you are in relationship with someone and something just doesn't feel right. You can consider the four possibilities and consider further self-exploration and, asking for feedback from others, or exploration of the other's issues. When you explore relationships like this, you are being "mindful" of your interactions with yourself and others.

MINDFUL RELATIONSHIPS

Mindful relationships happen when people who are in relationship practice mindfulness together. This births a dialogue, using honesty and loving kindness. The kinds of things that are discussed are:

- What you experience
- What you think and feel
- How all of the above affect the relationship

Sometimes things get too emotional in the moment to use this kind of sharing and one or all of the others need time to explore their experience and how they feel and think about the relationship. But, even if folks need to step away to regulate their emotions, a commitment needs to be made to come back when they are ready to continue the conversation.

THE BIG PICTURE

Ask yourself, who and what am I in relationship with in my current life? You are most likely in relationship with a lot of people, groups and much more. An easy way to do this is to create a relationship MindMap, or genogram, identifying: core relationships, family, friends, work, relationship to the world, media, music, movies and books.

Once you have everyone and everything laid out on your MindMap you can identify those that bring out the best in you, and those that don't. You can use colors, red for anger, blue for peaceful, yellow for stimulating etc. Create whatever color and image codes that make sense for you. Remember to use your values as guidelines, if Creativity is a high value for you, ask yourself, who do I feel creative with? Here is an example of a relationship MindMap.

Create your | 3.14a | **RELATIONSHIP MINDMAP** in the **MASTER CLASS WORKBOOK**.

I choose people who are willing to express themselves freely, are smart and curious about their interests, teach me new things and have a capacity for caring. Sometimes good relationships turn difficult. These are the ones that must be attended to as soon as possible. I also discovered when I made my relational MindMap that I began to think about values missing from my relationships and asked myself what I should do to create those kinds of relationships.

So how do you know who people are so you can choose wisely? Authenticity is critical because if someone isn't authentic you don't really know who you are

> For a relationship to stay alive, love is not enough. Without imagination, love stales into sentiment, duty, boredom.
> Relationships fail not because we have stopped loving but because we first stopped imagining.
>
> **JAMES HILLMAN**

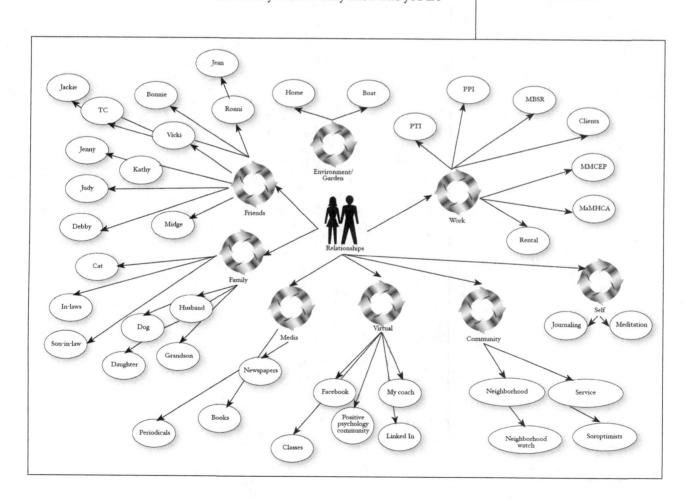

in relationship with. I also believe there needs to be some foundation of commonality so you have some place to relate from. Remember, the first and most important authentic relationship you need to build is the one with your SELF.

Because inner and outer relationships are a way of life, put some awareness into what you have now, and what you want for your future.

Please turn to | 3.14b | **RELATIONSHIP ASSESSMENT** in the **MASTER CLASS WORKBOOK** to complete your assessment.

It takes a great deal of bravery to stand up to our enemies, but just as much to stand up to our friends.

ALBUS DUMBLEDORE
In
Harry Potter and the Sorcerer's Stone

CHAPTER FIFTEEN

The Dance Arenas: Work As An Expression of Self

All labor that uplifts humanity has dignity and importance

and should be undertaken with painstaking excellence.

MARTIN LUTHER KING JR.

I remember my first job at age 13, as a babysitter. Being unclear on the concept of work, I was confused about whose priorities I needed to attend to – mine or the requirements of the job. Should I put the kids in front of the television and raid the refrigerator or find games for them to play? Later as an artist the struggle was, should I crank out the stuff people wanted to buy or create the work I loved? A few years ago, as a psychotherapist, I pondered, should I continue to be driven by the pathology based insurance industry or look at people in terms of their strengths and give them tools to build on? I believe the answers to all of these questions are obvious when the high road is taken, yet sometimes it's not always easy to take the high road.

Work issues have continued throughout my life, they simply change. I discovered that the more desperate I was (when I was a teen parent with no money) the less fulfilling the job I had was. I had to make it meaningful. As a receptionist in a restaurant I made a game out of how many people I could make laugh. While working in aerospace in a job that paid well, I discovered how more important it was to be interested in what I was doing than to get a big paycheck and amazing benefits. Being dissatisfied motivated me to go back to school. After graduating from college and going into the field of psychology, I finally discovered the joy of doing work I love and helping others. Work can be viewed on a spectrum. On one end is work that people hate and the other end is work as spiritual practice. In a lifetime people can crawl through jobs that make them money but give them no happiness. Hopefully, as they gain work experience, they learn what work means

> ❝
>
> The most powerful
> weapon on earth
> is the human soul
> on fire.
>
> ## FERDINAND FOCH

> ❝
>
> Nothing is secure but
> life, transition, the
> energizing spirit.
>
> ## RALPH WALDO EMERSON

to them, and what their ideal work life could be, until they are able to do what they love, are good at, and know what grows them.

Looking back on my work history, I see that I ran the gamut of work experiences from "Just get a job to pay the rent," to "Do I want to take this person as a client and be driven by their insurance?" I traveled from having a job that enabled me to support myself and my daughter to finding my professional calling and making a go of it. The journey, like most people's work lives, was a bumpy one. Remember, no matter what you do, it is a lot of WORK. Having a job you hate – and I have had more than a few -- is work, and it takes hard work, focus and dedication, to hear a calling for the work you love and to figure out how to make a living at it. Be very careful to not get stuck in a "safe" job you only do for the money. In today's world, there are no more safe jobs. If it's a job you hate, when it is gone, or over, you may have lost your spirit.

THE JOB

A job is work you do for money. If that is the only option open to you right now, there are ways to make it more palatable so the time will go by more quickly. One thing you can do to help you actually enjoy your work, even if you must get a job any job NOW, is to know your values and apply them in new ways as much as you can. Use the tools suggested in this book in your Values Assessment, Motivated Skills, and Personality Preferences.

Sometimes a person's vocation is obvious. I remember watching my daughter, at a very young age, delight in telling stories and entertaining people. When she told me she intended to major in communications in college, I thought it was a great match. Previously, she had thought she wanted to be a veterinarian because she had a wonderful affinity with animals and worked in a veterinarian hospital during high school. Eventually, she discovered that she loved the myth she had created around it but didn't much care for the reality of the business. She has flourished in her communications work and is very good at it because it matches her values, natural skills, and personal preferences. She now has her own business and is the teleprompter for corporate executives, politicians and media stars.

Sometimes it takes longer to find your calling.. I remember at age 18, I had to get a job to support myself and my daughter because my husband disappeared on a surfing trip. (He showed up several weeks later in a Mexican jail.) Friends told me, "Get a waitress job, they're everywhere." I practiced carrying lots of plates for a few days, then went to all the local restaurants and applied. Because I had never worked a day in my life, I had no idea how to start. One restaurant hired me as a hostess until a waitress slot opened up. Because this was my first real job, I was fortunate that my intuition told me that the way to make the day go by more quickly was to get to know the customers who came in the door and make then smile. I found them interesting and enjoyed talking to them about their day. It helped mine go by more smoothly. One of my highest values is curiosity and love of learning. As I got to know the regulars, we would talk about their work or life. Soon I became a waitress, and my job became a source of entertainment plus cheap food that I could take home for me and my daughter.

After a few months, I wanted to make more money and have health benefits. I looked in the newspaper and interviewed for a clerk job at a small loan company. I was hired and quickly discovered this was not a good move. I saw the same people every day, and many of them were not happy people. We made loans, but a lot of work was directed to collections as well. I found it unsettling to hear the stories of the collections agents about how they took someone's car or furniture away in the dead of night. I was soon promoted to vehicle registration clerk in the Department of Motor Vehicles. Now I not only saw the same people every day, I did the same thing every day. I actually found that I enjoyed problem solving because I could spend some time being creative looking for solutions. I was promoted to be the backup bookkeeper. The only problem I had was finding the $10 that was out of balance at the end of the day. I was making much better money, wearing nice clothes to work, had 9 to 5 hours – and was utterly miserable.

A friend of the family who knew of my plight got me an interview with an aerospace corporation. I was hired, as a clerk, but with better pay and benefits. Because the new facility was not up and running yet, I had to ride a bus for two hours every day to another location while our new offices were built. I was able to read during the trips back and forth. I love to read. I learned a new job and was surrounded by lots of people, who were a lot happier and successful. I stayed in that job for five years, but eventually I got bored there, too. I had risen to the position of methods analyst but not much was new or creative. The need for creativity and the potential for learning had dwindled. I did not see my future in aerospace. It was time for a career, not a new job.

> Happiness is like a butterfly which, when pursued is... beyond our grasp, but if you will sit down quietly, may alight upon you.

NATHANIEL HAWTHORNE

"

In case you wonder which way to follow, remember that your career won't wake up one morning to say that he doesn't love you.

LADY GAGA

THE CAREER

Lucky for me, while I was working in aerospace, I had a difficult personal relationship and a friend encouraged me to see a psychiatrist for help. I had tried to solve the problem on my own with my boyfriend and with a clergy counselor, but to no avail. After several months of seeing the Psychiatrist, I discovered I was fascinated by the field of psychology. I saw that there was much I didn't know about how people think, feel and create their own realities. I had never asked the question, "Who am I?" before. Relationships were mysteries in the past, but with increased awareness, relationships began to make sense to me as I learned about intimacy and communication. My driving values of the love of learning, curiosity and adventure were totally engaged. I wanted to learn and grow into a better, happier mother and individual with the potential for quality relationships. I began to ask myself if I could actually create a career for myself in that field. I decided to make the leap and left my job in aerospace and went to work for a psychiatrist. Dr. B was a Gestalt-based therapist who also loved to explore the leading edge of human potential. He invited leaders such as Alan Watts and Fritz Perls to his center to teach. I had the skills to run an office and he generously allowed his staff to participate in on-site training. Every week, he held a Gestalt therapy group for all the staff. I was in seventh heaven. My work was easy, there was much to be curious about, and I learned something new every day.

THE CALLING

Two years later, my world changed when his practice got smaller because of personal problems and I was the junior office member, so I was the first to be let go. I went on welfare but fortunately at the time, the state of California offered a benefit for single mothers on welfare that allowed me to work and go to school pursuing a nursing degree as a licensed psychiatric technician. I worked in a psychiatric hospital part-time and went to school full-time. I earned good money, had medical insurance for myself and my daughter and loved what I was learning. Then one day, I saw a film in a dance therapy class about Trudi Schoop, a dance therapist who worked with autistic children. As I watched the film, I found myself longing to do the work Trudi was showing us. She was able to gently and effectively connect and interact with people who had never before connected to another human being. She was creative, fun and very bright. I loved her willingness to go where others had given up and through her curiosity and engaging style was making a difference. I had found my calling.

Watching Trudi engage verbally and nonverbally with people who were clearly in distress warmed my heart. Looking back I believe I was most drawn to the person of Trudi. She was compassionate, interactive, intelligent and fun to be with. I wanted to grow up and be a professional like her. I knew I needed to learn more, gather experience, and grow personally to "be there," and I was committed. At the time I was working in a State Mental Hospital with the developmentally disabled. Years later, I transferred to an autistic unit at another hospital and pursued a degree in dance therapy. When I discovered how difficult it was to make a living as a dance therapist, rather than a licensed marriage family therapist, I completed the work needed to be licensed so I could be in private practice and be paid by insurance companies.

The professional journey from that calling to today has been long and interesting. The payoff has been beyond comprehension. I now work with clients and teach others how to create practices and businesses that provide a place for their calling to emerge. **My mission is to help professionals create practices that are as good for them as they are for the clients and communities they serve.**

When your work is an expression of who you are, and connects to your inner spirit, work becomes an integrated part of you and the rest of your life.

> "
>
> You are here to enable the divine purpose of the universe to unfold. That is how important you are!
>
> ECKHART TOLLE

YOUR WORK STORY

I've had many people come to see me because they hated their job or profession, and asked for guidance on the direction they should take. Besides having them do the Values, Motivated Skills and Personality Preferences Assessments, I also have them create a Work Story. This is the story of your work or roles going back as far as you can remember. Roles, such as being a parent, family caretaker, or Boy Scout leader also count. For each experience ask yourself:

- What age were you?
- What was the job?
- What skills were called on for this work?
- What did I most enjoy about the work?

- What did I not like about the work?
- What new skills did I learn while doing the work?

Create a Work Story Grid for yourself.

YOUR WORK STORY GRID

AGE _____

JOB _____

SKILLS EMPLOYED _____

ENJOYED ____

NOT ENJOYED ____

NEW SKILLS LEARNED _____

Once you have completed this assessment of your work history, look for patterns:

- What skills do you have that you are motivated to use?
- What have you consistently enjoyed?
- What have you consistently not enjoyed?
- What skills do you have that you want to use?

Looking at the Work Story Grid example above, it is clear that I enjoy creativity, learning, helping others and sharing ideas. I do not like paperwork, repetition or having limited time to do what I enjoy. This is a simple list. There were many more jobs and roles to analyze. You may discover patterns for yourself when you look at your Work Story.

Please turn to | 3.15a | **WORK STORY GRID** in the **MASTER CLASS WORKBOOK** to create your own work story.

WORK & LIFESTYLE

Your work definitely impacts your personal life and vice versa. If you are going though a divorce, are stressed for other reasons at home, or are ill, your work will suffer. If work is dragging you down, you are having problems with colleagues or have to work long hours, it affects your personal life. Rather than try to

> When you do things from your soul, you feel a river moving in you, a joy.
>
> RUMI

LifeDancing WORK STORY GRID

AGE	JOB	SKILLS REQUIRED	ENJOYED	NOT ENJOYED	NEW SKILLS
			YOUR NAME _____		
13	Babysitter	Childcare	New experience	Children's bad behavior	Behavioral skills
18	Waitress	Social, organizational	Meeting new people	Low pay	People skills
20	Collection agency	Organizational, bookkeeping	Learning new skills	Dealing with people's misery	Systems analysis
23	Aerospace method analyst	Computer skills, work flow assessment, form design	Learning many new skills; my boss	Daily repetition	Entrepreneurial skills
25	Clothing and jewelry designer	Clothing design, sewing, jewelry design	Creativity	Making the same thing over and over again; selling	Design
30	Psychiatric technician	Psych nursing	Helping others in a knowledgeable way	Having more needs than the job had resources	Learning many new skills; my boss
37	Private psychotherapy practice	Pscyhotherapy, business management, entrepreneurial	Running my own business on my own terms	24/7 responsibility	Entrepreneurial skills
42	Teaching	Public speaking, curriculum development	Sharing knowledge	Paperwork	Curriculum design
45	Author	Writing, editing	Writing	Creating the time to write and abandoning the rest of my life	Writing, publishing
60	Distance educator	Computer software, Internet tools	Reaching more people	Isolation	Connecting with people worldwide

> No eternal reward will forgive us now
> For wasting the dawn.
> **JIM MORRISON**
> From *The Wasp*

compartmentalize your home, relational and work lives, look for the connections and how you can enhance or balance one with the other.

Entrepreneurs often have the most difficulty keeping home and work life separate. They often start their business at home or in the garage, making it even more difficult to separate the two. They must pay attention to how they manage their home and work lives.

Ultimately, you must decide how much you can tolerate the merging or separation of the two – work and other arenas of your life. You may prefer a "job" so you can have a personal life not impacted by your work. You must make the choice.

Use the |3.15b| **WORK & LIFESTYLE PRIORITIES** checklist in **MASTER CLASS WORKBOOK** to get clear on your priorities.

"

Success usually comes to those who are too busy to be looking for it.

HENRY
DAVID
THOREAU

WORK & MINDFULNESS

Even if you are doing work you love, with today's busy world, it is easy to not be present and miss the joy of the days accomplishments. No matter what you do, work a job, pursue a career, or follow your calling, here are some tips to help you stay present and keep your stress level balanced.

THIRTEEN WAYS TO REDUCE STRESS
DURING THE WORKDAY

1. Take five to thirty minutes in the morning before work to meditate and be with yourself or find some way to have time for yourself, i.e., walk or be in nature in your garden or a local park.

2. If you drive to work, when you first get in the car, let it warm up while you take a few breaths to center yourself and prepare for the journey.

3. Give yourself enough time to allow the drive to be casual allowing extra time for traffic.

4. When you stop for stop signs, red lights, or pedestrians, drop down into your breath and let your shoulders relax.

5. When you arrive at work, check in with your body and see if tension is already starting. If so, notice it and relax if you can.

6. Take breaks, if you can, and use them to let go of previous stressors, relax, go for a short walk, or simply focus on your breath.

7. When you remember, face problems with a "beginner's mind," letting go of judgments and allowing yourself to think outside of the box.

8. Eat lunch away from your work site if you can. Eat mindfully and be with yourself. Take a walk.

9. At the end of the day reflect back on the day and identify at least three things that went well.

10. Make your list for things to do tomorrow that came up today.

11. Go into the bathroom and wash your hands with soap. As the water flows, imagine it taking all of today's stress and any toxic feelings down the drain so you can leave work cleanly.

12. When you pull into your driveway or park, let go of work and enter your home with the intention of "being home."

13. Change out of your work clothes as soon as possible and if others are there, connect by looking to their eyes.

WORKING FROM HOME

If you work at home, create some kind of transition ritual from home to your workspace and back again. You may not have to drive to get to work, but you need to be clear about when you are at home and when you are at work.

Your world of work is but one of your life arenas. Because it often is the arena that affects others – it's where you make the money to support yourself and others – and since this is an area where you spend a significant amount of time, it needs to be explored carefully and frequently. Also, if after exploration you discover that you want to make a change, that change must also be explored carefully to ensure a successful transition. Look at changing realities and trends in the workplace and in your field or profession. Do an Internet search on "business trends," subscribe to professional journals, subscribe to Google Keywords to stay abreast of media releases in your areas of interest. In this changing world your work will be impacted by the marketplace. It's best you see the changes coming before they hit you. If you are making a significant change, consult with a career specialist or coach to help you make a successful transition. If you are unhappy in your work, just knowing you have a plan for change can make each day easier.

Now assess where you stand in relation to work by completing your assessment with | 3.15c | **WORK ASSESSMENT** in the **MASTER CLASS WORKBOOK**.

> Your work is to discover your world and then with all your heart give yourself to it.
>
> **THE BUDDHA**

CHAPTER SIXTEEN

Home: The Heart of the Dancer

"The ache for home lives in all of us,
the safe place where we can go as we are and not be questioned."

MAYA ANGELOU

*H*ome is where the heart is" is a phrase most of us have heard and I believe is an ideal to move toward. There are many more one liners such as "A man's home is his castle." My favorite one-liner for women is "A woman's home needs a staff." Home can be a safe place inside of us or an environment we live in. The word "Home" then becomes a metaphor for safety, love and acceptance. Yet for many, home is not a safe place and some have no place to call home. We all have our unique home stories. I grew up with "home" as a movable feast. Consequently the concept of home, for me and maybe others, leans more toward a book rather than a one-liner.

A HOME STORY

What's your inner and outer home like? Take a moment and reflect back on your "home" experience. It has probably changed over your lifetime. In your **LIFEDANCING JOURNAL**, use the section titled Home, to explore your experiences. Be sure to explore your inner home as well as the environmental home/s. Here's a sample Home Story.

As a baby, I had the dubious distinction of accruing the most commercial air flight hours than any other infant under the age of one, as my mother followed after my Air Force father during World War II. Home was more the transitions between places than it was the places. Mom and Dad divorced when I was an infant and we moved from Texas to California to live with my maternal grandpar-

"

I long, as does every human being, to be at home wherever I find myself.

MAYA
ANGELOU

ents. Grandma and Grandpa and their house became home for me, and a wonderfully comfortable and loving home it was. Mom remarried and Father Number Two took us to a beautiful home in the hills above Silicon Valley in California. That home was beautiful as well, high up in the hills but there was a lot of anger in the house so home did not feel safe. That marriage collapsed into abuse, and it was back to Grandma and Grandpa, yea! A few years later Mother moved out on her own into an apartment. The space was small and dark and in no way could it could be called home. This was the beginning of serial apartment homes as we moved to where her next job was or her newest boyfriend lived. This began the growth of my internal home. Because the outer environment didn't qualify, I created an interior safe place. Mom remarried again and Father Number Three lured Mom to a small beach town. We had four apartments in Seal Beach, but I started to make friends at school so the town of Seal Beach became my home. Mother did the best she could but she was much more consumed with herself and her boyfriends to put energy into creating a home. When I was 16, I got pregnant to get out of the house that didn't feel like home and set up my own home in a series of apartments with my young husband. Home now became the stuff we schlepped from one apartment to another. There was the teak record cabinet, a television, couch and baby furniture that created the feeling of home wherever we went. Unfortunately, my young surfer husband temperamentally was not suited for the responsibility of a wife and child, so my daughter and I were off to live with a roommate, another single young mother. We lived in a beautiful home, in another beach community and that place became home for a time. This new home life came to an end when my roommate threw a large rock through the plate glass front of the house because her soon-to-be ex-husband was going to take the house in their divorce. I'd never seen a glass wall collapse before, it was impressive. It was clear my daughter and I needed to get out of there, so my most recent stepfather drove down from Northern California and took me to the home he'd made with my mother, once again I felt homeless, except for my inner home.

We stayed with my stepfather and my mother for a few weeks in a cramped space until a friend I had gone to school with contacted me. She needed a roommate to help her and her son make their expenses and invited us to move in with her. She had two children around my daughter's age, and we shared babysitting while each of us went to work. My daughter and I lived there for several years as she grew and I got better jobs. It felt like a home base, but it didn't feel like "my home." My roommate and I had a falling out over men (surprise!) so I moved into an apartment close to work. It was clean and safe, but it didn't feel like home. Because I had felt at home in Seal Beach, I looked for a year for an apartment there and finally found my nest in an apartment over a garage on an alley one block from the beach. I loved it there, it felt like home. We lived in that apartment for eight years while my daughter went to school.

Meanwhile, Seal Beach became more and more crowded with tourists and new homes, making the environment less comfortable for myself and my daughter. I had family living in the San Francisco area so we moved north to find a better place for us. We landed in a small northern California main street town that felt like home to both of us. It had a similar feeling to Seal Beach and the schools were much better. My daughter flourished in her new school. I found a job nearby in the local state mental hospital and we felt at home again. I bought a house with a new boyfriend but the house felt like it was his project rather than my home. It worked for a while, and then it didn't, so my daughter and I moved to an apartment that didn't feel like home. I saved my money and with what I received from the sale of the shared house, my daughter and I were able to buy our first house. This REALLY felt like home! A place of our own where we both felt safe. We lived there comfortably until I remarried and moved out and passed the house to my daughter, who still lives there and has made it her home. My new husband and I moved to a great condo complex where you could put your trash in a chute and never have to haul out a trash can to the curb. It was convenient and cozy but it didn't feel like home. Unfortunately, they didn't allow pets. Maybe that was why they asked us to move when the cat I had snuck in made a break for it while the landlord was standing in the hallway.

Then life happened and we moved to the Boston area, away from family and friends. We moved into the most beautiful house I had ever lived in, a three story Queen Ann Victorian with a full basement, yet it didn't feel like home. There was one add-on room that had been built during the Craftsman period with beautiful windows and a fireplace. Sometimes when it was snowing and I sat in that room I felt at home, but other than that, I did not.

We lived there fourteen years, and finally the call of California, my daughter and my ailing mother became very strong. I needed a home in California but

You can never go home again, but the truth is you can never leave home, so it's all right.
MAYA ANGELOU

Home is not where you live but where they understand you.
CHRISTIAN MORGENSTERN

> "
>
> Home is a place you grow up wanting to leave, and grow old wanting to get back to.
>
> **JOHN ED PEARCE**

didn't have the money to buy a second house, so I bought a boat to live on in a marina and moved to California. The yacht, LifeDancing, became home. While I was living on the boat, one day my daughter called. She had found a house during a garage sale event she went to. She told me I had to come over and see a great house I could afford. As I drove to the house, I had the feeling of coming home. It was a fixer-upper but had a wonderful backyard and was only two blocks off the water. Even though we bought a house in California, I've kept LifeDancing (my boat) and she is now my office and writing space. I don't feel like this last house will be my final home, but it'll do for now. My current mission is to downsize and simplify. No need for a large house to clean and maintain. It's time to look to sustainable living, community involvement and settling into the garden. We'll see what unfolds. After living in 23 apartments or` houses and a few homes, I can truly say that what has gone with me everywhere, is the home in my heart.

WHAT IS HOME FOR YOU?

Looking back, with my experience of twenty-plus living places, it's interesting to see when and where I felt at home. In some ways it had nothing to do with the house, a lot to do with the people and the community surrounding me. In today's world we also have the potential of a virtual home with an online community of people we feel at home with.

With all the movement in my life, I've become a firm believer that "home is where the heart is." As I was reflecting on the concept of home and looking for more perspectives, I found a study at West Virginia University, where the professors in the department of philosophy asked students, "What is home?" Here are their descriptions:

The place you live

Where your parents live

Where you keep your stuff

Where you spend your holidays

Where people you love are

Safety and security

Where you are accepted for who you are

A conference of like minds, face to face or virtual

Where your soul resides

Where your packages are delivered

Where your dogs are

Where you build your memories

Most of these are external homes. My experience tells me that there is an internal home, a place where your inner soul resides, the place to go to when all about you is changing or tumbling down.

Just as we need a physical place to call home, a place of safety, comfort, nourishment, familiarity, and warmth, we also need an inner home. Many create this space through spiritual practice, others know it intuitively. Just as we build, furnish, maintain, improve and occupy an outer home, the same needs to be done internally. We may need to wander the wilderness, find a cave and clear a place to build, it is well worth the work.

The inner dwelling is defined by our thoughts, emotions, senses and inner responses to the outer world. Even more than our physical home, the quality of our inner home determines the quality of our life. It is kept clean through meditation and conscience awareness.

To live in true comfort, we need a home where we feel loved and accepted. To improve our home we work toward our visions and dreams. When this is lacking, the home becomes abandoned and empty.

To keep the lights burning we need energy. The energy comes from inner well-being, happiness and inspiration.

Once our inner home feels safe and secure, we can invite guests. Our openness to and intimacy or connection with others brings the joy of laughter and love on which to build additional rooms and spaces until the inner and the outer worlds flow with ease.

Within all of us there can be a dialogue between inner and outer "home." Of the two, I believe the most critical is the inner home. It is a safe place that no one can take away from you. You don't need a mortgage or rent to be there. It doesn't have to be cleaned often if it is well-maintained. I know people who lived in the same house all their lives and call that home. I've seen some of them lose these homes or houses and be completely devastated. They were not able to find another place they felt at home in. I believe that if they had cultivated their inner home while they were growing into adulthood, they would have been able

> "
>
> Every house where love abides
> And friendship is a guest,
> Is surely home, and home sweet home
> For there the heart can rest.
>
> **HENRY VAN DYKE**

"

Man is a child of
his environment.

SUZUKI

to take their sense of home with them wherever they moved.

In the outer world, it is important to have a space where you feel safe and secure, where you can spend time with yourself, uninterrupted. This opportunity to have a space of one's own has long been acknowledged. In 1929, Virginia Woolf wrote an extended essay, "A Room of One's Own," based on a series of lectures she delivered at several colleges. She examined whether talented women were capable of producing quality literature who were being denied the same resources and opportunities men had access to. During Woolf's time, men worked, had private men's clubs, often a study at home and would never feel guilty about taking time and space for themselves. Women, on the other hand, being the keeper of the home, usually had no space they could call their own, and if they did, their space was still available to the household on an as-needed basis. To close and lock the door was considered odd or at least rude.

The world has changed considerably since 1929, yet today women still have more difficulty setting boundaries with family members and declaring a space of their own and time to themselves. I encourage both genders to make an effort to maintain an inner home, with time for reflection, as well as an outer space to inhabit alone.

HOME & OTHER ENVIRONMENTS

People have differing environmental awarenesses. My husband can live in total chaos and only notice it when he can't find his wallet or car keys. When I walk into a room, if the furniture is arranged so people can't engage in conversation, I feel uncomfortable. Needless to say, we have different relationships to our environments. His sense of being home, is where he can cable together all his computers and work on his train-board in peace. I love a spacious kitchen and a table where we can all sit, eat and chat. We've negotiated these things over the years, some spaces better than others, but have settled into a living space that works for both of us. His train-board is his "space." My space is my kitchen, home office with my yoga mat and meditation pillow, and then there's the boat. Having lived on a boat for awhile I know it is very different than living in a seven-bedroom Victorian with a full basement. Give yourself the luxury of asking yourself what your ideal home would be like. Here are a few questions to ask yourself:

Where would it be located?

What would it look like on the outside?

What kind of view does it have?

How many rooms will it have?

Kitchen	Cloakroom
Pantry	Conservatory
Bedroom/s	Drawing room
Bathroom/spa	Media room
Dining room	Mud room
Garage	Game room
Basement	Music room
Home studio	Sewing/train room
Home office	Library
Exercise room	Guest room
Outdoor room	Laundry or utility room
Garden	Other
Greenhouse	
Attic	
Ballroom	
Storage or box room	

How much or how little technology will it have, security system, i.e., cameras or motion detectors?

How will it be decorated?

How green or sustainable will it be?

Is it designed to include children and/or pets?

How easy will it be to clean?

What is the neighborhood like?

How close are you to friends or family?

A resource I have found to be an excellent guide in helping you create your ideal home is "The Emotional House" by Kathryn Robyn and Dawn Ritchie. The authors walk the reader through the process of designing and

> We see things not as they are, but as we are.
>
> **H. TOMLINSON**

"

I had rather be on my
farm than be
emperor of the world.

GEORGE
WASHINGTON

implementing the ideal home.

After identifying your priorities, go to | 3.16a | **THE IDEAL HOME** in
the **MASTER CLASS WORKBOOK** and write a description of your ideal
home.

Now, do an assessment of where you live, or call home now. Ideally, there
are some things that need to change. Turn to Chapter Eight to create a Mind-
Map and use the ideas from Chapter Nine to do problem solving that will
implement change. Use your **LIFEDANCING JOURNAL** to record your
thoughts and feelings about your project.

Before you burn down your current house because it is too awful or
overwhelmingly cluttered, there are things you can do before your ideal home
emerges.

DE-CLUTTERING

How about de-cluttering and simplifying? There are a lot of resources to
help you get started. Ones I like are "One Year to an Organized Life" by Regina
Leeds and "Scaling Down" by Judi Culbertson, George Booth and Marj Decker.
I'm no expert on clutter, but moving from a seven-bedroom Queen Anne Victorian, two-bath with a formal dining room and full basement to a two-bedroom
one-bath fixer-upper has created a downsizing challenge. As I write this, we are
about to empty our last storage container, and I feel like we are finally able to
identify the things we want to live with and remove the rest of the clutter. The
last holdouts are all the pictures and artwork we had on all those walls. A friend
of mine suggested I find a place to stack them all and rotate them throughout
the year.

If you find you really can't dig out from the clutter and have the resources,
I highly recommend hiring help. My friend Kimberly, who is a professional
organizer, has a gift. She took a home that was going to be torn down and had
homeless people living in it with no electric or plumbing, and turned it into a
showplace in three months – all on a reasonable budget. The house had "good
bones," she said. All it needed was design, hard work, love and attention.

Finally, when the clutter has been cleared and you are ready for the
finishing touches, I highly recommend a feng shui consultation. Feng shui is
"an ancient Chinese system of aesthetics believed to utilize the laws of both
heaven and earth to help one improve life by receiving positive Qi, or energy."

Westerners have embraced the ancient ideas and created an industry around it, helping people design environments that are soothing and healing. Landscape architects, interior designers, and architects have all used the ancient principles to these ends.

I had always been curious about feng shui, bought books and compasses and attempted to design rooms and other spaces to no avail. Then, when we were attempting to sell our house in Massachusetts -- yes the Victorian, and it had been on the market for six months -- I looked for help. In desperation I hired a feng shui consultant. She came to the house and walked every room with her pad in hand. After a few days, she came to me with a redesign plan. We moved furniture, and she sent me off with a list of purchases that cost less than $200. When we were done, the house looked and felt more inviting and cozy. The house sold in a week. Impressed with the results I did the same thing with my one-room office – with equal success. After the redesign I started asking new clients why they chose me as their therapist. They all said when they had to decide between other therapists they felt good about, the decision fell to me because they enjoyed coming to my office where they felt safe and secure. Hmmm, something like home?

So, yes, home is where the heart is, where the soul resides, and ideally in a beautiful, safe and secure environment that nourishes body, mind and spirit.

YOUR INNER IDEAL HOME

As I moved from place to place, I intuitively knew I needed to create an inner safe place. I didn't know it was my inner home until I was older. Building your inner home is much cheaper than an outer home. You only pay with time and inner cleansing. You can also remodel in the blink of an eye. As you create your ideal outer home, build one in your mind's eye as well. For example, my inner home is located on the side of a hill overlooking the sea but protected from the wind. It is covered with cedar shingles and there are a lot of windows and skylights to let in the sun and keep me connected to Mother Nature. The biggest room in my inner home is the kitchen. It faces the sea so I can watch it while I cook. It has a large center island where I can prepare food and visit with friends and family. There's also a flat panel screen where I can watch old movies while I cook. The bathroom has a walk-in steam shower and large Jacuzzi, also with a view, protected from prying eyes. The dining area is glassed-in with views

> Amidst all the clutter, beyond all the obstacles, aside from all the static, are the goals set. Put your head down, do the best job possible, let the flak pass, and work toward those goals.

DONALD RUMSFIELD

"

Invite the people you want to do business with or work with into your home environment and it will improve
the quality of your interaction and increase the depth of your relationships.

MITCH THROWER

"

Be thou the rainbow in the storms of life. The evening beam that smiles the clouds away,
and tints tomorrow with prophetic ray.

LORD BYRON

of the forest and the sea and has comfortable chairs so we can linger over food with good conversation. The garage is connected to the house and has automatic doors so I can enter the house with arms loaded with groceries. I have a home studio/office and exercise room with a Pilates Reformer. The outside garden connects to the greenhouse where I grow food as well as beautiful edible flowers. There is plenty of storage and a library that holds all of my books. The music/movie room has a large screen, good sound system, comfy furniture and a popcorn machine. We have one guest room so we won't get overloaded by house guests. My favorite room is my meditation room. It is private and opens up to its own small Japanese pond and garden. The space is quiet and tranquil and ready for me whenever I need it.

Wow, I just built that with no expense but time and attention. You can do the same in your **LIFEDANCING JOURNAL**.

Now assess where you stand in relation to home by completing your assessment with | 3.16b | **HOME ASSESSMENT** in the **MASTER CLASS WORKBOOK**.

CHAPTER SEVENTEEN

The Dance Arenas: Wholeness & Integration

LifeDancing means dancing in integral wholeness. It means commanding each stage of your life and keeping those arenas in balance. It takes a wholistic, systematic approach. LifeDance planning begins with taking responsibility for the quality of your life in every arena. In this chapter, you will step back so you can take an overview of your life, seeing all arenas.

As you go through each day, you may often become caught up in the demands and activities you believe you have to do. You get so busy, you often lose your perspective of the big picture. Life becomes "things to do" and "fire prevention," and you never see the results you want from your work, yourself or others. To maintain a balanced life you must create an integrated wholistic approach to your daily activities while always keeping an eye on your short and long-term goals.

Taking this wholistic approach to managing your life gives you the power to make smart decisions. Your life will change to one of higher quality, productivity and peace of mind.

Remember every day to keep an eye on the overall balance of your life. As you schedule your week and your day, make certain you are acting in accordance with your life vision. Schedule the activities that support your body, mind, emotions and spirit as well as your home, professional and social life congruent with your life plan. Then, live your life in the present, free from worry about the future because you have planned for its development and trust in the support you'll receive.

In the beginning, scheduling will seem like a lot of work. Like most things in life, you'll get better with practice. You'll begin to notice the knot in your stomach easing up and goals being met with more frequency. You'll discover that you can relax into the moment more easily because you don't have to worry anymore about all those things you SHOULD be doing, because you have them planned and scheduled. Use the **LIFE PLAN WORKSHEET** | 3.17 | you'll

"

Planning can make dreams
into reality.

MR. PROPHET

find in **MASTER CLASS WORKBOOK**. This worksheet provides one place to list all of your LifeDance goals and clarify which ones need more time than others to create the change you desire. You can use it as deeply as you want. You can divide your week into time chunks for different arenas or not. The most important part of this worksheet is creating an overview of your life and using your time as effectively as possible in the service of your Life Vision. I find that when I have a sense of how much time I want to give to something I don't enjoy doing very much, like filing, I do it early in the week so I can stop feeling guilty about not doing it. Customize the worksheet to your own needs, but please give it a try, not for me, *but for yourself*.

To deepen your Life Plan, use the | 3.17 | **LIFE PLAN WORKSHEET** in the **MASTER CLASS WORKBOOK**.

Step Four
PERFORMING: MASTERING LIFE'S MOVEMENT

Now, the dancer has become a master, tested in all of life's dance arenas. The dancer is now fully immersed and integrated with the movement of life, and dances in harmony in each arena. In this section, you'll learn how to fine-tune your LifeDance.

HARMONIC ORGANIZATION

Optimize your inner space and your outer environment to create harmony in your LifeDance. Harmonic organization supports your efforts to fulfill your vision.

RIDING CHANGE

Stay centered in the middle of uncertainty, and you'll have mastered the only constant force of life: Change.

THE DANCE OF EXCELLENCE

Ethics and excellence go together. That's because always doing your best and always honoring your values go hand in hand.

THE ART OF HAPPINESS

Create your own happy endings by cultivating the art of positive emotions. This is the joy of LifeDancing.

CHAPTER EIGHTEEN

Harmonic Organization

ONGRATULATIONS, you have your vision, goals, and plans in place, and have visited the arenas in your life. Now, let's optimize your environments to support your LifeDance. The ideal inner and outer environment is one that easily supports your efforts to realize your personal and professional missions. If that is the case, good work, if it is not, read on.

Can you see your LifeDancer having a morning like this?

She rises and wonders what day it is, oh right, Monday. Off to shower and feed the cat. Now what is she doing at work today, what should she wear? She'd love to wear those red pants, but where's the matching blouse? Oh well, she'll wear something else. She opens the refrigerator and realizes she's out of milk for coffee and cereal so decides to drive through a fast food place for breakfast. Now, where is that bag and what does she need to take today? Finally, ready to head out the door, and darn, where are those car keys?

Do you ever spend more time than you want looking for things, wondering what to wear, what to do next in your work day? When you are harmonically organized, you'll have the things you need close at hand and in a place where you know you can find them, even the keys to the car.

Often, the extent to which you are organized internally determines the way you arrange your life externally. People who have shaky or unrecognized inner organization arrange their environment in either a rigid, chaotic or less than optimal fashion. Inner structures include your definition of self, personality type and personal priorities (that is values, goals, motivators, mission). External fields include choices of what to pay attention to and your environments. The most functional way to be organized is by being aware of your internal organizational structures, your inner dancer, and arranging your outer world to reflect and facilitate your personal expression and work efforts. Some call it organizing from the inside out. I call it Harmonic Organization.

THE HARMONIOUS MIND

Harmonic Organization uses the tools you already have – your mind and your body. Your mind has two primary organizing processes. The right side of the brain takes in information in a wholistic manner, looking at the whole picture and adding information taken from all your senses. The left side arranges information in a linear format, prioritizing and making lists, clustering and filing data for use in the moment or saved for later. When looking for something, you either KNOW where it is, or you stop thinking about it and a few minutes later you remember, or move to, where it is.

THE HARMONIOUS BODY

Everyone possesses movement memory, proprioception which is the sense of the relative position of different body parts, such as how to get into and out of the shower safely, or remembering how you felt in a certain situation. When you enter a new environment, you scope it out, recognize it or not, connect it, or parts of it, with patterns you already know or feel scared or frightened about. The body remembers EVERYTHING about each of these experiences. This memory is what is sometimes called a "kinesthetic memory." This kinesthetic memory is a valuable tool for connecting to your inner knowing. A good example of this is my dog, Mo, a Yorkshire terrier. Mo is sacred of people who move too quickly. If you were to come to my house, and move too quickly, Mo would bite your ankles to slow you down. Everyone in my family, including the 5-year-old, knows that about Mo. The whole family knows we must move slowly or moderately when Mo is in the room. When they come through the front door, I notice that they change, they automatically slow down, their body remembers it has to slow down, before they even think of it.

You can use this body resource, it's a movement memory that organizes you and helps you know where to put and find your "stuff." As I've cultivated this resource, when I am leaving the house and doing the eternal "where are the keys" dance instead of trying to mentally remember where they are, I just tell my body to find them for me as quickly as possible and put it out of my mind.

Usually, around 95 percent of the time, within 10-15 minutes I've found my keys.

INNER/OUTER HARMONY

In order to organize your stuff – your thoughts, your actions, your material things – you need a framework that helps you devise a workable organizational system.

It's important to take a look at your inner organizational system and preferences before you create an outer organizational system. It is also important to be mindful of how the environment impacts your organizational system or preferences and collaborate with it to reach a win/win solution. Bring them into alignment to facilitate your actions and future success.

UNCOVERING YOUR INNER ORGANIZER

Everybody is organized to some extent. The question is how much and in what areas. Curious about what yours is? Try the following.

EXERCISE

PLAYING SHERLOCK HOLMES

Play Sherlock Holmes for a moment and and pretend you are a detective. Walk into your house or office as if for the first time. Your job is to identify the person who lives there. Is she organized, disorganized or a little bit of both? Would she immediately know where her keys are? What areas look well-organized or not? List them below.

Well-organized areas:

Not well-organized areas:

Who is this person?

Write a short narrative below describing what is, or is not, important to this person.

Where does she spend most of her time?

What does this environment say about the person who lives or works there?

Try to be as objective as possible, that means noncritical. Instead of "she's a complete neurotic who keeps everything too clean," you might say "she keeps her environment spotlessly clean in all rooms except her closet where it appears she

> First comes thought; then organization of that thought, into ideas and plans; then transformation of those plans into reality. The beginning, as you will observe, is in your imagination.
>
> # NAPOLEON HILL

"

Organize, don't agonize.

NANCY PELOSI

throws all of her clothes at the end of the day."

If you have discovered this person (you) is disorganized in any kind of way (be kind to yourself) complete the sentence below.

The good thing about having a disorganized (insert area) is:

_____

_____

_____

Example: The good thing about having a disorganized library is that when I'm looking for a book I get to relax, take my time, and look at a lot of books in my library while I'm finding the one I'm looking for.

List as as many ideas that come to you as quickly as you can without censoring any "silly" answers. Then try:

The things that bother me about having a disorganized (fill in area) is:

_____

_____

_____

Example: I often buy the same book twice because I can't find the first one. Have you learned anything about your relationship to organization? Write about it in your **LIFEDANCING JOURNAL**.

To realize harmonic organization, I suggest the following:

1 – Don't change a thing about how you organize; simply increase your awareness about how much stuff there is in your life and where you put things. Underneath all the chaos may be a perfectly functional organizational system. The way you organize could simply be so covered with "stuff" that you can't see it. You could have other issues, like hoarding or excessive cleanliness, which are simply indicators. Like most things, there is a spectrum of personal management to build on. If it isn't working, change the foundational structure. Take time to visualize and imagine what your ideally organized life would be like and write about it in your **LIFEDANCING JOURNAL** after you do the following visualization.

On one end, there is being buried in stuff and the other is attending to cleanliness so much it gets in the way of living. The first step is simply to increase your awareness of your situation, that means being more in the moment and seeing if you can get rid of the clutter. If you are on the edge of the spectrum on either end, I highly suggest asking for help. The best organizational system in the world does not stand up to piles of stuff. Take a good look at your attachment to your stuff. Your life will function much more smoothly if stuff isn't in your way. When you are ready to let go of the stuff that clutters your life, there are many excellent books on simplifying.

2 – Now that you have cleared away the clutter in some area of your life, what do you see underneath? Is there actually some sense to where you might put things? I'm guessing there is. Do you put clothes in the closet; food in the kitchen; towels in the bathroom? Those are pretty obvious organizational systems, and there may also be an obvious way in which you're organized but because you live with it every day you don't see it. Put on your "Sherlock" hat and step back and observe your organizational situation with more objective eyes. If you were an organizational consultant, what would you tell this person to do next?

A WAY OF LIFE

Getting organized is not a state you get to, it is a way of living. If you like what you see, then nothing needs to change. If you believe your personal organization system needs a change or upgrade, you are going to need to change the way you live and that won't be easy unless you are REALLY motivated to change. Take a look a the Stages of Change section in this book. There is a range of readiness to change, starting with being unaware of the need and ending with "What can I do NOW? I'm ready to act immediately."

No matter what stage you are at, you need to focus on one arena at a time to get organized so you can be effective, and, be able to see the changes you make. We all need feedback. How you are changing and working on a smaller focused area gives you more immediate success.

3 – OK, by now you have cleared the clutter (we can only hope) so you can see the underlying organizational structure that's already in place. Now, we want to build on that or if it isn't working, change the foundational structure. Take some time to visualize and imagine what your ideally organized life would be like and write about it in your **LIFEDANCING JOURNAL** in Harmonic Organization after you experience the following visualization.

> "
>
> NOW. This is it. The whole purpose and meaning for the existence of everything.
>
> **ZEN SAYING**

> Now if I do anything, it is to tune souls instead of instruments. To harmonize people instead of notes. If there is anything in my philosophy, it is the law of harmony: that one must put oneself in harmony with oneself and with others.

HAZRAT INAYAT KHAN

OPTIMAL HARMONY

Close your eyes and imagine what your life will be like when you are optimally organized. This means when everything you want and believe you need is easily available whenever you want it. You may want to do individual visualizations for the different environments you inhabit, i.e., home, office, boat.

AT HOME – When I walk in the door I want the entry way and stairs to be clear of clutter, with an intuitive place to put those pesky keys. This is doable! The next room I visit is the living and dining room. Yikes. OK, same theme here, I want the space to be clear of clutter. This is going to take some thought – how to manage periodicals, crafts, and that table where everything gets thrown that we used to call a dining room table. Then there's the issue of getting everyone else in the family to cooperate. Hmmmm.

AT WORK – When I walk in, I want it to be free of clutter, with paperwork, books, and office machines organized. Why do I have to always take stuff off the postage scale to use it? Where do I start? Because this is a smaller space and one I have most control over, I'll clean. Then I'll create a "leaving ritual" that tidies things up at the end of the day.

Note – I highly recommend reading the section on MindMapping, Project Planning and Problem Solving (Chapters Eight and Nine) when approaching a project or plan like this. When there is a lot of stuff to deal with, it might be a good idea to just write it all down, organize it, and then prioritize it. When you feel overloaded or flooded, walk towards the cannons, and don't run toward denial and safety, simply get all the information down and follow the Wholistic Problem Solving Process. Then, you'll know what to do first.

THE DANCE OF HARMONY

The theme of this book is that YOU are the expert in how to dance your life, and it continues here. I can offer suggestions on how to organize your life, but you are the ultimate decision maker and implementer. My job is to keep reminding you of that. I have way too many books on how to get organized, most of which I looked at when I bought them, and promptly put them on the shelf to read later. Yet, life goes on. What I've discovered is that it is my ongoing relationship to organization that is the key. The LifeDancing model works for me once I've cleared away the clutter, which is no small task.

HARMONIC ORGANIZATION PROCESS

I need or want something that I know I have and want it NOW. My mind does a search and sends me someplace to find it. I call this **"Inspiration."** If it is there, "Yea, if not, at least now I know WHERE IT SHOULD BE. The rest is the old story of **"The Search,"** which is a good thing because I always find something else I couldn't find before in the process of looking for something else. I call this phase **"Capture and Explore."** Either I discovered it was in its "right place," or not. If not, I now know where it belongs and when I find it, that's where it will be placed. Example: my grandson has a hearing loss in one ear and wears a hearing aid that we call his "ear toy." When he comes to visit, if he gets into water, he knows he must take his ear toy out so it won't get wet. You guessed it, each time he would take it out he put it someplace new, and when his parents came to pick him up it would take some time to track it down. One day a friend gave me a lovely crystal box and I dubbed it the Ear Toy Throne. Now, when Max takes his ear toy out he puts it in the Ear Toy Throne where we can all see it. This is the **"Change and Harmonize"** phase.

Using this process, if for some reason I want to reorganize a bigger project, like my closet or the desktop on my computer, I need a plan. Let's take on the closet. OK, I buy some kind of closet organizing kit, move all the clothes out of the closet, choose which clothes to keep, which to re-cycle, and which I can't let go of even though I haven't worn them for 20 years. I'm smack-dab in the middle of organizing the closet. Oh no, I have a work deadline and no time to finish the closet. Life has happened, and I need to move to another focus, yet NOT letting go of the first one, simply, prioritizing how important it is and putting it on my schedule. Because I can't find what to wear every morning, finishing the closet rises to the top of my list of priorities and schedule.

Whew, that was a lot of work, and that is often how "Getting Organized" goes. I have hired people to come in to organize for me, I love it after they leave, and after a few months I'm back to step 1 and changing their system to my own system. It's so much better when Harmonic Organization is simply a constant part of life. Here are the steps.

SEARCH - You look for something and can't find it, or it takes more time than you have allotted.

CAPTURE (or not) - You find it and wonder how it got there

> "
>
> It takes hands to build a house, but only hearts can build a home.
>
> # AUTHOR UNKNOWN

> "
>
> Courage is not
> simply one of the virtues,
> but the form of
> every virtue
> at the testing point.
>
> ## C. S. LEWIS

CHANGE AND HARMONIZE - You increase your awareness of where you automatically put things or organize things. Then you either change your habits, the environment, or both, so you can put things in natural places or the environment offers a way for you to put things where you can find them.

Being harmonically organized is a dynamic process, a part of your lifestyle. Life changes, where you put things changes, both internally and externally. If you believe you are disorganized, you are, if you believe that under all that stuff is a master organizational structure, there is.

Taking one step at a time, create a plan on how you are going to de-clutter and Harmonically Organize. If you get stuck here, hire or barter with someone who specializes in organization. This will give you a clean stage to move from. Check out the National Association of Professional Organizers (www.napo.net) for professional organizers..

The earlier scenario of someone rising in the morning, not knowing what to wear, no food for breakfast, no table to eat on, rushing to find what they need to take with them, changes to: Rising, moving to a staging area, dressing flawlessly for the day, making breakfast and eating calmly at the dining table. Being prepared for what you need to do, grabbing your bag, which you organized the night before, collecting car keys and dancing off confidently into the day. Yea!!!

Take the | 4.18 | **HARMONIC ORGANIZATION ASSESSMENT** in the **MASTER CLASS WORKBOOK** for a more detailed assessment of how well-organized your life is.

CHAPTER NINETEEN
Riding Change

"There is an unseen life that dreams us; it knows our true direction and destiny. We can trust ourselves more than we realize, and we need have no fear of change."

–JOHN O'DONOHUE

We live in a time when spaceships can reach speeds of 55,000 mph, yet one hundred years ago, the airplane was a new invention whose top speed was 100 miles per hour. Eight thousand years ago, the fastest form of transportation was the camel caravan, which averaged eight mph. You could turn, stop and get off any time you wanted. If it seems like change is happening at a dizzying pace these days, you're right. If you long for the security of knowing what you can count on, know that the one thing you absolutely can count on is that life is always changing. The dance of life is dynamic. We live our most dynamic lives when we dance cooperatively with change. Change is always within, and without. Mastering life's movement is available to us at every moment, every turn and every step of the way.

Life is either in the process of change – or not – that is, death. But change does not stop there, our bodies ultimately return to the earth. Some change is subtle, like the daily growth or decline of our bodies, and almost out of our awareness until something breaks. Sometimes change gathers momentum like a snowball rolling downhill such as losing a job and not being able to pay bills. Soon we are buried in the avalanche of a change that had a simple beginning. Our world is changing rapidly and moving more and more quickly every day. You've probably noticed that change has increased over the years you've been alive. Simply trying to keep up with technology is challenging. Just when I get my computer system or new mobile device figured out, it changes. Managing change is a skill everyone can learn.

"

They must often change,
who would be constant in
happiness or wisdom.

CONFUCIUS

"

The universe is
transformation; our life is
what our thoughts make it.

MARCUS
AURELIUS

With all the information we are confronted with on a daily basis, it is like having 40 different songs playing at once. To what tune do you dance? The solution is for the dancer to know what information or tune she needs to listen to or be informed by, so she can filter out the rest.

Staying centered in who you are is the best way to meet the challenge of rapid change. That way no matter what changes, you're centered and ready to move. For example, you can either be a surfer who watches the waves and prepares for "the big one." That's fear. Or, you can be the surfer who sits and lets herself be surprised and buried by a wave. That's denial. A centered dancer changes her center of gravity as movement fluctuates inside and out, and is guided by her inner wisdom and awareness of change. As the "big one" begins to build, she turns her awareness to the "big one" and adapts to the change as it unfolds. The keys are awareness, adaptability, and a willingness to engage with the change that's coming or taking place. Be ready, at the drop of a hat, to ride change successfully.

MASTERING CHANGE

The swirl of change around us presents constant challenges. When the external world is uncertain, we may hesitate to look deeply within for new ways of meeting our personal challenges. We begin to feel comfortable with examining personal change by understanding the types of change we face. Change happens in several different ways and we each choose which type of change management we're most comfortable with, or most used to.

A - Developmental Change - Improve on what you're doing and take it to a new different level.

B - Transitional Change - You take an old state progressively to a new state, steps 1-3

      1. Identify old state

      2. Know new state

      3. Set timetable for change

C - Transformational Change - You dismantle an old state before it self-destructs.

      1. There is no set timetable or pace

2. It can be driven by values or an ideal state

3. It can be managed as a series of transitions

D - Breakthrough - You know that you do not have the tools for the new state but jump to the new.

An example of the differences in these styles could be visioned via a trapeze artist.

The first trapeze artist climbs up the pole to her platform and practices day after day taking her skill growth to the next level slowly, as she feels comfortable. (Developmental)

The next trapeze artist sets timetables for her growth and pushes herself to reach these goals. (Transitional)

The third trapeze artist decides to learn these new skills via learning one aspect of the whole performance at a time and transforming the performance, before she is fired. (Transformational)

Finally, after much practice, the trapeze artist climbs up the pole to the platform after setting a fire at the bottom so she MUST jump to the NEW performance – or fall to a fiery death. (Breakthrough)

Which one of these styles resonates with you. Personally I vacillate between the Transformational and Breakthrough. I call it "playing edgies." I explore the new, walk around it, learn more and one day just make the leap.

STAGES OF CHANGE

In terms of personal change, there are stages everyone goes through. The stages of change are:

- **Pre-contemplation.** Not yet acknowledging that there is a problem, behavior that needs to be changed.

- **Contemplation.** Acknowledging that there is a problem but not yet ready or sure of wanting to make a change.

- **Preparation/Determination.** Getting ready to change.

- **Action/Willpower.** Changing behavior.

- **Maintenance.** Maintaining the behavior change and

- **Relapse.** Returning to older behaviors and abandoning the new changes.

> You must be on top of change or change will be on top of you.
>
> **MARK VICTOR HANSEN**

"

It is better to have less thunder in the mouth and more lightning in the hand.

APACHE SAYING

Homeostasis warning - As you change, others around you will consciously or unconsciously try to get you to go back to your old ways of doing things and try to keep things the way they were. They are comfortable with the old ways of being and even if the change is a positive one, they may not see it the same way you do.

For example, if you have always been one to seek others approval before you tried something new and you move toward trying new things without other's approval, they'll notice and may get annoyed with you. They'll offer guilt trips such as "why didn't you ask me before you ....?" "What were you thinking? "When were you going to tell me that ....?" and my most favorite "That was a stupid thing to do!" As you grow and change, you must always keep an eye out for other's discomfort/s with your new way of being. When you engage in a dialogue with them about what you're changing, you'll help them feel safe with the new you. That way you'll often find less resistance to your new ways of being. As you get on the Change Bus, you potentially can change together. Yet, sometimes folks just do not want us to change and we have to do it anyway!

PERSONAL CHANGE PROCESS

As you create change in your life your inner dancer changes as well. When you find yourself ready to create change in your life, here is the circle or cycle of personal change.

Today you are in your Comfort Zone.

1. You project a goal that will create a change that can re-create who you are today.

2. You face the **Unknown**, and a part of you contracts with **Fear**.

3. You create a **Glass Wall** to protect yourself from self-annihilation or a new sense of who you are.

4. You **Increase** your awareness and understanding of what you are changing into.

5. You accommodate or get to know your new Self.

Now you feel safe and your tension releases.

6. You develop an **Intuitional** functioning as you operate differently.

7. You become creative with your new Self.

8.   You realize your goal.

Now you have a new **Comfort Zone**.

Tomorrow you create a new **Goal**.

Return to #1.

This is a process that goes on and on. Something like the layers of an on-ion. You get through one layer and another magically presents itself. If you are actively changing something in your life, check-in with yourself and ask where in the cycle of implementation you stand. How has it changed who YOU are? Because who YOU are is simply a story you have created about yourself, now is the time to expand that story to include the changes that have happened.

Another example:

Several years ago I knew I had to move from Massachusetts to Califor-nia because of family commitments. I also knew my husband did not want to move and, for all of my efforts, he remained steadfast. I knew something had to change, but didn't know what or how. I struggled with making the change for seven years and finally reached the stage of Action. I was afraid of losing my husband, and knew that I had to move to California to care for my mother who had been diagnosed with Alzheimer's. How could I fulfill my responsibility to my mother and keep my marriage? I began by creating a transitional plan. I would find a low-cost house I could afford without my husband's commitment, which was outside of his comfort zone. I searched for two years for a solution, but to no avail. Then, I stepped outside of my comfort zone and decided to buy a boat and live on it because it would be much more affordable than a house. It was here that I moved into a Breakthrough model. I had no idea how to buy a boat but proceeded one step at a time, moving around obstacles and holding a vision of my new home in California. One day all the pieces fell together, I had a boat to live on, a slip to berth it in a marina close to my mother. My husband even enjoyed visiting the boat frequently. Uh oh, now I was on an adventure to create a new identity.

So you see, change may not be a linear journey. You can move around in Stages of Change, move into a new Type of Change and step back or forward in the Change process. As you clarify your vision, set your purpose and goals, plan and act, any or all of these might change. It is your job as your LifeDancer to always be aware of what changes are taking place, be in relationship to them as

"

It is utterly useless to try to change the outer world, for it is but a reflection of inner causes. The true seeker seeks to change himself.

VERNON HOWARD

"

There is no enlightenment outside of daily life.

THICH NHAT HANH

change unfolds, and know that change is a constant and an ever-moving dance of life. The key is to continue to be in touch with, and honor your inner truth. Yes, I could have gotten a divorce and moved to California, but I would have always wondered if I could have found another way. If, after exploring all the solutions I could imagine, my husband would not participate, that would have been the change. Not the change I would have chosen. But, stepping outside of my box or comfort zone and asking my "world" to support me, a win-win solution materialized.

DEVELOPMENTAL CHANGE MODELS THE DYNAMIC DANCER

You've watched babies grow into toddlers, then small children, teens, young adults and then full-fledged adults. This developmental growth is easy to observe because of the rapid physical change. Change doesn't stop there. Yes, we age and change physically, and we also change internally. Our brains are constantly growing as is our awarenesses and ways of being in the world. Knowing what these adult developmental models are helps us have a context for how we move through our lives. Here are a few of those models.

ERIKSON

Erik Erikson (1978) proposed a number of adult growth periods.

HOPE. Basic Trust vs. Mistrust - Infant stage. Does the child believe its caregivers to be reliable?

WILL. Autonomy vs. Shame and Doubt - Toddler stage. The child needs to learn to explore the world. It is difficult if the parent is too smothering or completely neglectful.

PURPOSE. Initiative vs. Guilt - Kindergarten - Can the child plan or do things on her own, such as dress herself. If "guilty" about making her own choices, the child will not function well. Erikson has a positive outlook on this stage, saying that most guilt is quickly compensated by a sense of accomplishment.

COMPETENCE. Industry vs. Inferiority - Around age 6 to puberty. The child compares self-worth to others (such as in a classroom environment).

The child can recognize major disparities in personal abilities relative to other children. Erikson places some emphasis on the teacher, who should ensure that children do not feel inferior.

FIDELITY. Identity vs. Role Confusion - Teenager. The questioning of self begins. Who am I, how do I fit in? Where am I going in life? Erikson be-lieves that if the parents allow the child to explore, they will conclude their own identity. However, if the parents continually push her to conform to their views, the teen will face identity confusion.

LOVE. (In intimate relationships, work and family.) Intimacy vs. Isolation - Young adult. Who do I want to be with or date, what am I going to do with my life? Will I settle down? This stage has begun to last longer as young adults choose to stay in school and not settle down.

CARING. Generativity vs. Stagnation - the Mid-life crisis. Measuring accomplishments/failures. Am I satisfied or not? The need to assist the younger generation. Stagnation is the feeling of not having done anything to help the next generation.

WISDOM. Ego Integrity vs. Despair - old age. Some handle aging and death well. Some can be bitter, unhappy, dissatisfied with what they accomplished or failed to accomplish in their life. They reflect on the past, and find satisfaction or despair. Erikson believed adults could have gotten stuck at any phase and then still need to continue their development to the final stage of wisdom during adulthood.

Progress has not followed a straight ascending line, but a spiral with rhythms of progress and retrogression, of evolution and dissolution.

JOHANN WOLFGANG VON GOETHE

MASLOW

Abraham Maslow proposed an adult "needs" hierarchy. He saw human beings' needs arranged like a pyramid. The most basic needs, at the bottom were PHYSICAL OR SURVIVAL NEEDS -- air, water, food, sleep. Then came SAFETY needs – security, stability -- followed by PSYCHOLOGICAL & SOCIAL needs – for belonging, love, and acceptance. Then, came SELF-ESTEEM needs – to feel achievement, status, responsi-bility, and reputation. At the top of it all were the SELF ACTUALIZING needs – the need to fulfill oneself, to become all that one is capable of becoming.

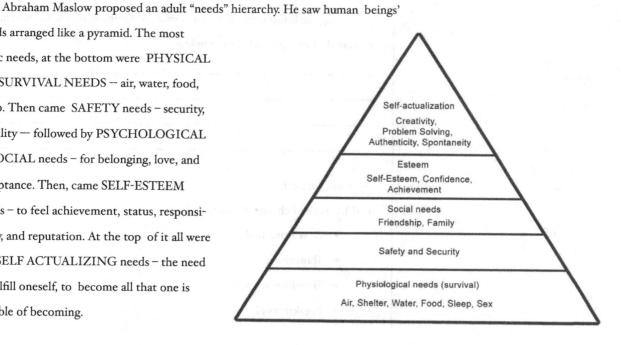

> "
> Develop an interest in life as you see it; the people, things, literature, music. The world is so rich, simply throbbing with rich treasures, beautiful souls and interesting people. Forget yourself.
>
> ## HENRY MILLER

The hierarchy looks something like this:

- SELF ACTUALIZATION
- SELF ESTEEM
- PSYCHOLOGICAL & SOCIAL NEEDS
- SAFETY
- SURVIVAL

Maslow felt that unfulfilled needs lower on the ladder would inhibit the person from climbing to the next step. Someone whose boyfriend just left will forget him quickly if she is dying of thirst.

The people who manage the higher needs are what Maslow calls self-actualizing people. Self-actualizing people tend to focus on problems outside of themselves, have a clear sense of what is true and what is phony, are spontaneous and creative and are not bound by social conventions.

Self-actualizing people have many peak experiences. Peak experiences are profound moments of love, understanding, happiness, or rapture, when a person feels more whole, alive, self-sufficient and yet a part of the world, more aware of truth, justice, harmony, goodness and so on.

EXERCISE
RIDING CHANGE

Using the information above, ask yourself some questions. Choose an issue you are dealing with and write it below.

_____

_____

_____

_____

Now, ask yourself:

1 What type of change do I usually implement?

- Developmental
- Transitional
- Transformational
- Breakthrough

2 What Stage of Change am I in:

- Pre-contemplation

- Contemplation

- Preparation/Determination

- Action/Willpower

- Maintenance

- Relapse

3 Where am I in my personal change process? Am I in a comfort zone?

4 Do any of the developmental models apply to me?

5 What do I need to do to move, with mastery, through my change process?

    Use this process for any change that seems to not be flowing easily. Remember, the one thing you can count on is change, why not be a master at it?

"

Change is good.

You go first.

DILBERT

CHAPTER TWENTY

The Dance of Excellence

"I think everybody has to be prepared in life for failure, disappointment, frustrated dreams, or even embarrassment. We must accommodate changing times and move with unchanging principles. What are the principles that don't change in your life? What principles help you build a new life, an expanded life, a better life, a more adventurous life?"

-- JIMMY CARTER

AS QUOTED IN SUCCESS BUILT TO LAST - CREATING A LIFE THAT MATTERS

*H*ow would you define an excellent life? Would it be getting everything you want? Finding Prince Charming? Raising beautiful children? Having a successful career? All of these are outcomes. They are goals we set for ourselves. I believe an excellent life is about how you live your life. The Dance of Life is measured in each beat of the dance. The Dance of Excellence is measured in how you move to that beat.

Our goals inform our steps – the way we dance – as we move toward more fulfilling, more joyful goals. When we dance toward these goals, and we dance with integrity, the journey becomes its own reward.

In LifeDancing, the Dance of Excellence is defined in every moment that you are doing the best you can with what you have to work with. You always stretch for your best way of moving in the moment.

Former President Jimmy Carter was eloquent in saying that it's not the events of life that matter, so much as it is the principles by which you live your life. These are the principles you live and operate by – your values. They are the heartbeat of your LifeDance.

Even though they reside solidly in your core, these principles are dynamic. They are constantly up for debate. We are constantly revising the dance. But

"

Eventually we have to 'settle up' and pay the price for our ethical violations. Just remember the old line that says, 'You can pay me now . . . or you can pay me later.'

Often you can buy some time, but when you 'pay later' you'll probably have to pay more.

PRICE PRITCHETT

"

First keep the peace within yourself, then you can also bring peace to others.

THOMAS KEMPIS

these principles are the solid, steady beat. They are your own personal standards for living your life. They inform your ethics.

MISSTEPS: ETHICAL CODES

Your own life is an ongoing process of writing your personal, internal code and your inner ethic is inseparable from the surrounding social moral code. The two are constantly intertwined.

When you dance away, even a few steps off, from your own personal ethic -- short of your standard of excellence or outside the sphere of your ethics, you often know with a deep inner knowing whether or not you are immediately conscious of it right in the moment.

When people dance outside their ethical comfort zones, they often:

- Lose sleep.
- Drink or eat too much.
- Take recreational drugs.
- Become irritable and suspicious.
- Find it difficult to relax.
- Notice they do not enjoy activities they usually enjoy.
- Fear getting caught.
- Find they cannot look people in the eye.
- Feel embarrassed with friends, family or colleagues.
- Get defensive and argumentative.
- Become belligerent in stating opinions.
- Desire confession, whether formally through a priest, less formally through a psychotherapist or trusted friend.
- Obsessively ruminating about the consequences of their decisions and actions.
- Say things like, "I could just kick myself."
- Continue to berate themselves.
- Look for excuses or scapegoats to blame.

Look over this list. Think about a time when something happened that challenged your personal ethic. How many of these were true for you in that situation? To explore your experience in more depth use the | 4.20a | **ETHICS**

ASSESSMENT in the **MASTER CLASS WORKBOOK**.

SHIFTING THE DANCE

How can you get back into the dance, when you misstep? Simple. Return to your personal ethic. To come back to your personal ethic though, first you must know what that is, through and through. Let's brainstorm for a minute about the ethics that most people have in their lives.

- Consideration of other people's well-being.

- Orienting your thinking toward community; thinking of yourself as a member of the community, not as an isolated individual.

- Obeying the law, yet not depending solely on the law to define your sense of what is right.

- Thinking of your life as part of a social whole.

- When you see something you believe is wrong, asking the question, "What sort of person would do such a thing?"

- When confronted with a moral dilemma, asking yourself, "What's the right thing to do here?"

- Respecting the customs of others, yet not at the expense of your own ethics.

Take a few minutes in your **LIFEDANCING JOURNAL** to add your own rules to complete this list.

EXCELLENCE

What is personal excellence? My definition is to live my life so that when I'm 104 and sitting in my rocking chair, I can look back on a life well-lived with no regrets. Personal excellence grows as you live your life based on your values, using your strengths, augmenting your weaknesses, and being present to life in every moment so you can constantly ask yourself, can I do this better? Some call this Continuous Quality Improvement (CQI) or Skillful Living. The term CQI was coined by William Edwards Deming, a business and industry analyst. You can bring CQI into your personal life and all arenas of your life to constantly improve the quality and excellence of how you live your life. Skillful living is a general concept about living life as if it was a skill you were developing with mindful, dedicated attention.

> "
>
> The truth is a beautiful and terrible thing, and should therefore be treated with caution.
>
> **ALBUS DUMBLEDORE**
>
> From *Harry Potter and The Sorcerer's Stone*

"

Live according to the
ethics of excellence, and you
can always stand proud. Pride
- not vanity, but dignity and
self-respect - should carry a
lot of weight in helping you
make decisions. Let pride
help you decide.

PRICE PRITCHETT

"

Bravery is stability, not of
legs and arms, but of courage
and the soul.

MICHEL DE MONTAIGNE

There will always be problems in life. When faced with a challenge, the task becomes figuring out what to do in a way that is good for you, those around you and does no harm to others. Rather than avoid, hide or run from mistakes, the high road is to be aware, acknowledge and, when called for, learn from your mistakes. Once you find you have made a mistake or chosen badly, you now have the opportunity to choose again.

Here is a formula for ethical decision making that walks you through the steps to an improved outcome.

1 - Clearly define the problem as if you are an investigative reporter, objectively and dispassionately.

2 - Ask yourself whose problem it is. Is it a personal problem, a role-defined problem, a work problem, an industry problem or a social problem?

3 - Determine if it is an ethical problem or simply a decision to be made.

4 - If it is an ethical or moral problem clarify the issue at hand.

5 - Ask yourself if it is a case of conflicting interests or a question of rights and/or fairness.

6 - Ask yourself what you want as an outcome.

7 - Who can help? Do you need technical, moral or spiritual consultation?

8 - Who is affected? Does it impact you only or are others involved? Do they need to be involved in the decision-making?

9. Reduce the number of alternatives to a manageable two or three; don't stumble all over the place.

10. Weigh the final alternatives.

11. Given each alternative, ask yourself if there is a law against it. Is it a violation of a clear moral rule (don't cheat, steal)? Is it an offense to local customs or mores?

12. Ask yourself how it makes you look to others. Does it accurately reflect the kind of person you are or want to be? ("Can I get away with it?" is not a step in ethical reasoning.)

13 - Make a decision and act. You may need to return to step 1, but you'll never know if you made the right choice if you don't act.

I have way too many examples of mistakes I've made in my life. When I realized the mistakes would continue, I decided I needed a way to problem solve when I realized what I had done badly, so at least I wouldn't make that mistake again. Sometimes it worked right away, and sometimes I had to remedy my ways more than once. In any case, at least I knew I was doing my best to be a better person and it felt good inside.

Remember, nobody's perfect, including you. The journey of life offers many opportunities to learn from our mistakes. It is those who do not learn, or choose to act differently, whose dance becomes a dance of fear, unhappiness, shame and defeat rather than joy and creativity. Use the | 4.20b | **ETHICAL PROBLEM SOLVING WORKSHEET** in the **MASTER CLASS WORKBOOK** to deal with any ethical conflicts you face today.

EXCELLENCE FULL CIRCLE

Clear, strong personal ethics are a foundation for the Dance of Excellence. As you dance through your life, keep your awareness on how you are interacting with yourself and others. Hold yourself to a standard of excellence you'll be able to use to manage LifeDance stumbles and bumps. Remember, it is not about the bumps; it is how you manage them. Everyone makes mistakes, the key is what you do about them. Do they change from bumps to points of change and adventure? You are the one who makes the difference!

A man without ethics
is a wild beast loosed upon
this world.

ALBERT CAMUS

The secret of joy in
work is contained in one
word – excellence. To know
how to do something well is
to enjoy it.

PEARL BUCK

CHAPTER TWENTY-ONE

The Art of Happiness

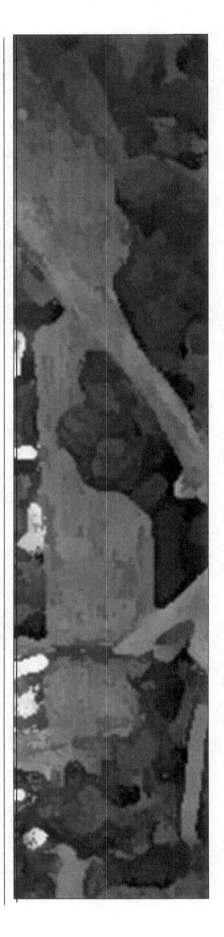

*T*here are many LifeDance themes, tragedies, mysteries and my favorite – the happy ending. Because you now know that you are the creator and director of your LifeDance, I'll assume you would prefer to create a happy dance rather than a sad one. I also assume you believe, like me, that the happy dance is the better of the two. Unfortunately, without the sad dance, you won't notice the happy dance. Because most lives are a mix of suffering and happiness, I ask you to allow for a moment, that whatever you feel, at any time, has the potential to be the "right" experience, or dance, for now. We all are the creators of our inner dialogue and dance of life stories. The degree to which we are attached to these narratives creates our level or suffering around them. There are, although, opportunities to lessen our unhappiness. Remember, there cannot be happiness without sadness. Unhappiness, or suffering is the ground or soil from which you can grow your happiness.

Human beings were not designed to be happy, they were designed to survive sometimes harsh and dangerous environments. Being happy, has emerged as culture has evolved to provide a foundation that allows for the pursuit of happiness. Unfortunately, the field of psychology, which should be able to provide us with tools and guidelines on how to create a good life, has fallen down on the job. Because its integration into the medical paradigm through Dr. Freud, psychiatry and psychology has focused, mostly, on what is wrong with people. There were mavericks along the way as seen in the work of Abraham Maslow, *Toward a Psychology of Being*, and Carl Rogers, *On Becoming A Person*, but as a whole, 90 percent of research money and focus is on pathology as opposed to well-being. In 1999, the new president of the American Psychological Association, Martin Seligman devoted his year in office to challenging his profession to

"

There is no way

to happiness,

happiness is the way.

THICH NHAT HANH

focus more on the traits and conditions that helped people feel happy. He was inspired to do this when one day, much to his dismay, his young daughter told him that he was always a grump. He decided then and there to make a personal change. Seligman began research on values, optimism and what made people happy. Eventually, he founded the Positive Psychology Center at the University of Pennsylvania and books and conferences emerged and established the field of positive psychology.

The field is in its infancy and is dynamic and growing. Basically the questions researchers are asking are:

INDIVIDUALLY

- What is the purpose of positive emotions such as joy, awe, happiness? (Fredrickson, Haidt, Isen)
- What are the inherent positive values and strengths of people? (Peterson, Park, Seligman)
- What makes people happy? (Diener, Myers, Seligman)
- How can people be happier? (Lyubomirsky, Peterson)
- Does happiness lead to success or success to happiness? (Diener, Lyubomirsky, King)
- What can people do to live happy lives? (Seligman)
- How can people use self-talk to succeed? (Seligman, Reivich, Gillham)

AT WORK

- How can people do what they most enjoy and do best at work? (Clifton, Rath)
- How can people get more involved in their activities and find flow states? (Csikszentmihalyi, Nakamura)
- How can one's work be a job, career or a calling? (Wrzesniewski)

When I was first exposed to Seligman's work in 2000, I felt like I had finally come home. I had never felt comfortable using the mental health field's bible – the DSM (Diagnostic and Statistical Manual) -- to label people with diseases such as depression and anxiety disorders. It always seemed that there was much more to a person than that. I hated that people called themselves bipolar or depressed when all that meant was they met the criteria in a book that was generated by insurance companies for payment purposes to doctors. The labels fenced people in, identifying them as though they were internally broken. It was like having a broken leg and always being called "the person with the broken leg."

Marty Seligman and Ed Diener[32] did a 10-year study on people's virtues, values and strengths. The results that came from their research provided a way of looking at people in terms of what was right with them. My professional work changed from fixing something that was broken to one of building and broadening on what was right. That made much more sense to me. The self-assessments and practices Seligman gave us helped me change how I approached my work and changed my inner dialogue and relationship with myself.

I was not alone in my aversion to only seeing pathology in people. In 2006, with the growth of this new field of research, Harvard University offered a class on Positive Psychology, only to have it become the most popular elective course in the history of the college. More than 800 students enrolled. When I took my first distance-learning class with Seligman, there were only a few books or workshops in the field; now there are thousands.

I believe the use of the tools and skills in positive psychology can change a life of sadness and distress to one of happiness and fulfillment.

Because this is a new field, there are many books on how to increase your happiness. The most recent one I have found to be helpful for myself and my clients is *Positivity* by Barbara Fredrickson (Crown, 2009). Because we are all familiar with the term negativity, and probably the experience of our own or others negativity, the term positivity makes sense.

Remember the story about the two boys and the pony? If not, here it is yet again, just a little different. The story illustrates how two people can be in the same place and time and have two very different experiences.

Remember two boys who desperately wanted a pony? Besides the one boy's envisioning a pony under a pile of horse poo, what are the characteristics of positive people? What the researchers have discovered is that they:

- Are optimistic.
- Look at crises and deep change as opportunities.
- View problems as temporary, not permanent states.
- Are resilient and bend in the face of change rather than break down.

> "
>
> Between stimulus and response there is a space. In that space is our power to choose our response. In our response lies our growth and our freedom.
>
> **VICTOR FRANKL**

Each morning when I open my eyes I say to myself: I, not events, have the power to make me happy or unhappy today. I can choose which it shall be. Yesterday is dead, tomorrow hasn't arrived yet. I have just one day, today, and I'm going to be happy in it.

GROUCHO MARX

- Look for solutions rather than sink in the problems.
- Have a sense of inner control over their fate.
- Have a full range of emotions and are able to manage their feelings creatively.
- Know what their personal values are and use them in different ways when they find their curiosity about life needs a boost.

Finally, when they are successful, they take credit for it. When they fail, they are able to assess the external circumstances and their role in creating the situation, their decisions in response to it, then take responsibility for the lessons to be learned so they can implement positive change. In other words, they turn lemons into lemonade.

There are some simple exercises you can do to increase your *Positivity*. Here are a few, and I also highly recommend using the book Positivity and following the exercises Fredrickson offers.

Fredrickson proposes that there is a tipping point where positivity outweighs negativity, making it easier and more natural to be positive. When you go to www.positivityratio.com you assess your positivity on a daily basis. Seligman proposes that we are all born with a set-point of our ability to be positive. The bad news is that there is a set-point, the good news is that it only determines a percentage of our ability to be happy. Other factors such as environment, relationship and personal practices can increase our ability to be happy. Remember, "neurons that fire together, wire together," so as you think more positively you rewire your brain for happiness.

Seligman's work offers other ways to increase an inner or subjective sense of happiness. He directs us to know our values and strengths and design our lives to use them frequently, and in new ways. Because I know I have a love of learning, it brings me great happiness to research a new idea or arena and share what I find with others. I also love being creative and enjoy designing an outfit, a new inner practice and a beautiful garden. If you didn't identify your personal values in the beginning of the book, go to www.authentichappiness.org and take the online VIA (Values In Action) assessment.

So why make the effort? It turns out that people who are happy actually live longer, are more productive and creative, enjoy better relationships and overall quality of life. It sounds good to me.

Here are the practices that have been found to be most helpful in creating an inner sense of happiness and a mental position of positivity.

1. Every night, right before you go to bed, think about or write down three things that went well that day. If it was a particularly difficult day, you have at least one thing to be proud of, you remembered to think about three positive things.

2. Use one of your values or strengths in a new way. Until you can remember your top five values, write them down on something you carry with you. When you have an opportunity at home, work or other arenas to choose activities, ask yourself how you can use your strengths in a new way.

3. Savor a good experience. Often, we have positive moments and are so distracted by thinking about the past or the future we simply miss the joy of the moment. When things are going well, take a deep breath and enjoy the moment using all of your senses. The act of being mindful has been found to increase happiness all by itself. It takes you out of worrying about the future and lamenting over the past. When you find yourself leaving the moment and bringing yourself down, come back to the moment, take a deep breath, and appreciate being fully alive. I find these moments frequently when I care for my grandson. He is five and a bundle of energy, curiosity and joy. When I'm able to be fully in the moment with him I'm able to see the world through the eyes of an innocent child and wonder in its curiosity and beauty. We take pictures together, color, create puppet stories and much more. I find being present with my dog and cat is a more nonverbal way of being non-judgmentally in the world. Life is all about the senses, what is going on in the environment and how you respond to it. Look for your opportunities to savor the moment. I recently was offered the exercise of savoring food more frequently. Often, I eat on the run and don't pay attention to what is going in my mouth. When I remember, I use the Mindful Eating method of:

- Savoring the first bite.
- Breathing fully and pondering where the food came from.
- Observing myself as an eater.
  - Deciding if what I'm eating is good for me, and the planet.
  - Choosing to continue eating or not.

> Some cause happiness wherever they go; others whenever they go.
>
> **OSCAR WILDE**

Waking up this morning,

I smile,

Twenty four brand new

hours are before me.

I vow to live fully in each

moment and to look at all

beings with eyes

of compassion.

**THICH
NHAT HANH**

Be content

with what you have;

Rejoice in the way

things are.

When you realize

there is nothing

lacking,

The whole world

belongs to you.

LAO TZU

- Noticing when I'm hungry, and when I'm full.
- Return to top.

What I discovered that was I often skip over step 1 entirely. Eating had become so automatic, just like life, that I often forgot to savor the moment.

4. Express gratitude to others whenever you have the opportunity. I had to ride the bus recently and was sitting right in back of the bus driver. She had a very sunny disposition and didn't let any of the public's antics, such as complaining about the schedule, bother her. One man came to the bus door and couldn't find his transfer ticket. He threw down his books and shoulder bag, cursing. She calmly said to him that many people couldn't find their tickets. They would buy them and stick them in a pocket or bag and forget where they were. "Just take your time and check all of your pockets and bags, you'll find it." He calmed down and did just that and eventually found his ticket and boarded the bus. When we finally reached our destination, when I was going out the door past her, I thanked her for her calm demeanor and gracious ways. It made us both feel better. The world is so used to telling us when we do things wrong, start today to let people know when they do something right. Start catching people doing something good.

5. Surround yourself with positive people. You may have family or friends who always find bad stuff to focus on. You may not be able to get them out of your life, but you don't have to spend a lot of time with them. You might even consider asking them to look for positive moments. Look for new friends who have a sunnier disposition and focus on family members who are more positive. You might even share what you're learning with them and check in with each other to see if you are remembering at the end of each day, the positive things.

Changing from a negative or unhappy position in life to a positive attitude takes time. Be patient with yourself, notice when you are off balance and negative and simply change your focus, increase your awareness of the moment, internally and externally, and reframe them to a positive stance. As you do, I promise you that your life will change for the better.

Let's hear a round of applause for your Happy LifeDance!!!!!!

Linda

APPENDIX A

RESOURCES

ALBERS, S. (2003). *Eating Mindfully: How to End Mindless Eating and Enjoy a Balanced Relationship With Food*. New Harbinger Publications.

ALBERS, S. (2009). *Eat, Drink, and be Mindful: How to End Your Struggle With Mindless Eating and Start Savoring Food With Intention and Joy*. New Harbinger Publications.

ALTMAN, D. (2002). *Art of the Inner Meal: The Power of Mindful Practices to Heal Our Food Cravings*, Revised and Expanded Edition (Revised and Expanded). Moon Lake Media.

ALTMAN, D. (2010). *The Mindfulness Code: Keys for Overcoming Stress, Anxiety, Fear, and Unhappiness*. New World Library.

AMEN, D. (2008). *Healing the Hardware of the Soul: Enhance Your Brain to Improve Your Work, Love, and Spiritual Life*. Free Press.

AMEN, D. G. (2006). *Making a Good Brain Great: The Amen Clinic Program for Achieving and Sustaining Optimal Mental Performance*. Three Rivers Press.

ANODEA, J. A. (2004). *Eastern Body, Western Mind: Psychology and the Chakra System as a Path to the Self* (Revised ed.). Celestial Arts.

BANDLER, R. (1979). *Using Your Brain – For a Change: Neuro-Linguistic Programming*.

BATESON, M. C. (2000). *Full Circles, Overlapping Lives: Culture and Generation in Transition*. Random House.

BAYS, J. C. (2009). *Mindful Eating: A Guide to Rediscovering a Healthy and Joyful Relationship With Food*. Includes CD. Shambhala.

BAYS, J. C. (2011). *How to Train a Wild Elephant: And Other Adventures in Mindfulness*. Shambhala.

BECK, M. (2002). *Finding Your Own North Star: Claiming the Life You Were Meant to Live*. Three Rivers Press.

BECK, R., & METRICK, S. B. (1995). *The Art of Ritual*. Celestial Arts Press.

BEN-SHAHAR, T. (2007). *Happier: Learn the Secrets to Daily Joy and Lasting Fulfillment*. McGraw-Hill.

BENSON, H., & KLIPPER, M.Z. (1976). *The Relaxation Response*. HarperTorch.

BIECH, E. (1994). *Tqm for Training*. McGraw-Hill.

BISWAS-DIENER, R., & DEAN, B. (2007). *Positive Psychology Coaching: Putting the Science of Happiness to Work for Your Clients*. Wiley & Sons.

BOLDT, L. G. (1999). *Zen and the Art of Making a Living: A Practical Guide to Creative Career Design* (Compass). Penguin (Non-Classics).

BOLDT, L. G. (1999). *The Tao of Abundance: Eight Ancient Principles for Abundant Living*, 1st ed. Penguin Books.

BOLEN, J. S. (1982). *The Tao of Psychology: Synchronicity and Self.* HarperSanFrancisco.

BOLT, M. (2004). *Pursuing Human Strengths: A Positive Psychology Guide*, 4th ed. Worth Publishers.

BORYSENKO, J. (1987). *Minding the Body, Mending the Mind*, 1st printing ed. Addison Wesley.

BORYSENKO, J. (1996). *A Woman's Book of Life*, 1st ed. Riverhead Hardcover.

BRACH, T. (2004). *Radical Acceptance: Embracing Your Life With the Heart of a Buddha.* Bantam.

BRIZENDINE, L. (2007). *The Female Brain.* Three Rivers Press.

BUCKINGHAM, M., & CLIFTON, D. O. (2001). *Now, Discover Your Strength.* Free Press.

BURNS, D. D. (1999). *The Feeling Good Handbook* (Revised ed.). Plume.

BUZAN, T. (1991). *Use Both Sides of Your Brain: New Mind-Mapping Techniques*, Third Edition (Plume) (Revised ed.). Plume.

BUZAN, T., & BUZAN, B. (1996). *The Mind Map Book: How to Use Radiant Thinking to Maximize Your Brain's Untapped Potential.* Plume.

CALVIN, W. (1990). *The Cerebral Symphony: Seashore Reflections on the Structure of Consciousness* (First Edition). Bantam.

CAMPBELL, D. (2001). *Mozart Effect: Tapping the Power of Music.* Avon.

CAMPBELL, J. (1973). *The Hero With a Thousand Faces.* Princeton Press.

CAPACCHIONE, L. (2000). *Visioning: Ten Steps to Designing the Life of Your Dreams.* Tarcher.

CARR, A. (2004). *Positive Psychology: The Science of Happiness and Human Strengths.* Routledge.

CHODRON, P. (2006). *Practicing Peace in Times of War* (1st edition, 1st Printing). Shambhala.

CHOPRA, D. (1989). *Quantum Healing: Exploring the Frontiers of Mind/Body Medicine* (1st printing). Bantam.

CHOPRA, D. (1997). *The Wisdom Within.* Harmony Books.

CHRISTAKIS, N. A., & FOWLER, J. H. (2009). *Connected: The Surprising Power of Our Social Networks and How They Shape Our Lives.* Little, Brown and Company.

COHEN, A. (2011). *Evolutionary Enlightenment: A New Path to Spiritual Awakening* (1st ed.). Select Books.

CONGER, J. P. (1994). *The Body in Recovery: Somatic Psychotherapy and the Self.* Frog Books.

COREY, L. M. K., & JONATHAN, H. (2002). *Flourishing: Positive Psychology and the Life Well-Lived* (1st ed.). American Psychological Association (APA).

COVEY, S. R. (1990). *The 7 Habits of Highly Effective People* (1st ed.). Free Press.

COVEY, S. R.; MERRILL, A. R., & MERRILL, R. R. (1994). *First Things First* (1st ed.). Simon & Schuster.

COZOLINO, L. (2002). *The Neuroscience of Psychotherapy: Building and Rebuilding the Human Brain* (1st ed.). W. W. Norton & Company.

CRUM, T. F. (2006). *Three Deep Breaths: Finding Power and Purpose in a Stressed-Out World.* Berrett-Koehler Publishers.

CSIKSZENTMIHALYI, M. (1990). *Flow: The Psychology of Optimal Experience.* Harper & Row.

CSIKSZENTMIHALYI, M. (1994). *The Evolving Self: A Psychology for the Third Millennium* (1st printing ed.). Harper Perennial.

CSIKSZENTMIHALYI, M. (1996). *Creativity: Flow and the Psychology of Discovery and Invention* (1st ed.). HarperCollins.

CSIKSZENTMIHALYI, M. (1997). *Finding Flow: The Psychology of Engagement With Everyday Life* (1st ed.). Basic Books.

CSIKSZENTMIHALYI, M., & CSIKSZENTMIHALYI, I. S. (2006). *A Life Worth Living: Contributions to Positive Psychology* (Series in Positive Psychology). Oxford University Press, USA.

DEMAREST, L. (1997). *Looking At Type in the Workplace (Looking At Type Series)*. Center for Applications of Psychological-Type.

DEROO, C., & DEROO, C. (2006). *What's Right With Me: Positive Ways to Celebrate Your Strengths, Build Self-Esteem and Reach Your Potential*. New Harbinger.

DERTOUZOS, M. L. (2001). *The Unfinished Revolution : Human-Centered Computers and What They Can Do for Us*. Harper-Audio.

DESALVO, L. (1999). *Writing as a Way of Healing: How Telling Our Stories Transforms Our Lives* (1st ed.). HarperOne.

DIENER, E., & BISWAS-DIENER, R. (2008). *Happiness: Unlocking the Mysteries of Psychological Wealth* (1st ed.). Wiley-Blackwell.

DOIDGE, N. (2007). *The Brain That Changes Itself: Stories of Personal Triumph From the Frontiers of Brain Science* (James H. Silberman Books) (1st ed.). Viking Adult.

DOMINGUEZ, J., & ROBIN, V. (1992). *Your Money or Your Life: Transforming Your Relationship With Money and Achieving Financial Independence*. Viking Press.

DOSSEY, L. (2001). *Healing Beyond the Body: Medicine and the Infinite Reach of the Mind* (1st ed.). Shambhala.

ELGIN, D. (1998). *Voluntary Simplicity: Toward a Way of Life That is Outwardly Simple, Inwardly Rich* (Revised Edition). Quill (William Morrow).

FOER, J. (2011). *Moonwalking With Einstein: The Art and Science of Remembering Everything* (UK Paperback ed.). Penguin.

FOWLER, J. W. (1995). *Stages of Faith: The Psychology of Human Development and the Quest for Meaning* (New edition). HarperOne.

FRATTAROLI, E. (2001). *Healing the Soul in the Age of the Brain: Becoming Conscious in an Unconscious World* (1st ed.). Viking Adult.

FREDRICKSON, B. (2009). *Positivity: Groundbreaking Research Reveals How to Embrace the Hidden Strength of Positive Emotions, Overcome Negativity, and Thrive* (1st Edition). Crown Archetype

FREEDMAN, R., & BARNOUIN, K. (2009). *Skinny Couple in a Box*. Running Press.

FRISCH, M. B. (2005). *Quality of Life Therapy: Applying a Life Satisfaction Approach to Positive Psychology and Cognitive Therapy*. Wiley.

GARDNER, H. E.; CSIKSZENTMIHALYI, M.; DAMON, W., & GARDNER, H. (2002). *Good Work: When Excellence and Ethics Meet*. Basic Books.

GERMER, C.K., PH.D.; SIEGEL, D., PSYD; & FULTON, P., ED.D., (2005). *Mindfulness and Psychotherapy* (1st ed.). The Guilford Press.

GILLIGAN, C. (2002). *The Birth of Pleasure* (1st ed.). Knopf.

GLADWELL, M. (2005). *Blink: The Power of Thinking Without Thinking* (Unabridged ed.). Hachette Audio.

GOLD, S. S. (2011). *Food: The Good Girl's Drug: How to Stop Using Food to Control Your Feelings*. Berkley Trade.

GOLEMAN, D. (1996). *The Meditative Mind: The Varieties of Meditative Experience*. Tarcher.

GOLEMAN, D. (1995). *Emotional Intelligence*. Bantam Books.

GONZALEZ, M., & BYRON, G. (2009). *The Mindful Investor: How a Calm Mind Can Bring You Inner Peace and Financial Security* (1st ed.). Wiley.

GROF, S., & BENNETT, H. Z. (1992). *The Holotropic Mind: The Three Levels of Human Consciousness and How They Shape Our Lives* (1st ed.). HarperCollins.

GRUDIN, R. (1988). *Time and the Art of Living*. Ticknor & Fields.

HAIDT, J. (2005). *The Happiness Hypothesis: Finding Modern Truth in Ancient Wisdom* (1st ed.). Basic Books.

HANLON, D. J., & GRAND, I., J. (1998). *The Body in Psychotherapy: Inquiries in Somatic Psychology (Body in Psychotherapy,* Vol 3). North Atlantic Books.

HANSON, R. (2009). *Buddha's Brain: The Practical Neuroscience of Happiness, Love, and Wisdom* (1st ed.). New Harbinger Publications.

HARRIS, B. (2002). *Thresholds of the Mind* (1st ed.). Centerpointe Press.

HARRIS, R. (2009). *Act Made Simple: An Easy-to-Read Primer on Acceptance and Commitment Therapy* (1st ed.). New Harbinger Publications.

HARRIS, T. A. (1948). *I'm OK, You're OK*. Harper Perennial

HAWKEN, P. (1994). *The Ecology of Commerce: A Declaration of Sustainability*. HarperBusiness.

HAYES, S. C., & SMITH, S. (2005). *Get Out of Your Mind and Into Your Life: The New Acceptance and Commitment Therapy* (1st ed.). New Harbinger Publications.

HENDRICKS, G. (2001). *Conscious Living: How to Create a Life of Your Own Design*. Harper.

HENDRICKS, G. (2009). *The Big Leap: Conquer Your Hidden Fear and Take Life to the Next Level*. HarperOne.

HILLMAN, J. (1983). *Healing Fiction*. Stationhill Press.

HOFSTADTER, D. R. (1980). *Godel, Escher, Bach: An Eternal Golden Braid*. Vintage.

HUBBARD, B. M. (1998). *Conscious Evolution: Awakening Our Social Potential*. 1st ed. New World Library.

HUBBARD, B. M. (2001). *Emergence: The Shift From Ego to Essence*. Hampton Roads Publishing.

HUFFINGTON, A. (1994). *Fourth Instinct: The Call of the Soul*. Simon & Schuster.

JACOBSON, J., & MADERA, K. C. (2010). *How to Meditate With Your Dog: An Introduction to Meditation for Dog Lovers*. Maui Media.

JOSEPH, S., & LINLEY, P. A. (2006). *Positive Therapy*. Routledge.

JUNG, C. J. (1938) *Psychology and Religion*. Yale University Press.

KABAT-ZINN, J. (1990). *Full Catastrophe Living: Using the Wisdom of Your Body and Mind to Face Stress, Pain, and Illness* (1st ed.). Delta.

KABAT-ZINN, J. (1994). *Guided Mindfulness: Series 1, 2, and 3*. Stress Reduction CDs, PO Box 547.

KABAT-ZINN, J. (2005). *Coming to Our Senses: Healing Ourselves and the World Through Mindfulness* (1st ed.). Hyperion.

KAHLE, L., R., & CHIAGOURIS, L. (1997). *Values, Lifestyles, and Psychographics* (Advertising and Consumer Psychology). Psychology Press.

KEEN, S., & VALLEY-FOX, A. (1989). *Your Mythic Journey: Finding Meaning in Your Life Through Writing and Storytelling* (Inner Work Book) (1st ed.). Tarcher.

KEGAN, R. (1982). *The Evolving Self: Problem and Process in Human Development.* (1st ed.). Harvard University Press.

KEGAN, R. (1998). *In Over Our Heads: The Mental Demands of Modern Life.* Harvard University Press.

KIMIECIK, J. C. (2002). *The Intrinsic Exerciser: Discovering the Joy of Exercise* (1st ed.). Mariner Books.

KLEIN, S. (2006). *The Science of Happiness: How Our Brains Make Us Happy – and What We Can Do to Get Happier.* Da Capo Press.

KLIPPER, M. Z., & BENSON, H. (2000). *The Relaxation Response* (Exp Upd ed.). William Morrow Paperbacks.

KOENIG, K. R. (2005). *The Rules of "Normal" Eating: A Commonsense Approach for Dieters, Overeaters, Undereaters, Emotional Eaters, and Everyone in Between!* (1st ed.). Gurze Books.

KORNFIELD, J. (1963). *A Path With Heart.* Bantam Books.

KORNFIELD, J. (2001). *After the Ecstasy, the Laundry: How the Heart Grows Wise on the Spiritual Path.* Bantam.

KORNFIELD, J. (2009). *The Wise Heart: A Guide to the Universal Teachings of Buddhist Psychology* (Reprint ed.). Bantam.

LAMA, T. D. (2003). *Stages of Meditation.* Snow Lion Publications.

LANGER, E. J. (1989). *Mindfulness.* Addison-Wesley.

LEPORE, S. J., & SMYTH, J. M. (2002). *The Writing Cure: How Expressive Writing Promotes Health and Emotional Well-Being* (1st ed.). American Psychological Association (APA).

LINLEY, A. P., & JOSEPH, S. (2004). *Positive Psychology in Practice* (1st ed.). Wiley.

LINN, D. (1998). *Quest* (1st U.S. Edition). Ballantine Books.

LIPTON, B. H. (2005). *The Biology of Belief: Unleashing the Power of Consciousness, Matter and Miracles.* Mountain of Love.

LOPEZ, S. J., & SNYDER, C., R. (2003). *Positive Psychological Assessment: A Handbook of Models and Measures* (1st ed.). American Psychological Association (APA).

LORING, S. T. (2010). *Eating With Fierce Kindness: A Mindful and Compassionate Guide to Losing Weight* (Reprint ed.). New Publications.

LUHRS, J. (1997). *The Simple Living Guide a Sourcebook for Less Stressful, More Joyful Living.* Broadway Books.

LYUBOMIRSKY, S. (2007). *The How of Happiness: A Scientific Approach to Getting the Life You Want* (1st ed.). Penguin Press.

MACE, C. (2007). *Mindfulness and Mental Health: Therapy, Theory and Science* (1st ed.). Routledge.

MACKENZIE, R. A., & MACKENZIE, A. (1975). *The Time Trap.* McGraw-Hill.

MARREWA, A. (2001). *The Feminine Warrior: A Woman's Guide to Physical, Emotional and Spritual Empowerment.* Citadel.

MASLOW, A. (1965). *Euphychian Management.* Dorsey Press.

MAY, M. (2011). *Eat What You Love, Love What You Eat: How to Break Your Eat-Repent-Repeat Cycle. Am I Hungry?* Publishing.

MCCULLOUGH, B. R. (1986). *Totally Organized: The Bonnie Mccullough Way.* St. Martin's Press.

MCGILCHRIST, I. (2010). *The Master and His Emissary: The Divided Brain and the Making of the Western World* (Reprint ed.) Yale University Press.

MCWILLIAMS, J.R.; McWILLIAMS, P.; & McWILLIAMS, J. R. (1991). *Do It! Let's Get Off Our Buts: A Guide to Living Your Dreams.* Bantam Dell Pub Group (Trd).

MEAD, A. (2008). *Wake Up to Your Weight Loss: Using the Art of Personal Narrative to Achieve Your Best Body* (1st ed.). A Storied Life Publishing.

MELLAN, O. (1995). *Money Harmony.* Walker & Company.

MILLER, J. B. (1987). *Toward a New Psychology of Women* (2nd ed.). Beacon Press.

MITCHELL, J. (1992). *Organized Serenity: A Practical Guide for Getting It Together.* Hci.

MOORE, T. (1994). *Care of the Soul : A Guide for Cultivating Depth and Sacredness in Everyday Life* (Reprint ed.). HarperPerennial.

NAIRN, R. (1999). *Diamond Mind* (1st Shambh ed.). Shambhala.

NEEDLEMAN, J. (1994). *Money and the Meaning of Life* (New edition). Doubleday.

ORIAH. (2006). *The Dance: Moving to the Deep Rhythms of Your Life.* HarperOne.

ORNSTEIN, R. (1991). *Evolution of Consciousness.* Pearson Ptr.

ORSBORN, C. (1992). *Inner Excellence: Spiritual Principles of Life-Driven Business.* New World Library.

PALMER, H. (1991). *The Enneagram: Understanding Yourself and the Others in Your Life* (1st ed.). HarperOne.

PELLETIER, D. K. R. (1994). *Sound Mind, Sound Body* (1st ed.). Simon & Schuster.

PETERS, T. J., & WATERMAN, R. H. (1982). *In Search of Excellence: Lessons From America's Best-Run Companies.* Harper & Row.

PETERS, T. (1999). *The Brand You 50 : Or : Fifty Ways to Transform Yourself From an 'Employee' Into a Brand That Shouts Distinction, Commitment, and Passion!* (1st ed.). Knopf.

PETERS, T., & AUSTIN, N. (1985). *A Passion for Excellence.* Random House.

PETERSON, C. (2006). *A Primer in Positive Psychology* (Oxford Positive Psychology Series) (1st ed.). Oxford University Press, USA.

PETERSON, C., & SELIGMAN, M. (2004). *Character Strengths and Virtues: A Handbook and Classification* (1st ed.). Oxford: Oxford University Press, USA.

PHILLIPS, M. (1996). *Honest Business* (Shambhala Pocket Editions) (1st ed.). Shambhala.

PINK, D. H. (2006). *A Whole New Mind: Why Right-Brainers Will Rule the Future.* Riverhead Trade.

PROCHASKA, J. (1994). *Changing for Good* (Abridged ed.). Sound Ideas.

PROCHASKA, J. O.; NORCROSS, J., & DICLEMENTE, C. (1995). *Changing for Good: A Revolutionary Six-Stage Program for Overcoming Bad Habits and Moving Your Life Positively Forward.* William Morrow Paperbacks.

PROGOFF, I. (1963). *The Symbolic & the Real.* McGraw Hill.

PSYD, S. A. (2009). *50 Ways to Soothe Yourself Without Food* (1st ed.). New Harbinger Publications.

RADIN, D. (2006). *Entangled Minds: Extrasensory Experiences in a Quantum Reality.* Paraview Pocket Books.

RAY, P. H., Ph.D, and S.R. ANDERSON (2000). *The Cultural Creatives: How 50 Million People Are Changing the World* (1st ed., 1st printing ed.). Harmony.

RAMDASS. (1974). *The Only Dance There Is*. Anchor.

RAMDASS. (1978). *Remember, Be Here Now*. Hanuman Foundation.

RATEY, J. J. (2008). *Spark: The Revolutionary New Science of Exercise and the Brain* (1st ed.). Little, Brown and Company.

RATH, T. (2007). *Strengthsfinder 2.0* (1st ed.). Gallup Press.

REISMAN, D. (2001). *The Lonely Crowd, Revised edition: A Study of the Changing American Character*. Yale University Press

RICHARDSON, C. (1999). *Take Time for Your Life: A Personal Coach's 7-Step Program for Creating the Life You Want* (1st ed.). Three Rivers Press.

RICHARDSON, C. (2002). *Stand Up for Your Life: Develop the Courage, Confidence, and Character to Fulfill Your Greatest Potential* (1st ed.). Free Press.

ROBERTS, H. (1993). *Quality is Personal: A Foundation for Total Quality Management* (1st ed.). Free Press.

ROBIN, V. (1999). *Your Money or Your Life: Transforming Your Relationship with Money and Achieving Financial Independence*. Penguin (Non-Classics).

ROBINSON, L. A. (2004). *Real Prosperity: Using the Power of Intuition to Create Financial and Spiritual Abundance*. Andrews McMeel Publishing.

ROBINSON, L. A. (2001). *Divine Intuition* (1st American Edition ed.). Hyperion.

ROEMER, L.R., Ph.D.; & ORSILLO, S. M. O., Ph.D., (2008). *Mindfulness- and Acceptance-Based Behavioral Therapies in Practice (Guides to Individualized Evidence-Based Treatment)* (1st ed.). The Guilford Press. ROTH, G. (2010). Women, Food and God: An Unexpected Path to Almost Everything. Scribner.

RUIZ, D. M. (1997). *The Four Agreements: A Practical Guide to Personal Freedom (a Toltec Wisdom Book)*. Amber-Allen Publishing.

RUIZ, D. M., & MILLS, J. (2000). *The Four Agreements Companion Book : Using the Four Agreements to Master the Dream of Your Life*. Amber-Allen Publishing.

RUTTER, V. B. (1993). *Woman Changing Woman: Feminine Psychology Re-Conceived Through Myth and Experience* (1st ed.). HarperCollins.

SANTORELLI, S. (2000). *Heal Thy Self: Lessons on Mindfulness in Medicine* (Reprint ed.). Three Rivers Press.

SCHULZ, M.L., M.D., Ph.D.,. (1998). *Awakening Intuition: Using Your Mind-Body Network for Insight and Healing* (1st ed.). Harmony.

SCHULZ, M. L. (2005). *The New Feminine Brain: How Women Can Develop Their Inner Strengths, Genius, and Intuition* (1st ed.). FreePress.

SELIGMAN, M. E. P. (1995). *What You Can Change and What You Can't: The Complete Guide to Successful Self-Improvement Learning to Accept Who You Are* (Fawcett Book) (First Ballantine Edition ed.). Ballantine Books.

SELIGMAN, M. E. P. (2002). *Authentic Happiness: Using the New Positive Psychology to Realize Your Potential for* Lasting Fulfillment (1st ed.). Free Press.

SENGE, P. M. (1994). *The Fifth Discipline: The Art & Practice of the Learning Organization* (4th ed.). Doubleday Business.

SENGE, P. M.; KLEINER, A.; ROBERTS, C.; ROSS, R.; & SMITH, B. (1994). The Fifth *Discipline Fieldbook: Strategies and Tools for Building a Learning Organization* (1st ed.). Crown Business

SERVAN-SCHREIBER, J.L. (1989). *The Art of Time.* Addison-Wesley.

SHATTE, A., & REIVICH, K. (2002). *The Resilience Factor: 7 Essential Skills for Overcoming Life's Inevitable Obstacles* (1st ed.). Broadway.

SHELTON, S. (1981). *Divine Dancer: A Biography of Ruth St. Denis.* Doubleday.

SIEGEL, D., & HARTZELL, M. (2004). *Parenting From the Inside Out* (1st ed.). Tarcher.

SIEGEL, D. J. (1999). *The Developing Mind: Toward a Neurobiology of Interpersonal Experience* (1st ed.). Guilford Press.

SIEGEL, D. J. (2007). *The Mindful Brain: Reflection and Attunement in the Cultivation of Well-Being* (1st ed.). W. W. Norton & Company.

SIEGEL, D. J. (2010). *Mindsight: The New Science of Personal Transformation* (1st ed.). Bantam.

SIEGEL, D. J. (2010). *The Mindful Therapist: A Clinician's Guide to Mindsight and Neural Integration* (Norton Series on Interpersonal Neurobiology) (1st ed.). W. W. Norton & Company.

SIMONS, T. R. (1996). *Feng Shui Step By Step : Arranging Your Home for Health and Happiness – With Personalized Astrological Charts* (Original ed.). Crown Trade Paperbacks.

SMITH, R. (2007). *The 7 Levels of Change: Different Thinking for Different Results* (3rd ed.). Tapestry Press.

SNEAD, G. L., & WYCOFF, J. (1997). *To Do Doing Done: A Creative Approach to Managing Projects & Effectively Finishing What Matters Most* (1st ed.). Touchstone.

SOMOV, P. G. (2008). *Eating the Moment: 141 Mindful Practices to Overcome Overeating One Meal At a Time* (1st ed.). New Harbinger Publications.

STAHL, B.S., Ph.D.; & GOLDSTEIN, E. (2010). *A Mindfulness-Based Stress Reduction Workbook* (Pap/MP3 Wk ed.). New Harbinger Publications.

STALLINGS, K. (2008). *Life is Mental: Think Thin to Live Thin* (1st ed.). Kelly Stallings.

STROZZI-HECKLER, R. (1997). *The Anatomy of Change: A Way to Move Through Life's Transitions* (2nd ed.). North Atlantic Books.

TOLLE, E. (1999). *The Power of Now: A Guide to Spiritual Enlightenment* (1st ed.). New World Library.

TRENT, J. (1994). *Lifemapping.* Focus on the Family Publications.

WEIL, A., & SMALL, G. (2007). *The Healthy Brain Kit: Clinically Proven Tools to Boost Your Memory, Sharpen Your Mind, and Keep Your Brain Young.* Sounds True, Incorporated.

WELWOOD, J. (2000). *Toward a Psychology of Awakening: Buddhism, Psychotherapy and the Path of Personal and Spiritual Transformation.* Shambhala.

WILBER, K.; PATTEN, T.; LEONARD, A.; & MORELLI, M. (2008). *Integral Life Practice: A 21st-Century Blueprint for Physical Health, Emotional Balance, Mental Clarity, and Spiritual Awakening.* Integral Books.

WINSTON, S. (1995). *Stephanie Winston's Best Organizing Tips: Quick, Simple Ways to Get Organized – and Get on With Your Life.*

Simon & Schuster.

WISE, N. (2002). *A Big New Free Happy Unusual Life: Self Expression and Spiritual Practice for Those Who Have Time for Neither* (1st ed.). Broadway.

ZANDER, R. S., & ZANDER, B. (2000). *The Art of Possibility: Transforming Professional and Personal Life* (1st ed.). Harvard School Press.

ZIMMERMAN, M. A. (2006). *Handbook of Community Psychology* (1st ed.). Springer.

ZUKAV, G. (1990). *The Seat of the Soul.* Free Press.

RESOURCES *by Category*

There are many, many more excellent resources for each of these categories currently, and more have emerged after printing this book. In an effort to not overwhelm you, I've:

- Only listed a few resources for each area, and of course only those I've personally explored.

- Tried to stay away from resources that are trying to just sell you something.

- Attempted to stay generic, or middle of the road, in an attempt to allow you your own exploration, realizing that my preferences leak through.

- Only listed sites that I believe have integrity and will not lead you astray to promote themselves.

- Invite you to send me resources I've missed so I can post the on the website. Send them to Linda@LifeDancing.com. In any case, I invite you to start your own resource list as you explore and learn more about each of these arenas.

Happy Resourcing!

Linda

P.S.: For a current listing of resources and active links to websites, please visit www.LifeDancing.com.

BODY

BOOKS

ANDERSON, B. (2000). *Stretching.* Shelter.

BENSON, H. (1976). *The Relaxation Response.* HarperTorch.

BORYSENKO, J. (1987). *Minding the Body, Mending the Mind* (1st printing ed.). Addison Wesley.

CONGER, J. P. (1994). *The Body in Recovery: Somatic Psychotherapy and the Self.* Frog Books.

DOSSEY, L. (2001). *Healing Beyond the Body: Medicine and the Infinite Reach of the Mind* (1st ed.). Shambhala.

DYCHTWALD, K. (1986). *Bodymind.* Tarcher, J. P.

HANLON, D. J., & GRAND, I., J. (1998). *The Body in Psychotherapy: Inquiries in Somatic Psychology (Body in Psychotherapy, Vol 3).* North Atlantic Books.

HUANG, A. H. (1988). *Embrace Tiger, Return to Mountain.* Celestial Arts Press.

KIMIECIK, J. C. (2002). *The Intrinsic Exerciser: Discovering the Joy of Exercise* (1st ed.). Mariner Books.

KLIPPER, M. Z., & BENSON, H. (2000). *The Relaxation Response* (Exp Upd ed.). William Morrow Paperbacks.

RATEY, J. J. (2008). *Spark: The Revolutionary New Science of Exercise and the Brain* (1st ed.). Little, Brown and Company.

SELL, C. (2003). *Yoga From the Inside Out: Making Peace With Your Body Through Yoga.* Hohm

WEBSITES

ALTERNATIVE MEDICINE - The National Center for Complementary and Alternative Medicine – http://nccam.nih.gov/health/decisions/talkingaboutcam.htm   Access date 2/4/14

DANCE THERAPY - http://en.wikipedia.org/wiki/Dance_therapy.   Access date 2/4/14

CHANGE

BOOKS

BECK, R., & METRICK, S. B. (1995). *The Art of Ritual.* Celestial Arts.

PROCHASKA, J. (1994). *Changing for Good* (Abridged ed.). Sound Ideas.

PROCHASKA, J. O., NORCROSS, J., & DICLEMENTE, C. (1995). *Changing for Good: A Revolutionary Six-Stage Program for Overcoming Bad Habits and Moving Your Life Positively Forward.* William Morrow Paperbacks.

SMITH, R. (2007). *The 7 Levels of Change: Different Thinking for Different Results 3rd Edition* (3rd ed.). Tapestry Press.

STROZZI-HECKLER, R. (1997). *The Anatomy of Change: A Way to Move Through Life's Transitions* (2nd ed.). North Atlantic Books.

YOUNG, A. M. (1992). *The Reflexive Universe: A Cosmological Paradigm.* Anodos Foundation.

WEBSITES

CHANGE MANAGEMENT - http://en.wikipedia.org/wiki/Change_management

Access date 2/4/14

DANCE

BOOKS

GARRIPOLI, G. (1999). *Qigong: Essence of the Healing Dance.* HCI.

ORIAH. (2006). *The Dance: Moving to the Deep Rhythms of Your Life.* HarperOne.

PALLARO, P. (Ed.). (1999). *Authentic Movement: Essays by Mary Starks Whitehouse, Janet Adler and Joan Chodorow.* Jessica Kingsley Pub.

ROTH, G. (1998). *Maps to Ecstasy* (2nd ed.). New World Library.

SHELTON, S. (1981). *Divine Dancer: A Biography of Ruth St. Denis.* Doubleday.

WISE, N. (2002). *A Big New Free Happy Unusual Life: Self Expression and Spiritual Practice for Those Who Have Time for Neither* (1st ed.). Broadway.

WEBSITES Access date 2/4/14

DANCE & HEALING

http://www.medicinenet.com/script/main/art.asp?articlekey=50647

http://healing.about.com/od/dance/Movement_Therapy.htm

DEVELOPMENTAL MODELS

BOOKS

KALL, R. V., CAVANAUGH, J. C. (2008) *Human Development: A Life-Span View.* (5th ed.) Wadsworth Publishing

KEGAN, R. (1982). *The Evolving Self: Problem and Process in Human Development* (1st ed.). Harvard University Press.

KEGAN, R. (1998). *In Over Our Heads: The Mental Demands of Modern Life.* Harvard University Press.

MASLOW, A. H. (1962). *Toward a Psychology of Being.* D. Van Nostrand Co.

ORNSTEIN, R. (1991). *Evolution of Consciousness.* Pearson Ptr.

WELWOOD, J. (2000). *Toward a Psychology of Awakening: Buddhism, Psychotherapy and the Path of Personal and Spiritual Transformation.* Shambhala.

WEBSITES

HUMAN DEVELOPMENT

https://en.wikipedia.org/wiki/Developmental_psychology Access date 7/13/2015

EMOTIONS

BOOKS

BURNS, D. D. (1999). *The Feeling Good Handbook* (Revised ed.). Plume.

GOLEMAN, D. (1995). *Emotional Intelligence*. Bantam Books.

ENVIRONMENTS

BOOKS

SIMONS, T. R. (1996). *Feng Shui Step By Step : Arranging Your Home for Health and Happiness--With Personalized Astrological Charts* (Original ed.). Crown Trade Paperbacks.

EXCELLENCE

BOOKS

BIECH, E. (1994). *TQM for Training*. McGraw-Hill.

FRISCH, M. B. (2005). *Quality of Life Therapy: Applying a Life Satisfaction Approach to Positive Psychology and Cognitive Therapy*. Wiley.

GARDNER, H. E., CSIKSZENTMIHALYI, M., DAMON, W., & GARDNER, H. (2002). *Good Work: When Excellence and Ethics Meet*. Basic Books.

ORSBORN, C. (1992). *Inner Excellence: Spiritual Principles of Life-Driven Business*. New World Library.

PETERS, T. J., & WATERMAN, R. H. (1982). *In Search of Excellence: Lessons From America's Best-Run Companies*. Harper & Row.

PETERS, T., & AUSTIN, N. (1985). *A Passion for Excellence*. Random House.

ROBERTS, H. (1993). *Quality is Personal: A Foundation for Total Quality Management* (1st ed.). Free Press.

FINANCES

BOOKS

BOLDT, L. G. (1999). *The Tao of Abundance: Eight Ancient Principles for Abundant Living* (1st ed.). Penguin Books.

DOMINGUEZ, J., & ROBIN, V. (1992). *Your Money or Your Life: Transforming Your Relationship With Money and Achieving Financial Independence*. Viking Press.

GONZALEZ, M., & BYRON, G. (2009). *The Mindful Investor: How a Calm Mind Can Bring You Inner Peace and Financial Security* (1st ed.). Wiley.

HAWKEN, P. (1994). *The Ecology of Commerce: A Declaration of Sustainability*. HarperBusiness.

MILLER, J. B. (1987). *Toward a New Psychology of Women* (2nd ed.). Beacon Press.

NEEDLEMAN, J. (1994). *Money and the Meaning of Life* (New edition). Doubleday.

ROBIN, V. (1999). *Your Money or Your Life: Transforming Your Relationship With Money and Achieving Financial Independence*. Penguin (Non-Classics).

SOFTWARE

INVESTMENT EDUCATION - http://www.betterinvesting.org/public/default.htm   Access date 07/13/2015

NOTE

Many software products and cloud-based websites help you manage your finances. I suggest you do a web search for the solution that best suits your needs. Use key words "personal financial management" and see what you can explore. I'm cautious about recommending anything personally because I know how personal and private managing money can be. Always be an educated consumer!

HAPPINESS

BOOKS

AMERICAN PSYCHOLOGICAL ASSOCIATION (2002). *Flourishing: Positive Psychology and the Life Well-Lived*.

BEN-SHAHAR, Tal (2007). *Happier: Learn the Secrets to Daily Joy and Lasting Fulfillment*, McGraw-Hill.

BOLDT, L. G. (1999). *The Tao of Abundance: Eight Ancient Principles for Abundant Living* (1st ed.). Penguin Books.

CARR, Alan (2004). *Positive Psychology: The Science of Happiness and Human Strengths*, Routledge.

CSIKSZENTMIHALYI, Mihaly and SELEGA, Isabella (2006). *A Life Worth Living*, Oxford Univ. Pr 2006.

DIENER, Ed and BISWAS-DIENER, Robert (2008). *Happiness: Unlocking the Mysteries of Psychological Wealth*, Wiley-Blackwell.

DOMINGUEZ, J., & ROBIN, V. (1992). *Your Money or Your Life: Transforming Your Relationship With Money and Achieving Financial Independence*. Viking Press.

FREDRICKSON, Barbara (2009). *Positivity: Groundbreaking Research Reveals How to Embrace the Hidden Strength of Positive Emotions, Overcome Negativity, and Thrive*, Crown.

GONZALEZ, M., & BYRON, G. (2009). *The Mindful Investor: How a Calm Mind Can Bring You Inner Peace and Financial Security* (1st ed.). Wiley.

HAIDT, Jonathan (2006). *The Happiness Hypothesis: Finding Modern Truth in Ancient Wisdom*, Basic Books.

HAWKEN, P. (1994). *The Ecology of Commerce: A Declaration of Sustainability*. HarperBusiness.

KLEIN, Stefan (2006). *The Science of Happiness: How Our Brains Make Us Happy-and What We Can Do to Get Happier*, Da Capo Press.

LYUBOMIRSKY, Sonja (2008). *The How of Happiness: A New Approach to Getting the Life You Want*, Penguin.

MILLER, J. B. (1987). *Toward a New Psychology of Women* (2nd ed.). Beacon Press.

NEEDLEMAN, J. (1994). *Money and the Meaning of Life* (New edition). Doubleday.

PETERSON, Christopher (2006). *A Primer in Positive Psychology*, Oxford University Press, USA.

ROBIN, V. (1999). *Your Money or Your Life: Transforming Your Relationship With Money and Achieving Financial Independence*. Penguin (Non-Classics).

SELIGMAN, Martin (2004). *Authentic Happiness: Using the New Positive Psychology to Realize Your Potential for Lasting Fulfillment*, Free Press.

SELIGMAN, Martin and PETERSON, Christopher (2004). *Character Strengths and Virtues: A Handbook and Classification*, Oxford University Press, USA.

WEBSITES

AUTHENTIC HAPPINESS - https://www.authentichappiness.sas.upenn.edu Access date 7/13/2015

GAMES - https://company.zynga.com Access date 7/13/2015

HAPPINESS ASSESSMENTS - http://www.authentichappiness.sas.upenn.edu/Default.aspx   Access date 7/13/2015

POSITIVE PSYCHOLOGY - http://www.positivityratio.com   Access date 7/13/2015

STRENGTHS FINDER - Gallup Strengths finder, http://www.strengthsfinder.com/home.aspx Access date 7/13/2015

VIA INSTITUTE - http://www.viacharacter.org/www/   Access date 7/13/2015

INTEGRATION

BOOKS

CHOPRA, D. (1989). *Quantum Healing: Exploring the Frontiers of Mind/Body Medicine* (1st printing ed.). Bantam.

HARRIS, B. (2002). *Thresholds of the Mind* (1st edition). Centerpointe Press.

HENDRICKS, G. (2009). *The Big Leap: Conquer Your Hidden Fear and Take Life to the Next Level*. HarperOne.

ORIAH. (2006). *The Dance: Moving to the Deep Rhythms of Your Life*. HarperOne.

PELLETIER, D. K. R. (1994). *Sound Mind, Sound Body* (1st ed.). Simon & Schuster.

WILBER, K., PATTEN, T., LEONARD, A., & MORELLI, M. (2008). *Integral Life Practice: A 21st-Century Blueprint for Physical Health, Emotional Balance, Mental Clarity, and Spiritual Awakening*. Integral Books.

WEBSITES

http://www.lifedancing.com/   Access date 7/13/2015

http://www.essortment.com/jungian-psychology-personality-integration-16771.html   Access date 7/13/2015

INTUITION

BOOKS

HUFFINGTON, A. (1994). *Fourth Instinct: The Call of the Soul*. Simon & Schuster.

RADIN, D. (2006). *Entangled Minds: Extrasensory Experiences in a Quantum Reality*. Paraview Pocket Books.

ROBINSON, L. (2004). *Real Prosperity: Using the Power of Intuition to Create Financial and Spiritual Abundance*. Andrews McMeel Publishing.

ROBINSON, L. A. (2001). *Divine Intuition* (1st American Edition). Hyperion.

SCHULZ, MONA LISA, M.D., Ph.D. (1998). *Awakening Intuition: Using Your Mind-Body Network for Insight and Healing* (1st ed.). Harmony.

VAUGHAN, F. E. (1979). *Awakening Intuition*. Anchor.

JOURNALING

BOOKS

DESALVO, L. (1999). *Writing as a Way of Healing: How Telling Our Stories Transforms Our Lives* (1st ed.). HarperOne.

HILLMAN, J. (1983). *Healing Fiction*. Stationhill Press.

LEPORE, S. J., & SMYTH, J. M. (2002). *The Writing Cure: How Expressive Writing Promotes Health and Emotional Well-Being*

BAYS, J. C. (2009). *Mindful Eating: A Guide to Rediscovering a Healthy and Joyful Relationship With Food--Includes CD* (1st ed.) American Psychological Association (APA).

MEAD, A. (2008). *Wake Up to Your Weight Loss: Using the Art of Personal Narrative to Achieve Your Best Body* (1st ed.). A Storied Life Publishing.

PROGOFF, I. (1963). *The Symbolic & the Real.* McGraw Hill.

PROGOFF, I. (1992) *At a Journal Workshop: Writing to Access the Power of the Unconscious and Evoke Creative Ability.* Tarcher.

NOTE

There are many excellent books on Journaling. A search of the Amazon site using the key word "Journaling" finds many good books and many excellent resources.

WEBSITES Access date 7/13/2015

http://www.lifejournal.com/   Access date 7/13/2015

http://syniumsoftware.com/   Access date 7/13

MIND

BOOKS

AMEN, D. (2008). *Healing the Hardware of the Soul: Enhance Your Brain to Improve Your Work, Love, and Spiritual Life* (Reprint ed.). Free Press.

AMEN, D. G. (2006). *Making a Good Brain Great: The Amen Clinic Program for Achieving and Sustaining Optimal Mental Performance* (1st ed.). Three Rivers Press.

BUZAN, T. (1991). *Use Both Sides of Your Brain: New Mind-Mapping Techniques, Third Edition.* (Revised ed.). Plume.

BUZAN, T., & BUZAN, B. (1996). *The Mind Map Book: How to Use Radiant Thinking to Maximize Your Brain's Untapped Potential.* Plume.

COZOLINO, L. (2002). *The Neuroscience of Psychotherapy: Building and Rebuilding the Human Brain* (1st ed.). W. W. Norton & Company.

DOIDGE, N. (2007). *The Brain That Changes Itself: Stories of Personal Triumph From the Frontiers of Brain Science* (James H. Silberman Books) (1st ed.). Viking Adult.

FOER, J. (2011). *Moonwalking With Einstein: The Art and Science of Remembering Everything* (UK Paperback ed.). Penguin Press.

FRATTAROLI, E. (2001). *Healing the Soul in the Age of the Brain: Becoming Conscious in an Unconscious World* (1st ed.). Viking Adult.

GLADWELL, M. (2005). *Blink: The Power of Thinking Without Thinking* (Unabridged ed.). Hachette Audio.

GROF, S., & BENNETT, H. Z. (1992). *The Holotropic Mind: The Three Levels of Human Consciousness and How They Shape Our Lives* (1st ed.). HarperCollins.

LIPTON, B. H. (2005). *The Biology of Belief: Unleashing the Power of Consciousness, Matter and Miracles*. Mountain of Love.

MCGILCHRIST, I. (2010). *The Master and His Emissary: The Divided Brain and the Making of the Western World* (Reprint ed.). Yale University Press.

ORNSTEIN, R. (1991). *Evolution of Consciousness*. Pearson Ptr.

PINK, D. H. (2006). *A Whole New Mind: Why Right-Brainers Will Rule the Future*. Riverhead Trade.

SIEGEL, D., & HARTZELL, M. (2004). *Parenting From the Inside Out* (1st ed.). Tarcher.

SIEGEL, D. J. (1999). *The Developing Mind: Toward a Neurobiology of Interpersonal Experience* (1st ed.). Guilford Press.

SIEGEL, D. J. (2007). *The Mindful Brain: Reflection and Attunement in the Cultivation of Well-Being* (1st ed.). W. W. Norton & Company.

SIEGEL, D. J. (2010). *Mindsight: The New Science of Personal Transformation* (1st ed.). Bantam.

SIEGEL, D. J. (2010). *The Mindful Therapist: A Clinician's Guide to Mindsight and Neural Integration* (Norton Series on Interpersonal Neurobiology, 1st ed.). W. W. Norton & Company.

WEIL, A., & SMALL, G. (2007). *The Healthy Brain Kit: Clinically Proven Tools to Boost Your Memory, Sharpen Your Mind, and Keep Your Brain Young*. Sounds True Inc.

WEBSITES

http://www.bbc.co.uk/science/humanbody/ Access date 7/13/2015

http://www.investigatingthemind.org Access date 7/13/2015

National Center for Complementary and Alternative Medicine https://nccih.nih.gov/health/meditation/overview.htm

NOTE

Advances in research on the human mind are expanding at an ever-faster pace as our research protocols and tools become more sophisticated. The websites that I've referenced can be trusted to stay current in their references. This is another arena that I encourage you to continue to explore as we learn more and more about what it is to be human.

MINDFUL EATING

BOOKS

ALBERS, S. (2009). *50 Ways to Soothe Yourself Without Food* (1st ed.). New Harbinger Publications.

ALBERS, S. (2003). *Eating Mindfully: How to End Mindless Eating and Enjoy a Balanced Relationship With Food* (1st ed.). New Harbinger Publications.

ALBERS, S. (2009). *Eat, Drink, and be Mindful: How to End Your Struggle With Mindless Eating and Start Savoring Food With Intention and Joy* (1st ed.). New Harbinger Publications.

ALTMAN, D. (2002). *Art of the Inner Meal: The Power of Mindful Practices to Heal Our Food Cravings, Revised and Expanded Edi-*

ed.). Shambhala.

FREEDMAN, R., & BARNOUIN, K. (2009). *Skinny Couple in a Box*. Running Press.

GOLD, S. S. (2011). *Food: The Good Girl's Drug: How to Stop Using Food to Control Your Feelings*. Berkley Trade.

KOENIG, K. R. (2005). *The Rules of "Normal" Eating: A Commonsense Approach for Dieters, Overeaters, Undereaters, Emotional Eaters, and Everyone in Between!* (1st ed.). Gurze Books.

LORING, S. T. (2010). *Eating With Fierce Kindness: A Mindful and Compassionate Guide to Losing Weight* (Reprint ed.). New Harbinger Publications.

MAY, M. (2011). *Eat What You Love, Love What You Eat: How to Break Your Eat-Repent-Repeat Cycle*. Am I Hungry? Publishing.

ROTH, G. (2010). *Women Food and God: An Unexpected Path to Almost Everything*. Scribner.

SOMOV, P. G. (2008). *Eating the Moment: 141 Mindful Practices to Overcome Overeating One Meal At a Time* (1st ed.). New Harbinger Publications.

STALLINGS, K. (2008). *Life is Mental: Think Thin to Live Thin* (1st ed.). Kelly Stallings.

WEBSITES

http://www.tcme.org/   Access date 7/13/2015

MINDFULNESS/MEDITATION

BOOKS

ALTMAN, D. (2010). *The Mindfulness Code: Keys for Overcoming Stress, Anxiety, Fear, and Unhappiness*. New World Library.

BAYS, J. C. (2011). *How to Train a Wild Elephant: And Other Adventures in Mindfulness*. Shambhala.

BRACH, T. (2004). *Radical Acceptance: Embracing Your Life With the Heart of a Buddha*. Bantam.

CALVIN, W. (1990). *The Cerebral Symphony: Seashore Reflections on the Structure of Consciousness* (1st ed.). Bantam.

CHODRON, P. (2006). *Practicing Peace in Times of War* (1st ed., 1st printing.). Shambhala.

GERMER, C.K., Ph.D., SIEGEL, D.R., Psy.D., & FULTON, P.R., Ed.D., (2005). *Mindfulness and Psychotherapy* (1st ed.). The Guilford Press.

GOLEMAN, D. (1996). *The Meditative Mind: The Varieties of Meditative Experience*. Tarcher.

JACOBSON, J., & MADERA, K. C. (2010). *How to Meditate With Your Dog: An Introduction to Meditation for Dog Lovers*. Maui Media.

KABAT-ZINN, J. (1990). *Full Catastrophe Living: Using the Wisdom of Your Body and Mind to Face Stress, Pain, and Illness* (1st ed.). Delta.

KABAT-ZINN, J. (1994). *Guided Mindfulness Meditation: Series 1, 2, and 3*. Stress Reduction CDs, PO Box 547.

KABAT-ZINN, J. (2005). *Coming to Our Senses: Healing Ourselves and the World Through Mindfulness* (1st ed.). Hyperion.

LANGER, E. J. (1989). *Mindfulness*. Addison-Wesley.

MACE, C. (2007). *Mindfulness and Mental Health: Therapy, Theory and Science* (1st ed.). Routledge.

NAIRN, R. (1999). *Diamond Mind* (1st Shambhala ed.). Shambhala.

ROEMER L., Ph.D., & ORSILLO, S. M., Ph.D. (2008). *Mindfulness- and Acceptance-Based Behavioral Therapies in Practice (Guides to Individualized Evidence-Based Treatment)* (1st ed.). The Guilford Press.

SANTORELLI, S. (2000). *Heal Thy Self: Lessons on Mindfulness in Medicine* (Reprint ed.). Three Rivers Press.

STAHL, B. S., Ph.D, & GOLDSTEIN, E. (2010). *A Mindfulness-Based Stress Reduction Workbook* (Pap/MP3 Wk ed.). New Harbinger Publications.

WEBSITES

http://www.contemplativemind.org/   Access date 7/13/2015

http://www.mindandlife.org/   Access date 7/13/2015

MBSR - http://www.umassmed.edu/cfm/stress/index.aspx   Access date 7/13/2015

http://nccam.nih.gov/health/meditation Access date 7/13/2015

OPTIMAL PERFORMANCE

BOOKS

COVEY, S. R. (1990). *The 7 Habits of Highly Effective People* (1st ed.). Free Press.

COVEY, S. R., MERRILL, A. R., & MERRILL, R. R. (1994). *First Things First* (1st ed.). Simon & Schuster.

GRUDIN, R. (1988). *Time and the Art of Living*. Ticknor & Fields.

MACKENZIE, R. A., & MACKENZIE, A. (1975). *The Time Trap*. McGraw-Hill.

McWILLIAMS, J.R., McWILLIAMS, P., & McWILLIAMS, J. R. (1991). *Do It! Let's Get Off Our Buts: A Guide to Living Your Dreams*. Bantam Dell Pub Group (Trd).

RICHARDSON, C. (1999). *Take Time for Your Life: A Personal Coach's 7-Step Program for Creating the Life You Want* (1st ed.). Three Rivers Press.

RICHARDSON, C. (2002). *Stand Up for Your Life: Develop the Courage, Confidence, and Character to Fulfill Your Greatest Potential* (1st ed.). Free Press.

SENGE, P. M. (1994). *The Fifth Discipline: The Art & Practice of the Learning Organization*. Doubleday Business.

SENGE, P. M., KLEINER, A., ROBERTS, C., ROSS, R., & SMITH, B. (1994). *The Fifth Discipline Fieldbook: Strategies and Tools for Building a Learning Organization* (1st ed.). Crown Business.

SERVAN-SCHREIBER, J.-L. (1989). *The Art of Time*. Addison-Wesley.

SNEAD, G. L., & WYCOFF, J. (1997). *To Do Doing Done: A Creative Approach to Managing Projects & Effectively Finishing What Matters Most* (1st printing ed.). Touchstone.

TRENT, J. (1994). *Lifemapping*. Focus on the Family Publications.

WEBSITES

As I searched for website for Optimal Performance, I discovered most of them are trying to sell you something, so please do your own search and see if any of the resources you find appear to fill your needs.

ORGANIZATION

BOOKS

ELGIN, D. (1998). *Voluntary Simplicity: Toward a Way of Life That is Outwardly Simple, Inwardly Rich* (Revised Edition) (Revised ed.). Quill (William Morrow).

GLADWELL, M. (2005). *Blink: The Power of Thinking Without Thinking* (Unabridged ed.). Hachette Audio.

MCCULLOUGH, B. R. (1986). *Totally Organized: The Bonnie Mccullough Way.* St. Martin's Press.

MITCHELL, J. (1992). *Organized Serenity: A Practical Guide for Getting it Together.* Hci.

WINSTON, S. (1995). *Stephanie Winston's Best Organizing Tips: Quick, Simple Ways to Get Organized-and Get on With Your Life.* Simon & Schuster.

WEBSITES   Access date 2/4/14

http://www.wikihow.com/Category:Time-Management-%26-Personal-Organization   Access date 7/13/2015

Self Organizing Systems - http://en.wikipedia.org/wiki/Self-organization   Access date 7/13/2015

NOTES

Many kinds of organizational systems are out there. Always keep in mind that you have your own unique organizational system. If you are new to this concept, start by trying other's systems and find what works and does not work for you. LifeDancing offers self-management and organizational tools to get you started.

PERSONALITY

BOOKS

DEMAREST, L. (1997). *Looking At Type in the Workplace* (Looking At Type Series). Center for Applications of Psychological Type.

KEIRSEY, D. (1998) *Please Understand Me II: Temperament, Character, Intelligence. Prometheus Nemesis Book C.*

PALMER, H. (1991). *The Enneagram: Understanding Yourself and the Others in Your Life* (1st ed.). HarperOne.

POSITIVE PSYCHOLOGY

BOOKS

BEN-SHAHAR, T. (2007). *Happier: Learn the Secrets to Daily Joy and Lasting Fulfillment* (1st ed.). McGraw-Hill.

BISWAS-DIENER, R., & DEAN, B. (2007). *Positive Psychology Coaching: Putting the Science of Happiness to Work for Your Clients* (1st ed.). Wiley.

BOLT, M. (2004). *Pursuing Human Strengths: A Positive Psychology Guide.* Worth Publishers.

BUCKINGHAM, M., & CLIFTON, D. O. (2001). *Now, Discover Your Strengths* (1st ed.). Free Press

CARR, A. (2004). *Positive Psychology: The Science of Happiness and Human Strengths.* Routledge.

COREY, L. M. K., & JONATHAN, H. (2002). *Flourishing: Positive Psychology and the Life Well-Lived* (1st ed.). American Psychological Association (APA).

CSIKSZENTMIHALYI, M. (1990). *Flow: The Psychology of Optimal Experience.* Harper & Row.

CSIKSZENTMIHALYI, M. (1994). *The Evolving Self: A Psychology for the Third Millennium* (1st ed.). Harper Perennial.

CSIKSZENTMIHALYI, M. (1996). *Creativity: Flow and the Psychology of Discovery and Invention* (1st ed.). HarperCollins.

CSIKSZENTMIHALYI, M. (1997). Finding Flow: The Psychology of Engagement With Everyday Life (1st ed.). Basic Books.

CSIKSZENTMIHALYI, M., & CSIKSZENTMIHALYI, I. S. (2006). *A Life Worth Living: Contributions to Positive Psychology* (Series in Positive Psychology). Oxford University Press, USA.

DEROO, C., & DEROO, C. (2006). *What's Right With Me: Positive Ways to Celebrate Your Strengths*, Build S

DIENER, E., & BISWAS-DIENER, R. (2008). *Happiness: Unlocking the Mysteries of Psychological Wealth* (1st ed.). Wiley-Blackwell.

FREDRICKSON, B. (2009). *Positivity: Groundbreaking Research Reveals How to Embrace the Hidden Strength of Positive Emotions, Overcome Negativity, and Thrive* (1st ed.). Crown Archetype.

HAIDT, J. (2005). *The Happiness Hypothesis: Finding Modern Truth in Ancient Wisdom* (1st ed.). Basic Books.

HANSON, R. (2009). *Buddha's Brain: The Practical Neuroscience of Happiness, Love, and Wisdom* (1st ed.). New Harbinger Publications.

JOSEPH, S., & LINLEY, P. A. (2006). *Positive Therapy.* Routledge.

KAHLE, L. R., & CHIAGOURIS, L. (1997). *Values, Lifestyles, and Psychographics* (Advertising and Consumer Psychology). Psychology Press.

KLEIN, S. (2006). *The Science of Happiness: How Our Brains Make Us Happy-and What We Can Do to Get Happier* (Tra ed.). Da Capo Press.

LINLEY, A. P., & JOSEPH, S. (2004). *Positive Psychology in Practice* (1st ed.). Wiley.

LOPEZ, S. J., & SNYDER, C., R. (2003). *Positive Psychological Assessment: A Handbook of Models and Measures* (1st ed.). American Psychological Association (APA).

PETERSON, C. (2006). A Primer in Positive Psychology (Oxford Positive Psychology Series) (1st ed.). Oxford University Press, USA.

PETERSON, C., & SELIGMAN, M. (2004). Character Strengths and Virtues: A Handbook and Classification (1st ed.). Oxford: Oxford University Press, USA.

SELIGMAN, M. E. P. (1995). What You Can Change and What You Can't: The Complete Guide to Successful Self-Improvement

Learning to Accept Who You Are (Fawcett Book) (First Ballantine Edition ed.). Ballantine Books.

SELIGMAN, M. E. P. (2002). *Authentic Happiness : Using the New Positive Psychology to Realize Your Potential for Lasting Fulfillment* (1st ed.). Free Press.

WEBSITES   Access date 7/13/2015

University of Pennsylvania Positive Psychology Center - http://www.ppc.sas.upenn.edu/

RELATIONSHIPS

BOOKS

BATESON, M. C. (2000). *Full Circles, Overlapping Lives: Culture and Generation in Transition* (1st ed.). Random House. CHRIS-
TAKIS, N. A., & FOWLER, J. H. (2009). *Connected: The Surprising Power of Our Social Networks and How They Shape
Our Lives*. Little, Brown and Company.

GOTTMAN, J. (2002) *The Relationship Cure: A 5 Step Guide to Strengthening Your Marriage, Family, and Friendships*. Three Rivers Press

ZIMMERMAN, M. A. (2006). *Handbook of Community Psychology* (1st ed.). Springer.

NOTE: Remember the most important relationship you have is the one you have with yourself!

SPIRITUALITY

BOOKS

COHEN, A. (2011). *Evolutionary Enlightenment: A New Path to Spiritual Awakening* (1st ed.). Select Books.

FOWLER, J. W. (1995). *Stages of Faith: The Psychology of Human Development and the Quest for Meaning* (New ed.). HarperOne.

KORNFIELD, J. (1963). *A Path With Heart*. Bantam Books.

KORNFIELD, J. (2001). *After the Ecstasy, the Laundry: How the Heart Grows Wise on the Spiritual Path*. Bantam.

KORNFIELD, J. (2009). *The Wise Heart: A Guide to the Universal Teachings of Buddhist Psychology* (Reprint ed.). Bantam.

LAMA, T. D. (2003). *Stages of Meditation*. Snow Lion Publications.

MOORE, T. (1994). *Care of the Soul : A Guide for Cultivating Depth and Sacredness in Everyday Life* (Reprint ed.).
HarperPerennial.

RAMDASS. (1974). *The Only Dance There Is*. Anchor.

RAMDASS. (1978). *Remember, Be Here Now)*. Hanuman Foundation.

TOLLE, E. (1999). *The Power of Now: A Guide to Spiritual Enlightenment* (1st ed.). New World Library.

ZUKAV, G. (1990). *The Seat of the Soul* . Free Press.

VISIONING

BOOKS

BECK, M. (2002). *Finding Your Own North Star: Claiming the Life You Were Meant to Live*. Three Rivers Press.

CAPACCHIONE, L. (2000). *Visioning: Ten Steps to Designing the Life of Your Dreams*. Tarcher.

KEEN, S., & VALLEY-FOX, A. (1989). *Your Mythic Journey: Finding Meaning in Your Life Through Writing and Storytelling* (Inner Work Book) (1st ed). Tarcher.

LINN, D. (1998). *Quest* (1st U.S. Edition). Ballantine Books.

ZANDER, R. S., & ZANDER, B. (2000). *The Art of Possibility: Transforming Professional and Personal Life* (1st ed.). Harvard Business School Press.

WOMEN

BOOKS

BORYSENKO, J. (1996). *A Woman's Book of Life* (1st ed.). Riverhead Hardcover.

BRIZENDINE, L. (2007). *The Female Brain*. Three Rivers Press.

GILLIGAN, C. (2002). *The Birth of Pleasure* (1st ed.). Knopf.

MARREWA, A. (2001). *The Feminine Warrior: A Woman's Guide to Physical, Emotional and Spritual Empowerment*. Citadel.

RUTTER, V. B. (1993). *Woman Changing Woman: Feminine Psychology Re-Conceived Through Myth and Experience* (1st ed.). HarperCollins.

SCHULZ, M. L. (2005). *The New Feminine Brain: How Women Can Develop Their Inner Strengths, Genius, and Intuition* (1st ed). Free Press.

WORK

BOOKS

BOLDT, L. G. (1999). *Zen and the Art of Making a Living: A Practical Guide to Creative Career Design* (Compass) (Rev Exp ed.). Penguin (Non-Classics).

MASLOW, A. (1965). *Euphychian Management*. Homewood, Il: Dorsey Press.

PHILLIPS, M. (1996). *Honest Business* (Shambhala Pocket Editions) (1st ed.). Shambhala.

RATH, T. (2007). *Strengthsfinder 2.0* (1st ed.). Gallup Press.

NOTE

For a current listing of resources and active links to websites, please visit www.LifeDancing.com.

APPENDIX B

FORMS

The goal of LifeDancing is to integrate the right and left sides of the brain, the wholistic, intuitive functions with the linear concrete functions, so you can use ALL the best parts of yourself and create positive change. I have used a personal organizing system for years and don't know how folks function these days without one. There are many on the market and my two favorites are Levenger and Franklin systems. Over the years I have found it helpful to make my own forms and thought I would use those in LifeDancing. You can use these exclusively or incorporate any you find useful in your current system.

The forms that follow are offered to help you become more self-directed and better manage your time, money and energy. They are here alphabetically and you may copy them for your use or order pre-printed copies for yourself at http://www.lifedancing.com/   If you do use an organizer, I suggest you organize the forms in the following order:

1 - Cover Page

Behind the cover page, for each arena include:

2 - Foundations

3 - MindMap Worksheet

4 - Project Worksheet

5- Wholistic Problem Solving

6 - Strategic Plan

7 - Action Form

Calendars and Scheduling - Depending on how busy you are, or whether or not you are traveling, you can use any or all of the following forms. I highly suggest having a master calendar for your ideal life to work from. The reason you don't put your calendar at the front of your organizer is to make you look at what you really are working toward before making a commitment for something. It is often too easy to say yes to something that will take time away from something else that is more important.

8 - Monthly Schedule

LifeDancing ACTION

PROJECT NAME				

PRIORITY	TO DO	EST. TIME	DUE	STATUS
				☐ current ☐ scheduled☐ following up☐ delegated ☐ cancelled ☐ completed
				☐ current ☐ scheduled☐ following up☐ delegated ☐ cancelled ☐ completed
				☐ current ☐ scheduled☐ following up☐ delegated ☐ cancelled ☐ completed
				☐ current ☐ scheduled☐ following up☐ delegated ☐ cancelled ☐ completed
				☐ current ☐ scheduled☐ following up☐ delegated ☐ cancelled ☐ completed
				☐ current ☐ scheduled☐ following up☐ delegated ☐ cancelled ☐ completed
				☐ current ☐ scheduled☐ following up☐ delegated ☐ cancelled ☐ completed
				☐ current ☐ scheduled☐ following up☐ delegated ☐ cancelled ☐ completed
				☐ current ☐ scheduled☐ following up☐ delegated ☐ cancelled ☐ completed
				☐ current ☐ scheduled☐ following up☐ delegated ☐ cancelled ☐ completed
				☐ current ☐ scheduled☐ following up☐ delegated ☐ cancelled ☐ completed
				☐ current ☐ scheduled☐ following up☐ delegated ☐ cancelled ☐ completed
				☐ current ☐ scheduled☐ following up☐ delegated ☐ cancelled ☐ completed
				☐ current ☐ scheduled☐ following up☐ delegated ☐ cancelled ☐ completed
				☐ current ☐ scheduled☐ following up☐ delegated ☐ cancelled ☐ completed
				☐ current ☐ scheduled☐ following up☐ delegated ☐ cancelled ☐ completed
				☐ current ☐ scheduled☐ following up☐ delegated ☐ cancelled ☐ completed
				☐ current ☐ scheduled☐ following up☐ delegated ☐ cancelled ☐ completed
				☐ current ☐ scheduled☐ following up☐ delegated ☐ cancelled ☐ completed
				☐ current ☐ scheduled☐ following up☐ delegated ☐ cancelled ☐ completed
				☐ current ☐ scheduled☐ following up☐ delegated ☐ cancelled ☐ completed
				☐ current ☐ scheduled☐ following up☐ delegated ☐ cancelled ☐ completed
				☐ current ☐ scheduled☐ following up☐ delegated ☐ cancelled ☐ completed

LifeDancing COVER PAGE

MASTERING LIFE'S MOVEMENT

NAME	
CONTACT INFORMATION	
MAILING ADDRESS	
TELEPHONE(S)	
FAX	
EMAIL	
WEBSITE(S)	

Reward if found $_____

VITAL INFORMATION	
MEDICAL	
LEGAL	
OTHER	

LifeDancing EXPENSES - WEEKLY

EVENT								YEAR _____
		WEEKLY EXPENSES FOR _____ THROUGH _____						
				(date)				(date)
	SUNDAY	MONDAY	TUESDAY	WEDNESDAY	THURSDAY	FRIDAY	SATURDAY	TOTALS
Breakfast								
Lunch								
Dinner								
Groceries								
Supplies								
Education								
Entertainment								
Gifts								
Travel								
Parking/tolls								
Gas & oil								
Mileage end								
Mileage start								
Mileage total								
Mileage at fill-up								
Gallons								
TOTALS								

LifeDancing FOUNDATIONS

_____
arena

	DATE
NEEDS	
VALUES	
SKILLS	
PREFERENCES	
MISSION(S)	

LifeDancing JOURNAL LOG

LIFE ARENA

BODY

MIND

SPIRIT

HOME

RELATION-SHIPS

EMOTIONS

WORK

OTHER

LifeDancing JOURNAL LOG

LIFE ARENA

BODY

MIND

SPIRIT

HOME

RELATION-SHIPS

EMOTIONS

WORK

OTHER

Life Dancing LIFESTYLE CHANGE

NEW DAILY HABITS

HABIT	ARENA	MONTH	1	2	3	4	5	6	7	8	9	10	11	12	13	14	15	16	17	18	19	20	21	22	23	24	25	26	27	28	29	30	31
1																																		
2																																		
3																																		
4																																		
5																																		
6																																		
7																																		
8																																		
9																																		
10																																		
11																																		
12																																		
13																																		
14																																		
15																																		
16																																		
17																																		
18																																		
19																																		
20																																		
21																																		
22																																		

LifeDancing MIND MAP WORKSHEET

ISSUE

_____

Completion Date:_____

MIND MAP

Write the name of your project in a circle in the middle of the page and brainstorm ideas about what you'll need to do.

LifeDancing PROJECT WORKSHEET

Name of Project _____Date _____

DRIVING VALUES

1   _____

2   _____

3   _____

4   _____

5   _____

VISION/MISSION

Benefits for:

Myself _____

Others _____

GOALS

Due Date   Goal

1 _____   _____

2 _____   _____

3 _____   _____

4 _____   _____

5 _____   _____

REMEMBER

Goals must be decided by YOU and be congruent with your personal values.

Goals must be worthy.

Goals must be stated in the present tense.

Goals must be realistic and attainable.

Goals must have target dates.

Goals must be written.

LifeDancing SCHEDULE - DAILY   MASTER _____

TODAY'S DATE		SCHEDULED EVENTS	
TODAY'S FOCUS			

1 2 3	TO DO	DUE	ARENAS									
											7:00	
											7:30	
											8:00	
											8:30	
											9:00	
											9:30	
											10:00	
											10:30	
											11:00	
											11:30	
											noon	
											12:30	
											1:00	
											1:30	
											2:00	
											2:30	
											3:00	
											3:30	
											4:00	
											4:30	
											5:00	
											5:30	
											6:00	
											6:30	
											7:00	
											7:30	
											8:00	
											8:30	
											9:00	

NOTES	SUPPLIES NEEDED

LifeDancing SCHEDULE-DAILY DETAILED

																DATE
	Arena	Miles	Code	ODOMETER Begin-End	Vehicle #	Prkg/Tolls	TRAVEL				MEALS/ ENTERTAINMENT				JOURNAL ENTRY	
							Air	Rental	Lodging	Other	Breakfast	Lunch	Dinner	Ent.		
SCHEDULED EVENTS																
7:00																
7:30																
8:00																
8:30																
9:00																
9:30																
10:00																
10:30																
11:00																
11:30																
noon																
12:30																
1:00																
1:30																
2:00																
2:30																
3:00																
3:30																
4:00																
4:30																
5:00																
5:30																
6:00																
6:30																
7:00																
7:30																
8:00																
8:30																
9:00																

CODES

B-Business P-Personal C-Commute

Vehicles #1 _____ #2 _____ #3 _____

Arenas R-Relationships B-Body S-Spirit M-Mind E-Emotions
H-Home W-Work Wh-Wholeness

LifeDancing SCHEDULE - MONTHLY

	SUNDAY	MONDAY	TUESDAY	WEDNESDAY	THURSDAY	FRIDAY	SATURDAY

LifeDancing SCHEDULE - WEEKLY

TIME	SUNDAY	MONDAY	TUESDAY	WEDNESDAY	THURSDAY	FRIDAY	SATURDAY
7:00							
7:30							
8:00							
8:30							
9:00							
9:30							
10:00							
10:30							
11:00							
11:30							
noon							
12:30							
1:00							
1:30							
2:00							
2:30							
3:00							
3:30							
4:00							
4:30							
5:00							
5:30							
6:00							
6:30							
7:00							

LifeDancing **STRATEGIC PLAN**

ARENA	JANUARY	FEBRUARY	MARCH	APRIL	MAY	JUNE	JULY	AUGUST	SEPTEMBER	OCTOBER	NOVEMBER	DECEMBER
☐ body ☐ mind ☐ emotions ☐ spirit ☐ relationships ☐ work ☐ home ☐ wholeness												
☐ body ☐ mind ☐ emotions ☐ spirit ☐ relationships ☐ work ☐ home ☐ wholeness												
☐ body ☐ mind ☐ emotions ☐ spirit ☐ relationships ☐ work ☐ home ☐ wholeness												
☐ body ☐ mind ☐ emotions ☐ spirit ☐ relationships ☐ work ☐ home ☐ wholeness												
☐ body ☐ mind ☐ emotions ☐ spirit ☐ relationships ☐ work ☐ home ☐ wholeness												
☐ body ☐ mind ☐ emotions ☐ spirit ☐ relationships ☐ work ☐ home ☐ wholeness												
☐ body ☐ mind ☐ emotions ☐ spirit ☐ relationships ☐ work ☐ home ☐ wholeness												
☐ body ☐ mind ☐ emotions ☐ spirit ☐ relationships ☐ work ☐ home ☐ wholeness												

LifeDancing TIME LOG

TIME ASSESSMENT

Keep track of each 30-minute increment of your day to see how you really spend your time.

Reason for assessment			Body	Mind	Emotions	Spirit	Relationships	Work	Home	Wholeness
TIME	ACTIVITY	THOUGHTS & FEELINGS	ARENAS							

2.9a
WHOLISTIC INTEGRATIVE PROBLEM-SOLVING WORKSHEET

What problem or obstacle are you facing? Describe it in here. This is only a focusing statement, not a solution.

_____

_____

Make a Mind Map on the back of this page. (See Exercise 2.8a.)

List the ideas that came up in your Mind Map. Don't worry about the order.

_____

_____

Use the step-by-step process and prioritize your ideas and action items.

___ _____ ___ _____

___ _____ ___ _____

___ _____ ___ _____

Explore inner and outer obstacles.

_____

_____

Schedule your action items.

___ _____ ___ _____

___ _____ ___ _____

___ _____ ___ _____

If you schedule something and DON'T ACT, break the item down into smaller pieces here.

_____

_____

_____

What problem or obstacle are you facing? Describe it in here. This is only a focusing statement, not a solution.

_____

_____

Make a Mind Map on the back of this page. (See Exercise 2.8a.)

List the ideas that came up in your Mind Map. Don't worry about the order.

_____

_____

Use the step-by-step process and prioritize your ideas and action items.

_____   _____   _____   _____

_____   _____   _____   _____

_____   _____   _____   _____

Explore inner and outer obstacles.

_____

_____

Schedule your action items.

_____   _____   _____   _____

_____   _____   _____   _____

_____   _____   _____   _____

If you schedule something and DON'T ACT, break the item down into smaller pieces here.

_____

_____

INDEX

FOOT NOTES

[1] http://stress.about.com/od/generaltechniques/p/profilejournal.htm
The Benefits of Journang for Stress Management By Elizabeth Scott, M.S.

[2] *Character Strengths and Virtues: A Handbook and Classification*, Christopher Peterson and Martin Seligman.
(See Appendix A, bibliography.)

[3] http://www.myersbriggs.org/
Find more Myers-Briggs resources

[4] http://www.apple.com/ilife/iphoto/
Find more iPhoto information and
http://www.nuance.com/dragon/index.htm
Find more Dragon Speech information

[5] http://www.capt.org/catalog/archetype-assessment-personal.htm

[6] *Dance, Dance Evolution* - APA Monitor April 2010 Vo. 41 - No. 4 pg. 40

[7] *The Mindful Brain: Reflection and Attunement in the Cultivation of Well-Being*, Daniel J. Siegel.
(See Appendix A, bibliography.)

[8] http://www.centerpointe.com/

[9] http://www.mindfulnesscds.com/

[10] *A Whole New Mind,* Daniel Pink.
(See Appendix A, bibliography.)

[11] Albert Einstein. (n.d.). Retrieved December 8, 2010, from BrainyQuote site at
http://www.brainyquote.com/quotes/quotes/a/alberteins138241.html

[12] Lao Tzu. (n.d.). Retrieved December 8, 2010, from BrainyQuote site at
http://www.brainyquote.com/quotes/quotes/l/laotzu151139.html

[13] *Empowerment Theory*, M.A. Zimmerman, M.A. Eds., J. Rappaport & E. Seidman.
Handbook of community psychology. (See Appendix A, bibliography.)

[14] *Flow: The Psychology of Optimal Experience*, Mikalyi Csikszentmihalyi.
(See Appendix A, bibliography.)

[15] *Positive Psychology Coaching: Putting the Science of Happiness to Work for Your Clients.*.
R. Biswas-Diener & Ben Dean. (See Appendix A, bibliography.)

[16] http://www.fordfound.org/

[17] http://www.icisf.org/news/myers.html

[18] http://www.inspiration.com/

[19] http://www.sensorimotorpsychotherapy.org/referral.html

[20] *Full Catastrophe Living: Using the Wisdom of Your Body and Mind to Face Stress, Pain, and Illness*, Jon Kabat-Zinn.
(See Appendix A, bibliography.)

[21] *The Relaxation Response*, Herbert Benson, Miriam Z Klipper.
(See Appendix A, bibliography.)

[22] *The Mindful Brain: Reflection and Attunement in the Cultivation of Well-Being*, Daniel J. Siegel.
(See Appendix A, bibliography.)

[23] *The Female Brain*, Louann Brizendine.
(See Appendix A, bibliography.)

[24] *Flow: The Psychology of Optimal Experience*, Mikalyi Csikszentmihalyi.
(See Appendix A, bibliography.)

[25] *Mindsight: The New Science of Personal Transformation*, Daniel Siegel (2010). (1st ed.). Bantam

[26] Eye Movement Desensitization and Reprocessing Therapy Institute – http://www.emdr.com

[27] http://www.sensorimotorpsychotherapy.org/home/index.html

[28] *Emotional Intelligence*, Daniel Goleman. (See Appendix A, bibliography.)

[29] *Emotional Intelligence*, Daniel Goleman. (See Appendix A, bibliography.)

[30] *Psychology and Religion*, Carl G Jung. (See Appendix A, bibliography.)

[31] Luft, J.; Ingham, H. (1955). "The Johari window, a graphic model of interpersonal awareness". Proceedings of the western training laboratory in group development (Los Angeles: UCLA).

[32] *Character Strengths and Virtues: A Handbook and Classification*, Christopher Peterson, Martin Seligman.
(See Appendix A, bibliography.)

"

There's only one reason why you're not experiencing bliss at this present moment, and it's because you're thinking or focusing on what you don't have....But, right now you have everything you need to be in bliss.

ANTHONY DE MELLO